No Remorse

Johan Ulvenlöv   Matti Palm   Anders Larsson

No Remorse

Gustaf Ekström
The SS volunteer who
founded the Sweden Democrats

Vaktel förlag

Vaktel förlag
Box 3027
630 03 Eskilstuna
Sweden
vaktelforlag.se
vaktelforlag@gmail.com

English edition © 2019
First Swedish edition © 2017
Johan Ulvenlöv, Matti Palm & Anders Larsson
Translation from Swedish: Neil Betteridge
First English edition, First printing
Cover: Matti Palm
Design: Matti Palm
Printon Printing House, Estonia
ISBN 978-91-88441-46-1

"It all happened so fast. The ghetto. The deportation. The sealed cattle car. The fiery altar upon which the history of our people and the future of mankind were meant to be sacrificed."

Elie Wiesel, author and Holocaust survivor. Extract from his acceptance speech on being awarded the 1986 Nobel Peace Prize.

Inside jacket cover shows general maps of the German railway network from 2 November 1942. The locations in the clippings at the front and back of the book include, respectively, Berlin, Theresienstadt and Auschwitz; and Sobibor, Belzec and Malkinia, the station closest to Treblinka. (Übersichtskarte zum 14. Verzeichnis der SF-Züge. Stand: 2. November 1942. Kursbuchbüro der Generalbetriebsleitung Ost (Hrsg.), Deutsche Reichsbahn, 1942. Original in the authors' personal archive.)

Content

Authors' foreword	8
Foreword	11
Introduction	15
1. Between the old and the new	19
2. The emigrant	27
3. The nursing home on Lützowstrasse	35
4. Nazi youth Secretary and soldier in the depot	39
5. Racial theory on the agenda	55
6. A telephone directory reveals its secrets	79
7. An organisation built for terror	82
8. There were 256 of them	85
9. At the SS-Hauptamt	92
10. Irene Heim	96
11. Propaganda at the front	99
12. The transports east	120
13. Amongst the houses in Grunewald	130
14. Towards Theresienstadt	140
15. Encounter with a traitor	166
16. From Lützowstrasse to the Holocaust	172
17. Nuremberg	183
18. Nazis old and new	192
19. From SS to SD	222
20. Triumph	227
Epilogue	229
Appendix	239
The residents of Lützowstrasse 48/49	240
Interviews and memoranda from the security police files	273
Some key years	285
Gustaf Ekström's political engagement	287
List of illustrations	289
References	298
Acknowledgements	320
Index	321

Authors' foreword to the English edition

The Sweden Democrats are probably unique from an international perspective. Few modern parties have the same kind of Nazi, neo-Nazi and White-Power origins as the Sweden Democrats, and even fewer far-right or nationalistic parties have grown so quickly. The Sweden Democrats emerged from the 2018 general election as one of the largest parties in the country. The Sweden Democrats' Nazi roots have split political alliances and redrawn the political map in Sweden, and are consequently of immediate topical concern. This book is about one such root: Gustaf Ekström – collaborator, Nazi and co-founder of the Sweden Democrats.

The authors
Jerusalem, 5 December 2018

Authors' foreword to the second revised and expanded Swedish edition

Many people have written to us since the publication of the first Swedish edition of this book. Some of them are still seeking the truth about what happened to their relatives at one or other of Berlin's Jewish nursing homes, despite its being 72 years since the end of the War. Might we have a name on one of our lists? We didn't. But since an ever-growing volume of Holocaust material is becoming searchable in new digital archives, many such questers will probably discover the truth in the end. Others who have contacted us have provided further details of Ekström's doings in the Sweden Democrats. Small details, admittedly, but combined with what we have already written they give us a clearer picture of how active Gustaf Ekström was in the party. It turns out that his engagement continued longer than we thought when we wrote the first edition of this book.

We also managed, finally, to make contact with a Jewish person of relevance to our story who survived the flight from Germany when he was a child. His mother worked in one of the properties, Sanatorium Grunewald, that the SS eventually stole from the Jewish family; it was here, at Hagenstrasse 39–47 in Berlin's most exclusive district, where Gustaf Ekström, founder of the Sweden

Democrats, served for the SS-Hauptamt Germanische Leitstelle.

We have also obtained new documents from archives in Germany and the USA since the printing of the first edition.

All in all, this new information prompted us to produce a revised and expanded edition of the book.

The authors, November 2017

Foreword

In November 2015, my attention was drawn to a documentary about the Sweden Democrats that LO (the Swedish Trade Union Confederation) had produced and that was published on Facebook, where it has been viewed, at the time of writing, over 1.6 million times. This was at the end of the dramatic refugee crisis, a year in which there were numerous attacks on asylum centres, when the public debate on immigration and minorities was at its fiercest and, not least, when the Sweden Democrats nudged 20 to 25 per cent in the opinion polls and were well on the way to become Sweden's second largest, if not largest party. The film, which bears the title *The Sweden Democrats – Ett parti som alla andra?* (literally: the Sweden Democrats – A party like any other?) depicts a party living in symbiosis with social media hate speech and with the right-wing radical "alternative media" that flourishes in cyberspace; but also a party that has direct racist roots. Much of this is old news. What made the film stick out was how well researched it was, and the due prominence it gave to the currently relatively unknown Gustaf Ekström.

Two years later, Johan Ulvenlöv, Matti Palm and Anders Larsson publish this book. Based on extensive and thorough research in archives and libraries in Sweden, Germany, Israel and elsewhere, the book leaves no doubt that Ekström personifies in effect the 20th century history of Sweden's far right, from his joining Sveriges Fascistiska Kamporganisation (roughly Swedish Fascist Movement) in the 1920s to his founding of the Sweden Democrats in the 1990s – and signing up to many other Swedish and German fascist organisations in between. Ekström was a member of Nationalsocialistiska Arbetarpartiet (the National Socialist Workers Party), which was the largest Swedish Nazi party until its dissolution in 1950. He was also active in the West German SRP until its proscription in 1952, and in the Nationaldemokratische Partei Deutschland (NPD), the biggest West German post-war far-right party. The NPD still exists, even though most of its voter base have defected to the right-wing populist party, Alternative für Deutschland.

This said, the book is not just a political biography of a relatively obscure Swedish far-right extremist who never abandoned his political beliefs or his political involvement, and who during the war enlisted in the Waffen-SS. Ulvenlöv, Palm and Larsson's book is also about all those who had once lived at the Jewish nursing home at Lützowstrasse 48/49 in Berlin, which the Nazis expropriated and turned into an SS headquarters, and where Ekström was to serve as an SS volunteer. At the same time as Ekström has his office at Lützowstrasse 48/49, the evicted elderly German-Jewish residents are deported to the ghettos and camps in the East, where they are murdered or left to die. By the end of the war, all but seven of these elderly people have passed away. The book reveals that Ekström is saved from a bomb-wrecked Germany and from falling into the hands of the Allied troops by a Nazi official at the Swedish Ministry for Foreign Affairs who secures a place for him on one of the Red Cross's White buses. To posterity, however, the white buses have mainly been seen as a rescue operation for the Jews who were still in the concentration camps at the end of the war; moreover, Ekström was not the only Swedish Nazi to remain in the Third Reich until the bitter end and who "got a lift home" in one of the white buses.

After the war, Ekström was probably involved in helping Nazis and fascists flee and emigrate to South America and was eventually instrumental in the founding of the Sweden Democrats in 1988. In the party's early years he was the executive committee's auditor. Ekström's story is therefore also one of Sweden's own past and present, and of the systematic mass-murder of German and European Jews in which Ekström was complicit as a cog in the Nazi propaganda machine. Ekström finally appeared only once in public when he agreed to be interviewed for SVT's documentary Blågul nazism (roughly: Swedish Nazism) in 1993, in which he denied the fact of the very same genocide of which he himself had been part.

Tobias Hübinette

Lecturer and researcher at Karlstad University, co-founder of Expo, and researcher for Bosse Schön's documentaries and books on the Swedish SS volunteers.

"Of course, the terrible things I heard from the Nuremberg Trials, about the six million Jews and the people from other races who were killed, were facts that shocked me deeply. But I wasn't able to see the connection with my own past.

I was satisfied that I wasn't personally to blame and that I hadn't known about those things. I wasn't aware of the extent. But one day I went past the memorial plaque which had been put up for Sophie Scholl in Franz Josef Strasse, and I saw that she was born the same year as me, and she was executed the same year I started working for Hitler. And at that moment I actually sensed that it was no excuse to be young, and that it would have been possible to find things out."

Traudl Junge, Hitler's personal secretary 1942–1945. Quoted from the documentary *Im toten Winkel – Hitlers Sekretärin*, 2002.

"No sensible person believed a word about these concentration camps. We all understood it to be war propaganda. It had started already during and before the war and persisted after the war. So every sensible person was highly sceptical towards these horror stories."

Gustaf Ekström, volunteer in the Waffen-SS 1941–1943. Quoted from the documentary *Blågul nazism*, 1993.

Introduction

Gustaf Ekström was never a prominent Nazi. He was never a great leader and never distinguished himself. But during his long life, he was in or in touch with many of the most influential Swedish and German Nazi organisations before, during and after the War. Always in some middle position – as secretary of the youth association, as a local SA leader, as a non-commissioned officer of the Waffen-SS and finally an auditor when he helped to found the Sweden Democrats. That was his final political deed of any substance. The history of Gustaf Ekström is the history of Nazism, in Sweden as much as in Germany.

The Sweden Democrats are a party with Nazi roots, and one of the reasons for this is that Nazis were amongst its founders. This book explores one of these roots in detail.

We first came across the Nazi and SS-volunteer Gustaf Ekström when we were making a documentary about the Sweden Democrats in the autumn of 2015. Our researches took us to Berlin and Lützowstrasse 48/49, the site of the former premises of the SS-Hauptamt (SS Main Office), one of the most important SS organisations and employer of Swede Gustaf Ekström. There was nothing left of the building when we arrived, having been bombed by the Allies in 1943 or 44. Today, a 1980s apartment block stands in its stead. Our journey could have ended here. We had the footage we had come to film. But something was not quite right, and it pricked our curiosity.

The address of the SS-Hauptamt, Lützowstrasse 48/49 we obtained from a librarian at the Topographie des Terrors (The Topography of Terror), a museum of Nazi crimes built upon the ruins of the Gestapo/SS joint headquarters in Berlin. The librarian produced letters and telephone directories from 1930s and 1940s Berlin, and through them we were able to trace the office at which Gustaf Ekström was employed. In the 1941 Berlin telephone directory we learned that the SS-Hauptamt was at Lützowstrasse 48/49. But the Berlin directory of addresses from that same year said something completely different: "Jüdisches Altersheim e.V. Lützowstrasse 48/49". Would a Jewish nursing home and an SS office have shared the same building? Hardly, but what did it mean?

This, in other words, was not the end of our journey but the start. Every discovery presented a new mystery. Every stone we turned revealed another that we wanted to turn, and again another. And with each stone, Gustaf Ekström's story grew ever murkier.

That autumn we collected an extensive bank of material comprising hundreds of documents, and counting. With each response to our inquires from different archives came new details, photos, letters, lists or brief margin notes. A humble telephone bill from Berlin at the time of Ekström's employment could prove a vital piece of our puzzle. What did Ekström actually do during the Second World War? Where was he deployed? Who crossed his path? Why did he volunteer to enlist for the Waffen-SS and how did his time in the SS inform his political choices later in life? Every answer that landed in our letter box sparked new ideas. Let's send a request to another archive! Maybe we can find a postcard or a photo of that building or place in some records somewhere or in an antiquarian bookshop! Or why not visit this important place and see what it looks like today?

We sought the answers to many questions: Who were the residents of the Jewish nursing home in Berlin? He was a rising SS official. But where were they headed? The more we endeavoured to discover what became of these people, the more obvious it was that the Nazis intended the victims' stories to die with them. The Holocaust is the Nazi ideology in action. The nursing home is therefore an important part of the story of Gustaf Ekström's life. Despite the Nazis' efforts to eradicate even the very memory of their victims, we eventually found several sources that laid the foundations of this book. They include the Nazis' own detailed chronicle of their crimes and disparate testimonies. Yet given how many victims of persecution there were during the War, the sources are sometimes frustratingly scant.

As we worked, we became fascinated by how the small details shaped the greater whole. Lists, addresses, names, dates, years, scribbled margin notes and things lurking in the background of photographs can be of major significance. An old telephone directory can say more than a thesis, a letterhead with an address and telephone number says more than yet another book about some general.

We have taken a systematic, source-critical approach to our material, and with Gustaf Ekström's activities constantly in mind, have identified names, places and times, and what he and others undertook to do. Piece by piece, we have built up an ever more comprehensive picture.

We pursued our researches as we wrote. Or perhaps our researches pursued us. There are constantly many loose threads to follow and many stones to turn, while the slow passage of documents from archives around the world to our desks never seems to end. We therefore hope that his book does not mark the end of the story, but the beginning of something else. The fact is that owing to digitalisation and the gradual erosion by time of the principles of secrecy, it is nowadays easier than ever to dig around old archives. As recently as 7 January 2017 a new digital archive from the International Tracing Service was opened, allowing 30 million documents on Nazi deeds searchable by anyone with an internet connection. We hope that this book and its discoveries will serve as inspiration to seekers, letter-writers and hasslers of helpful archivists. Feel free to pick up where we have left off.

During our investigations we encountered scepticism from many quarters. One objection has been that the book market is saturated with literature about the Second World War, everything from psychological analyses of Hitler and Stalin to chilling accounts of the cruelties of war. So why another one? Often we, as readers, are served the sweeping, broad perspectives. A life becomes a statistic, commas separate one death sentence from another, famous generals wreak devastation with a mark on a map. Our story is the opposite. In it, we let one person's life be the thread running through 70 years of European Nazism.

Another objection has been, why dig up the past? What does it matter what an old man did in his youth? It was all so long ago. The answer to that question is that it matters a great deal. There can be no doubting that a straight line can be traced from the very first fascist and Nazi organisations in Sweden to our current political situation. And Gustaf Ekström is one of the men who tie everything together. Letting the past remain in the past is a frequent argument used by Nazis seeking to belittle or excuse the most horrific crime against humanity the world has ever seen: the Holocaust.

Chapter 1
Between the old and the new

Gustaf Ekström's mother, Hilda Michelson, found herself in the little village of Färila in Hälsingland at the time of his arrival on 9 October 1907. She had actually moved to Stockholm, where she lived with her husband, Samuel Ekström, and Gustaf's three elder siblings in a newly procured apartment in the up-market Östermalm district of Stockholm. The address was Linnégatan 32.

Gustaf Ekström's parents had followed the lead of many others at the end of the 1800s, and moved to Stockholm to live a more modern life than that of their parents. Samuel Ekström was the son of pastor Johan Sacharias Ekström and Hilda Michelson's father was a forester.

The young family arrives in a city in the throes of transformation. Stockholm's population has expanded to 300,000 and the city is steeped in optimism. Society has declared war on the widespread health problems that overcrowding brings and is intent on cleaning away the filth of the 19th century. Children are organised to exterminate the city's rats for 60 öre per tail submitted; parks are laid and trees are planted along the wider streets and avenues; clean market halls rise as a modern alternative to the grime of the outdoor marketplaces.

Samuel Ekström is a gymnastics trainer, the equivalent of our modern physiotherapist, at Stockholm's Institute of Orthopaedics. Modern Swedish gymnastics leads the world and is widely exported. The idea is to make people healthier, to prevent disease and help improve public health. Motion becomes a "folk" movement in the same way as the abstinence movement sobered Swedes up and the revivalist movement ensured their salvation.

Now, new political movements and ideologies start to emerge. The working class organises itself in trade unions and social democracy spreads. In tandem with the modern political movements, national romanticism and nationalism start to thrive around the turn of the century as a reaction to contemporary progress. The Skansen open-air museum opens its gates in Stockholm, nursery books teach children about the Vikings and the hero kings. In 1910 Gustaf Cederström completes his painting "Segern vid Narva" (The Victory at Narva), which romanticises the defeat of the Russians at the hands of King Karl XII.

However, life in 20th century Sweden is not just one of progress and development. Fresh conflicts also flare up. Poverty is rife and the income gap between rich and poor generates tension. Women do not have the vote and even men's voting rights are limited. In 1909, the employers try to stem the first advances of the labour movement. Their aim is to lower wages in the textile factories and sawmills. The union movement responds by bringing 300,000 workers out on what has come to be known as the Great Strike. The strategy fails, however, and the employers advance their positions. There is, in consequence, a resurgence of emigration to America. Life in Sweden is too paltry.

Gustaf Ekström's first setback in life occurs when he is only one year old. His parent's marriage comes to an end and he has to move from Linnégatan.

Divorces at this time were very rare, and for vicar's son Samuel Ekström to dissolve his marriage was scandalous. Nevertheless, the family was well-off, which helped matters. The solution was for Hilda Ekström to move to Lindesberg outside Örebro with two of their four children, Gustaf and Bengt, while daughter Britta and eldest son Sven stayed behind in Stockholm with their father.

At this time, only one in a thousand women divorce, and to be the child of a single mother could bring social ostracisation. But Gustaf Ekström is not left wanting. His mother is listed in the 1910 census as a "capitalist", which means that in the eyes of the authorities she has been left with enough money from the divorce that she can live off the interest. The house to which they move is a charming stone edifice on Lindesberg's main street at Kungsgatan 10, right next to Lindesjön lake. Lindesberg was also home to Gustaf Ekström's maternal uncle, court photographer Alfred Michelson, which could have been the reason why the recently divorced mother chose to move here.

As a child, Gustaf Ekström pays frequent visits to Färila, the town in which his parents were born and raised. Since he makes these journeys in the school holidays, it is possible that he was there on that fateful day of 28 July 1914 when the First World War broke out. After years of rearmament, ultimatums and military alliances, the war was seen by European heads of state as inevitable. Four years later, once the gunpowder smoke has settled, many millions of people lie dead on the battlefields or of the disease and hardship that has followed in the wake of the war. The bloodbath was without compare, no one had ever seen anything like it.

Sweden had managed to dodge the war. A decision on neutrality had been made early on by the Swedish government, and its Nordic neighbours followed suit. Nonetheless, the war left deep scars on society as galloping prices and shortages of import goods hit the Swedish population. To make matters worse, the war also coincided with poor harvests. 1917 was a particularly bad year.

Over and above the far-reaching social issues, politics was dominated by the great dispute over the size of Sweden's defences, an issue that was hotly debated even before the outbreak of war. This defence controversy forms the hotbed in which the early fascist and later Nazi organisations can take root, including the first fascist organisation that Gustaf Ekström will join.

Prior to the First World War, Karl Staaf's liberal government had decided to cut the defence budget, a move that was condemned by powerful forces in society and that prompted the famous explorer and Swedish academician Sven Hedin to travel the country campaigning for a stronger national defence. In February 1914, King Gustaf V holds his Courtyard Speech, which Hedin has written for him. With the King calling for armament, the government is forced to resign. The defence question remains in focus, with the liberal and social democrat politicians in one corner and the conservative right, with its links to the military and the palace, in the other.

The conflict over defence was at least just as much about the emergence of a burgeoning democracy. If the advocates of democracy want to dismantle the nation's defences, it proves that democracy does not work, argued the right. At the same time, there was such popular support for the defence forces that it was a given issue to pursue for the anti-democracy forces.

The 1917 Russian revolution is another event that had ramifications in Sweden. One of Europe's oldest royal houses, the Romanov dynasty, had been dethroned and a new political ideology and a new political system installed in its stead. In Finland, the repercussions were dramatic when the country was plunged into civil war between the Red Guards and the Whites.

In 1923, Gustaf Ekström enters his final year at the municipal middle school in Lindesberg. The first extant photograph of him is from this time, with his uncle Alfred Michelson the likely person behind the camera. Dressed in the school's sports kit with LiKM on the breast, he poses proudly for the photographer along with 21 schoolmates and their besuited teacher.

On 2 June 1923, Gustaf Ekström takes his secondary school exams. He obtains the best grades in the natural sciences and history. But all in all, he was neither top nor bottom of his class. His grades, however, are adequate, for Gustaf Ekström is given a chance granted to only a few in Sweden: he may continue his studies. In 1924 he enrols at Örebro technical gymnasium, where he is joined by middle brother Bengt a few years later. Both brothers will leave with a qualification in chemical engineering.

In 1924, Gustaf Ekström's eldest brother, Sven, also moves to Örebro, where he begins his military career. He has applied, on leaving Hersby gymnasium on Lidingö with middling grades, to join the Life Grenadiers Regiment in Örebro. Perhaps he wants to be closer to his mother and two brothers. 16 years after their parents' divorce, the brothers are together again. Their sister, Britta, remains in Stockholm, however, where she marries surveyor Albin Edlund in 1928.

On 26 May 1925, the government announced cuts in defence spending. The right had lost its battle against parliamentarianism and democracy, for which the defence appropriation was an important symbolic issue. The Liberals and Social Democrats judged Germany to have been weakened by the Treaty of Versailles and trusted the newly formed League of Nations, the forerunner of the UN, to mitigate the risk of war. They also believed the threat from the infant Soviet Union to have waned. Finland, Estonia, Latvia and Lithuania, which had once belonged to Russia, had become independent and thus formed a buffer between Sweden and the USSR. The conclusion was that Sweden was no longer under military threat. The right and the army, however, were of a different opinion, and regarded Soviet Bolshevism as a new, major threat to Europe.

The Swedish Fascist Movement, Sveriges Fascistiska Kamporganisation (SFKO) is founded in 1926 through a call to arms against the defence decision. It is one of the first fascist organisations in Sweden. Initially, inspiration is drawn from Mussolini's fascists in Italy, its members favouring the black shirt, shoulder strap, jodhpurs and boots look. But there is one point on which Swedish and Italian fascism differ: the former is immersed in anti-Semitism and racial ideology. Many of Sweden's young fascists are schooled in the SFKO, amongst them gymnasium student Per Engdahl and one sergeant Sven Olov Lindholm, who was to be instrumental during the 1930s in the birth of a purely Swedish Nazi party. The organisation won sympathisers amongst the military but also recruited other gymnasium students. Shortly after its founding, the organisation accepts into its ranks Gustaf Ekström, aged 19.

The government's decision to slash defence spending by 41 per cent, which meant the closure of several regiments, affected Gustaf Ekström's brother Sven Ekström. Even if I3, where Sven served, was not on the list of doomed regiments, it is not difficult to imagine the insecurity that must have haunted professional soldiers. The discussions in the officers' clubs, soldiers' messes and barracks around Sweden were presumably heated, as many an officer was doubtlessly incensed by the decision. The tone in nationalist circles was even more strident. Or as one of Sweden's most notorious Nazis, Per Engdahl, put it in an interview in 1993 when explaining why he joined the SFKO:

"[...] the disarmament decision of 1925 [went on] to prove extremely momentous by causing massive indignation in wide national circles. And to a certain extent, the SFKO was born as an expression of protest against the very fact of disarmament."

The protests of the national movement are not only against the defence cuts. An appeal published in the SFKO's own organ, *Spöknippet* (literally The Rod Bundle, in reference to the symbol adopted by the Italian fascists), embeds the protest more firmly in ideology and embodies many of the components that came to define Nazism: a hatred and fear of Communism, explicit anti-Semitism and the belief in the blood inheritance of national traits. Consider the following extract from *Spöknippet*:

"Swedish men and women!

Slowly but surely, Moscow-paid demagogues are seeking to cast our ancient culture into the pit of Bolshevism. In hatred and discord we fail to notice that its hired minions will soon lead us to moral and financial ruin. With mendacious and ambiguous words, Swedes and turned against Swedes. It is merely a matter of time before we are 'blighted' by Russian illiterates and nomadised parasites of Jewish lineage. It is merely a matter of time before Sweden's domains are controlled by the parliament of the street, where crime is a boon, and true Swedish customs are trampled underfoot. It is merely a matter of time before our Swedish flag – the emblem of our childhoods' Sweden – the flag, which our forefathers rallied around in times good and bad – completely vanishes from our minds.

Swedes! Are we not duty-bound to sustain and protect the Sweden that our forefathers built and for which they gave their lives and blood?

Swedish fascism will lift the nation from out of chaos. Rally as one around King and flag! Become a Swedish fascist!

Swedish Fascist Movement ."

The SFKO's text paints an almost mythically ideological picture of a nation on the brink of collapse and ruin. The country is in chaos and fascism is the solution.

Despite the fascistic name, the SFKO is closer to German Nazism, and is already attending the Nazis' Nuremburg rallies in August 1929. The trip, which is led by former non-commissioned officer Konrad Hallgren, who had served in the German army during the First World War, doubtlessly made a lasting impact on the Swedish delegation. By the end of the year, the SFKO has changed its name to the National Socialist People's Party (SNFP) – a decision taken at its first congress in the presence of delegates from the German Nazi party.

Another Nazi organisation founded at this time is the Swedish National Socialist Freedom Party, also known as the Furugård Movement. The organisation started in Värmland back in 1924 and was quick to forge strong links with the German Nazi party. The year previously, in July 1923, brothers Gunnar and Sigurd Furugård met Adolf Hitler for the first time. In 1928, Birger Furugård meets Adolf Hitler and Joseph Goebbels.

Gustaf Ekström's studies are interrupted when he is drafted into the I2 regiment in Karlstad on 15 June 1927. Six months later, Ekström is discharged with an exemplary service record and resumes his studies, which he completes in the spring of 1928. A photograph from the school's yearbook shows him wearing a smart blazer, his striped tie neatly knotted and his hair well-groomed. His exam results are nothing exceptional and his grades are average for the class. He has scored a B in almost every subject. The higher grades he gets for languages; he receives an upper B for English, German and Swedish.

Another photo of Ekström from this time is taken on the veranda of his uncle's house, which stands at the intersection of Smedjegatan and Kristinavägen in Lindesberg. Through the window we can see trees in full leaf, under which family and friends have gathered for some feast or other. On the far right sits Alfred Michelson, to his left a woman who is probably Gustaf Ekström's mother, and to her left Ekström himself. All are wearing their Sunday best and on the table stand crystal carafes, champagne glasses and a bottle of champagne. The photo shows us that Ekström's youth is securely anchored in the upper middle class.

But it does not take long after leaving school for Gustaf Ekström to decide that his future does not lie in Sweden. When a few months' additional military service comes to an end on 10 October 1928, he is granted an exit permit to the USA. With him in his baggage is a gymnasium qualification in engineering and a decent knowledge of English.

Chapter 2
The emigrant

On Tuesday 5 February 1929 Gustaf Ekström steps ashore at the Swedish-America Line's pier 97 next to 57th street in New York. He has 125 dollars in his pocket in initial capital, a sum equivalent to about 13,000 kronor in today's money. He is one of the last of the 1.3 million emigrant Swedes who moved to the USA between 1830 and 1930.

The cause of the emigration is usually said to have been starvation, hardship and population expansion. The number of Swedes had increased as a consequence of a combination of factors, including smallpox vaccination, potato cultivation and the years of peace. There is much truth in this. But if you ask the Swedes who emigrated, you actually get different answers. The national Emigration Report that was released in 1913 after a six-year investigation does just this. As part of the investigation, 289 letters were published from Swedes in North America. One A G explains in letter 280 why he moved from Gävleborg County to Canada in 1903:

"I was born in Hälsingland to poor parents. ... When I reached the age of 21, I started to wonder whether I should go forth to defend King and country. What would I do that for? I didn't have as much as a handful of soil. Indeed, I knew that I was destined to fight and die for those who did nothing but demand that I pay them tax. Pay them for risking my life for them; it's dreadful when you think that the poor man, who owns nothing, shall go forth whether he like it or not and defend the life and wealth of his tormentors. No, it shall not be!

Let every man go out and defend what he owns and remove the differences of rank, and I think things will be different. Let the poor man vote with the rich and do not trample him underfoot. Circumstances are different here in this country. Here, everyone is equal, high and low, rich or poor. I do not even need to tip my hat to the consul if I should meet him or if I enter his house, I do not even need to remove it. No, create an America in Sweden, and I believe that your sons and daughters will stay at home, otherwise not. Shorten the lengthy conscription time, give people the vote, distribute the land that lies untended, and do away with some of all these salary-takers who live only on the worker and of what he earns."

Similar accounts can be found in many of the anonymous letters from and interviews with Swedish emigrants. Many blame their refusal to return on the hard, long terms of conscription, the lack of universal suffrage and the differences in income. But Gustaf Ekström was no normal emigrant to the USA. He wasn't fleeing an arduous existence bereft of hope.

Ekström's journey to a new life in the USA begins on 26 January 1929. He boards M/S Gripsholm in Gothenburg with a visa indicating that the expensive ticket, costing 449 kronor (about 12,000 kronor in today's money), had been paid for by his uncle Michelson.

The ship in which he sails was launched just over three years earlier and was one of the world's most modern ocean-going vessels. The decor on the ship, which was dubbed "the floating palace" was of an extravagant older style. There were copies of paintings from Gripsholm palace on board, for example, and the first-class passengers even had a swimming pool. In third class, where Gustaf Ekström is travelling, three-course meals are served in the dining room. In the manifest we find Gustaf Ekström listed with his new title: engineer. The other third-class passengers have stated such professions as farmer, house-worker, seamstress or simply wife. The young Ekström is one of the most highly educated passengers amongst them.

Ekström's destination is the industrial town of Schenectady in New York state, the home of his 12-year older friend Sven Rystedt and his wife Elsie Rystedt, who live on 1593 Rugby Road. The house has six rooms and two bathrooms and was built in 1905. Sven and Elsie travelled to the USA in May and November 1920. They married in 1923 and Sven now works as an engineer at Adirondack light, heat and power company. The company has several Swedes on its payroll, so it seems that Ekström and his friend Rystedt are not alone in seeking their fortune in Schenectady. The town's industries have been thriving of late and there is a desperate need for skilled labour.

When Gustaf Ekström arrives in the USA in early February 1929 he finds a country aglow with optimism. There is ample work, the entire 1920s having been a time of prosperity. Consumption is at a high and the industrial machine is going flat out. The middle class is growing. A new idea that anyone can become rich starts to spread, not least through the agency of the banks, whose adverts entice the public to purchase shares. The stock market on Wall Street shoots up in value and soon millions of Americans have become shareholders. In 1928, the year before Ekström's arrival, the market rises by 50 per cent.

For Gustaf Ekström, the gay 20s prove short-lived. Just a few months after his disembarking, the bubble bursts and on 24 October 1929, Black Thursday, the market starts to plummet. People around the USA who have bought shares queue up outside brokers' offices demanding to know what is going on. The crash is a reality. Many people, having bought shares on credit, lose everything they own.

His journey to Schenectady is not the success that Gustaf Ekström has pinned his hopes on. General Electric, one of the town's main employers, is hit badly by the crash. When Gustaf Ekström steps off the ship, the GE share is trading at 396 dollars. A few years later, it is worth a mere 8.5 dollars.

On 1 April 1930 we find Gustaf Ekström residing at 5 Crescent Avenue in Jersey City in New Jersey. He has left the Rystedts' in Schenectady, and the district where he is now living has grown up over the past 30 years. Shortly after the turn of the century, most of the developments here were wooden two-storey houses. When Ekström arrives, Jersey City is a town of brick and part of Greater New York. On the other side of the Hudson River is southern Manhattan, where the crash began just a few months earlier. The George Washington Bridge is under construction, and when it is inaugurated eighteen months later it is the world's longest suspension bridge, despite the savings in construction material occasioned by the austerity of the Depression. The bridge's large steel towers still remain to be clad in concrete and granite as originally intended.

At the time of the 1930 census, there are 13,360 Swedish-born residents of New Jersey. Between 1900 and 1923 nine Swedish Lutheran churches are opened in the state. As bastions of Swedish language, culture and customs, the churches try to stoke young people's interest in their old homeland. The congregations sing Swedish songs and celebrate Swedish festivals.

On Crescent Avenue Gustaf Ekström rents a room from siblings Ada Wagner, 59, and Frantz Eckler, 77. Ada Wagner works as an auxiliary nurse while her 18-year older brother is a retired pharmacist. Another family lives in the house in which Ekström lodges. The father of the family is unemployed, having once been a chauffeur for a funeral parlour; the daughter of the family is the only one with a job. She works on a telephone switchboard.

Unemployment has not only hit the family in the house where

Ekström is living, but the whole of the USA. Slums appear in the vicinity of Jersey City, shanty towns settled by unemployed bachelors and families start to spread. Social exclusion, unemployed demonstrations and long queues for whatever temporary labour was available define the townscape.

Despite mounting unemployment, Gustaf Ekström has managed to find work with the city's oil industry. Perhaps he works at the nearby Bayway Refinery in Linden, founded by John D Rockefeller's Standard Oil 20 years previously. Work at the refineries at this time is hard, dirty and dangerous. Accidents are many. On 18 February 1930, there is a huge explosion at the Bayway Refinery. The newspapers report ten dead and some three-score injured. The accident comes just over a week after an explosion at another refinery in neighbouring Bayonne.

The stock market crash of 1929 had led to a serious economic depression in the USA. Prior to the crash, in 1928, unemployment was 4.2 per cent. By 1930 it had more than doubled to 8.7 per cent. But things would get much worse. In November 1931, Dagens Nyheter back home in Sweden reports that at over 25 per cent, Jersey City has the sixth highest rate of unemployment in the whole USA.

The economic crisis becomes pandemic. For years, the USA had been lending money to Germany, which was hard pressed after the reparations imposed on it by the Treaty of Versailles. After the 1929 crash, the USA demanded its money back. Consequently, unemployment in Germany skyrocketed. In 1932 it was 30 per cent.

Many people seek scapegoats for the crash and the ensuing depression. Anti-Semitism has been growing ever stronger in the USA throughout the 1920s, with Jews being blamed for everything from the Great War to the Russian Revolution; they are also accused of controlling the global economy, and when the crash and the subsequent depression hit, some people hold them to be the product of a Jewish conspiracy.

More then 60 years later when interviewed for Swedish Television, Gustaf Ekström will refer back to this idea of a Jewish "enemy of the people". He explains why he and other Nazis vilified the entire Jewish race in this way:

"If we'd said, for example, that the enemy of the people is Rothschild, or Roosevelt or Rockefeller, the greater masses wouldn't have understood. So we needed an adversary, the identity of which the people could comprehend."

Ekström names here Rothschild and his European banking dynasty, along with Rockefeller, who founded the refinery at which he worked during his stay in New Jersey. He also names Roosevelt, who became the American president in 1933. While neither the industrialist Rockefeller nor Roosevelt was Jewish, they are often mentioned in similar anti-Semitic conspiracy theories as "crypto-Jews" or covert Jews. Amongst other things, in the 1930s the American Nazis were known to call Roosevelt by the more Jewish-sounding name Rosenfeld. They also changed the name of Roosevelt's reform programme to reduce unemployment from "The New Deal" to "The Jew Deal".

During the turbulence as the 1920s becomes the 1930s, a Nazi movement starts to emerge in New Jersey, which perhaps is not the first place that springs to mind when discussing Nazism, which is usually considered an altogether European phenomenon. We do not know if Gustaf Ekström joins some organisation during his US years, but the fact is that if he wished to transfer his Nazi allegiance from a Swedish to an American organisation, New Jersey presents him with ample opportunity to do so.

Back in 1924 Fritz Gissibl and three other German citizens founded the Free Society of Teutonia in Chicago. Fritz Gissibl was already a hardened Nazi, and a year previously had been involved in Hitler's failed Beer Hall Putsch in Munich. At first, the organisation had only 500 or 600 members. But more would join.

One of the states in the USA in which Teutonia was active was none other than New Jersey. One of its missions was to raise funds for the Nazi party in Germany. Adolf Hitler himself wrote to Teutonia in 1926, thanking them for their birthday greetings. In similar letters from 1928 and 1929, the German Nazi party thank Teutonia for their donations. Over time, the organisation grew ever more militant and explicitly anti-Semitic. Many of members of this first wave of Nazis in the USA came from Germany or had German roots, and were to run into difficulties with the migration authorities. Some even had their American citizenship revoked and were held in confinement during the war.

Teutonia was the first of several national socialist organisations established in the USA. Another Nazi organisation that was active in New Jersey and New York was the Friends of New Germany. Whoever wanted to join the Friends of New Germany was required, for example, to sign a membership card confirming that they were not Jewish, a Freemason or of "coloured blood". Amongst other operations, the Friends of New Germany endeavoured to infiltrate non-political German-American societies and arrange boycotts of Jewish shops in areas with many German immigrants, including Manhattan's Yorkville.

The Nazi movement continued to grow in the USA during the 1930s after Gustaf Ekström's departure back to Sweden. In 1935, the Friends of New Germany transformed itself into yet another new organisation, the German American Bund, which according to reliable estimates had 25,000 paid-up members, 8,000 of whom were SA men or, as they were called in the USA, Storm Troopers.

On 20 February 1939 the organisation mustered its largest demonstration. It had hired New York's Madison Square Garden and drew between 18,000 and 20,000 devotees. Perched high above the stage was the German Imperial Eagle. The arena had been decorated with banderols bearing swastikas and slogans such as "Stop Jewish Domination of Christian Americans". The audience cheered their leader Fritz Kuhn as he delivered his address. With his German accent, not unlike that of the classic Hollywood baddie, Kuhn condemns "Jewish Communism". The catcalls reached a peak when he named congressman Samuel Dickstein, who chaired many of the anti-Nazi hearings of the House of Representatives Special Committee on Un-American Activities. Dickstein was also a Jew, which probably fuelled their antipathy. At the rally, Fritz Kuhn declaimed:

"If you listen to Dickstein and other political hounds in the pay of a Jewish camarilla you will have absolutely the most false impression of our organisation."

But the Madison Square Garden rally is held long after Gustaf Ekström's departure from the USA. His time in the USA was not particularly long, despite his intention of settling there permanently, as is evident from his visa. He also applied for naturalisation (i.e. to become an American citizen) but he travelled home to Sweden too early for his citizenship to be granted. Maybe he too became unemployed.

By April 1931, the economic crisis had ravaged New Jersey. Two state banks, the Linden National Bank and the State Bank of Linden, were forced into closure. Soup kitchens and bread lines became a commonplace feature of Jersey City. From having doubled between 1928 and 1930, unemployment in the USA climbed even higher; by 1932, 23.6 per cent of Americans were without work.

Gustaf Ekström's emigration to the USA did not turn out as he had planned. Unlike the Rystedts, who have children, work and live in the USA, Gustaf Ekström gives up. His starting capital of 125 dollars has run dry. He cannot even afford a ticket home to Sweden, and has to work on board to compensate. On 21 April 1932 he is able to enlist on the smaller and simpler of the America ships, S/S Drottningholm. In the spring of 1932 he disembarks onto the quayside in Gothenburg. His emigration to the USA has come to nothing.

Chapter 3
The nursing home on Lützowstrasse

Many people who have visited Berlin are probably familiar with the KaDeWe department store, or Kaufhaus des Westens to give it its proper name. It is one of the world's largest and most distinguished department stores and was founded back in 1907 by Jewish businessman and board of trade member Adolf Jandorf. In the early 1930s, Rabbi Dr Martin Salomonski is director of the non-profit association Jüdische Altersheim e.V., which runs nursing homes for elderly Jews in Berlin and its environs. On 20 August 1933, he officially opens the new home at Lützowstrasse 48/49 in memory of Adolf Jandorf, who died on 12 January 1932. The home is in Berlin's Tiergarten district, not far from Lützowplatz with its pretty fountains and statues. A short walk northwards via the Hercules Bridge takes you over the Landwehrkanal and into the delightful surroundings of Tiergarten park. And two blocks eastward from the home, on the same street, is a synagogue with a magnificent organ and room for over 1,800 visitors.

At this time there are over 160,000 Jews living in Berlin, almost one third of the German Jewish population. The city's Jewish community, Jüdische Gemeinde, operates some two dozen nursing homes around the city, as well as schools, children's homes and libraries. A social network has been set up so that people can take care of each other. Besides its own establishments, the community is also active through non-profit associations, such as the nursing home on Lützowstrasse.

The address Lützowstrasse 48/49 will prove central to Gustaf Ekström's story. When we realised this, we searched for months for photographs of the building, including from the time before Ekström had anything to do with it. We scoured archives, image banks and shops selling postcards and old photographs. Finally, we find a whole album of pictures of the home in Heinrich Stahl's private collection in the Leo Beck Institute archive in New York. Heinrich Stahl was chairman of the Jewish community in Berlin and was given the album by the nursing home's director, Martin Salomonski.

The photographs were taken in early September 1933, just after the opening. The black-and-white pictures, which have been lovingly glued into the album, show the facade and premises, with brief descriptions accompanying each one. This album is probably the only extant collection of photographs of pre-war Lützowstrasse 48/49, before much of the city was destroyed. They actually constitute some of the few physical items that have been preserved for posterity from the nursing home. But they are not mere photographs; they are testimony to what life was like for many people, all of whom would shortly disappear. The first photograph shows the building's facade, five storeys high with bay windows overlooking Lützowstrasse, where tram 98 rattles by. The entrance looks modest but the evidence in the album makes it clear that the home is an object of pride for Salomonski. It is tempting even to say that at the time of its opening, the nursing home on Lützowstrasse is one of the most modern in Berlin.

The home on Lützowstrasse was also equipped with a lift and a telephone. In the archive of the Centrum Judaicum in Berlin we find a leasing contract for a newly installed telephone system with a loud ring signal. The leasee is the Jüdische Altersheim e.V.

association and the supplier is AG Gesellchaft für automatische Telephonie. The contract was signed on 2 June 1933, just over two months before the official opening. In the 1936 Berlin telephone directory, we find the number: switchboard B2 Lützow 19 20.

The communal refectory has space for 42 diners. Tables have been laid for a three course meal. Other photographs from the album show furnished single rooms, a general kitchen, laundry and mangle room for bed linen, and a day-room where the elderly could sit reading newspapers and books. The bedrooms were furnished with a bed and bedside table, a small desk and chair, an armchair and a wardrobe.

One photograph shows the assembly room. Hanging here is a portrait of Adolf Jandorf, the man in whose memory the home was opened. He is posing with one hand cradling a cigarette and the other in his trouser pocket. There is also a commemorative plaque of the official opening and a devotional niche containing two candles and a Star of David, where the residents could conduct their own services. The assembly room, which is on the second floor, has leaded windows adorned with stained glass images of Jewish symbols. In one window is a Star of David, in another the symbol of Moses' tablets bearing the Ten Commandments, and in a third the Jewish seven-armed menorah. In August 1933, seven months after Hitler comes to power, a Jewish nursing home could still proclaim its identity to the world. But it was just a matter of months before things would change. Soon, Nazi swastikas will be billowing on the quarter's facades.

In the day-room hang three newspapers, the 1 September 1933 issue of *Jüdische Rundschau*, *Der Israelit* and *Jüdisch liberale Zeitung*. All the newspapers will soon be forbidden. Jüdisch liberale Zeitung contains articles with such headlines as "Austrian government sets Anti-Semitic course?" and "Stateless non-Aryan brokers no longer allowed to work in Berlin commodity exchange". We can also read that Jews are being barred from entering Munich's exhibition hall during the October Festival, while another article reports on the various bathing bans for Jews around Germany.

The advertisement pages are crammed with offers for trips to Palestine and the USA.

Anti-Semitism, the hatred of Jews, has a history in Germany that began long before the Nazis came to power. But during the Nazi regime, the hatred will take a new turn. For the vast majority of Berlin's Jewish population, the coming decade will be a horrific journey into a heart of darkness. Already at the end of 1933, the segregation and persecution of Jews had started to become increasingly visible. Many of those who could fled the country; hence all the travel advertisements in the Jewish papers. It was above all the young and those with a stronger position in society, who chose to depart, leaving behind the elderly, the poor and otherwise unable to emigrate. It was also rational to count on being able to ride out the storm. No one could have imagined what was going to happen. For it had never happened before.

Yet still, in 1933, neither Gustaf Ekström nor the elderly residents on Lützowstrasse are aware that their paths will soon cross.

Chapter 4
Nazi youth Secretary and soldier in the depot

Gustaf Ekström de-enlists from S/S Drottningholm and steps ashore in Gothenburg on 1 May 1932. Now, after returning from his unsuccessful attempt to emigrate to the USA, his political engagement becomes an ever more explicit and central part of his life. While he has been in the USA, the Swedish Nazi movement has congealed into a party.

Prior to the 1930s, Swedish fascism and Nazism had comprised a motley collection of small organisations and newspapers, and the same people often featured in more than one of them. In April 1930, the SFKO finally merged with the Furugård Movement. With a new manifesto and headed by party leader Birger Furugård and his deputy Sven Olov Lindholm, the new organisation calls itself the Swedish National Socialist Party (SNSP).

The movement now has sufficient resources to forge ahead. Local branches are opened and daily public meetings and actions are arranged around the country. With grand plans in store, they turned their gaze on the ever-greater successes of German Nazism. One problem that will dog the Nazis in every election, however, is that most of its members are too young to vote. The links to Germany are extensive. There is a German representative in attendance at the 1931 party congress and its organ Vår kamp (Our struggle) publishes a series of articles written by Adolf Hitler. In September 1932 the party stands for election for the first time but fails to win a seat in the Riksdag, having accrued only 15,167 votes.

Gustaf Ekström briefly recounts his joining the SNSP in an interview in the documentary *Blågul nazism* filmed in 1993 by Karl-Axel Jansson and Ingemar Schmidt for Swedish Television:

"I travelled down to Gothenburg and signed up to join the SNSP, Sweden's national socialist party. It was led by Birger Furugård up in Deje in Värmland and his deputy Sven Olov Lindholm in Gothenburg."

Throughout its short life, the SNSP was beset by intrigue and internal power struggles. Barely three years after the party was founded it split up. In January 1933 deputy party leader Sven Olov Lindholm founds his own rival Nazi party, the National Socialist Workers' Party (NSAP), also known as the "Lindholmers" or the "Lindholm Movement". Eventually, the NSAP becomes the largest and most active Swedish Nazi party. Ekström recalls the split between Lindholm and Furugård and his decision to join Lindholm's party in the interview from 1993:

"I'd met Lindholm in the beginning of his time as party leader, the spring of 1933 it was, and I got the impression that he had sound motives and wanted to take the thing further. He also claimed that purely practical measures had played a big part in his split with Furugård in that Furugård lived weeks and months up in Finnskogarna in Värmland and so was absent from the daily struggle on the streets of our cities and towns."

What Ekström does not mention is the bitter power struggle between Lindholm and Furugård. Countless articles, leaflets and meetings were devoted to attacking Furugård and depicting him as an alcoholic who failed to pay his bills and frittered away the party cash. The NSAP's youth organisation, Nordisk Ungdom (the Nordic Youth) were particularly keen distributers of leaflets libelling Furugård, and in 1935, Ekström is made its secretary. The mid-winter 1935 issue of the NSAP's youth organ *Stormfacklan* (Storm torch) carries a Christmas greeting from its executive in Gothenburg; Ekström's name is one of seven.

At the same time as Ekström is choosing sides in the in-fighting plaguing Sweden's Nazi parties, Adolf Hitler seizes control of Germany. On 30 January 1933, one of Europe's most populous countries is led by a Nazi party and a Nazi chancellor. Sven Olov Lindholm, Gustaf Ekström and the Swedish Nazis turn their gaze towards Germany and feel that they too have the wind in their sails. The Swedish Nazis make frequent visits to their German brethren in the 1930s. Sven Olov Lindholm himself makes several trips to Germany and gives a frank account of his experiences in his book *Svensk Frihetskamp*, published by the Nazi publisher NS-Press in 1943. He sums up his meetings with Adolf Hitler:

"During my two visits, which took place before the National Socialists came to power, I had the opportunity to meet Adolf Hitler. During our conversations he showed a particular interest in the Nordic idea from a race perspective and maintained (1932) that Europe even then actually formed a certain political kinship."

Networks were created and links forged between, above all, SS commander Heinrich Himmler and Sven Olov Lindholm. A key figure in the relations between the Swedish and German Nazis is the German Nazi and businessman Max Pferdekämpfer. He was an early member of the German Nazi party, one of the first in fact, having joined the NSDAP back in 1919. Pferdekämpfer had a reputation amongst the German Nazis as a first-rate Scandinavia expert. In the Workers' Movement archive, in John Takman's collections, are photostats of correspondence from 1930–1933 between

Heinrich Himmler and Max Pferdekämpfer concerning relations with, amongst others, Sven Olov Lindholm and the Swedish Nazis. Pferdekämpfer is described by historian Heléne Lööw as a close friend of Sven Olov Lindholm's.

Pferdekämpfer's contributions to Swedish Nazism do not stop at mail correspondence. According to Lööw, Pferdekämpfer helps the Lindholm Movement to identify, through a lawyers' practice in Jönköping, anti-Nazis in Sweden. Pferdekämpfer also helps to procure rooms for the Ortsgrupp, the local branch of the NSAP, in Berlin, which it continues to occupy throughout the war. The office was located in a property shared with the DAF (Deutsche Arbeitsfront), the Nazi equivalent of a trade union, on Immelmannstrasse 10, a stone's throw from Tempelhof airport. It later becomes an important place for the Swedish Nazis who take it upon themselves to volunteer for the Waffen-SS. The Swedish Nazis also maintain a journalist and correspondent at the office, Thorolf Hillblad, who would later crown himself the "National leader" of Swedish Nazis in Germany – at least, that is the title he demands of the party in Sweden in a letter to the party headquarters on Markvardsgatan in Stockholm. Ekström will also visit the office at Immelmannstrasse 10 for reasons that we will return to later.

Author and journalist Bosse Schön has spent decades writing about and researching Swedish SS veterans. He shows us a photograph of Gustaf Ekström in the extensive archive that he has amassed over the years. It was probably taken around 1933–1935, perhaps during the time when Ekström was secretary of the Nordic Youth. The black-and-white photograph is a group shot that was presumably published in some Nazi tract or pamphlet. In it we see 27 uniformed men with shoulder straps, armbands and jodhpurs posing for the camera. They are proud and most are staring squarely into the lens. Some of the men seem, like Ekström, to be in their late 20s, while others look no more than adolescents. This was how the movement wanted to depict itself: strong, self-assured, young and fearless. Ekström, who is sitting furthest to the right in the front row has twisted his arm so that the red armband with the yellow swastika on its blue background is extra visible. His expression is resolute and self-satisfied. In the background we glimpse what we can assume to be the party flag, the last letters of the party abbreviation NSAP and the sunshine yellow swastika just visible in the blue flag's centre.

In 1935 Ekström lives in Gothenburg, at the junction of Storgatan 41 and Chalmersgatan 3, and works as an engineer. It is now that he is appointed to his first official post, the secretary of the Nordic Youth. As part of its executive he thus took part in the planning of the organisation's activities. They held processions *(uppmarscher)*, effectively public rallies, at which they sang songs, marched to a band, shouted slogans and handed out fliers. At such gatherings, members – who were also known as "national recruits" – could deliver harangues on such themes as "What measures should be taken against the Jews". Violence and its glorification were part of the organisation's activities and ethos. In 1939 it broke into the offices of the socialist organisation Clarté and stole the members register and details of refugees in hiding. The scandal broke when it emerged that the Nordic Youth was responsible. The attention and adverse publicity the organisation received prompted it to temporarily change its name to the Wasa Youth Movement. It resumes its former name in 1941.

The society's organ, *Stormfacklan*, is crude in tone and describes the society's activities in glowing terms. Articles on hikes and camping rub shoulders with essays on race biology and eugenics, descriptions of the Swedish disposition and attacks on SSU (the Swedish Social Democratic Youth League) and LO (the Swedish Trade Union Confederation). Articles call for social upheaval. Freemasons, jazz music and Jews are repudiated as signs of decadence. Other newspapers are accused of being mendacious and of hiding the truth from the Swedish people. Only the National Socialist movement can rescue Sweden from the great conspiracy. And running through everything that *Stormfacklan* publishes is that harsh and vulgar anti-Semitism. An example from 1 March 1936:

"The Jewish question in Sweden is exceedingly important. ... The Jew holds far too influential a position in our country. He is not of our blood and consequently is unable to react in the same way as one of our people's own sons. The status of the Jew in society must not be the same as that of the Nordic Swede. The Jew is to be considered a temporary guest in our country who must, on account of mistakes made, be tolerated but who may not arrogate to himself any power over the host nation."

Sven Olov Lindholm himself writes in a text entitled "The youth struggle against the Jews" from April 1936:

"The name Nordic Youth itself embodies a protest against the alien parasites who systematically poison our blood and turn us into a mongrel hotchpotch. ... Racial renewal first requires the Jewish peril and all its toxic fruits to be crushed."

The tone and content are fully in keeping with the anti-Semitic tirades and theses that Adolf Hitler spouts in *Mein Kampf*, which must be regarded as one of the most important sources for understanding Nazism. In *Mein Kampf* Hitler writes:

"If... twelve or fifteen thousand of these Hebrew corrupters of the people had been held under poison gas... the sacrifice of millions at the front would not have been in vain."

Hitler expresses himself with even greater clarity in a Reichstag speech from 30 January 1939:

"Today I will once more be a prophet: if the international Jewish financiers in and outside Europe should succeed in plunging the nations once more into a world war, then the result will not be the Bolshevizing of the Earth, and thus the victory of Jewry, but the annihilation of the Jewish race in Europe!"

Hitler repeats this maxim in his speech at the 19th anniversary of the Beer Hall Putsch in Munich. By this time, the deportations and the planning of the Holocaust had begun. Hitler and Lindholm, the Swedish and the German Nazis are united in their blind racial hatred and their conviction that the Jews are the root of all evil and that good can only be achieved if that evil is "annihilated" (Hitler) or "crushed" (Lindholm). In all their simplicity, the two brief, brutal quotes articulate the heart of the Nazi ideology. Historian Saul Friedländer has described the foundation of Nazism as a "redeeming anti-Semitism". The core of the ideology is this very hatred of the Jews and the power of violence to redeem and save the people. Lindholm also imports the German Nazi anthems "Horst Wessel Lied" and "Volk ans Gewehr" into his own movement, supplying them with Swedish lyrics. In Lindholm's version, "Horst Wessel Lied" becomes "Awaken, our people" and contains the following anti-Semitic lines:

"Friends face up to Marxism's den of Jews ... The swastika standards and freedom's oath are now raised The destiny of the world spring from Nordic blood!"

There is also an anti-Semitic streak to Lindholm's Swedish lyrics to "Volk ans Gewehr", which he retitles "People, to arms!":

"The Northmen's budding future land /ascending from the golden skies / here against the Jewish hordes we stand /that from our woods and towns arise."

Today both songs are banned from public performance in Germany. The original German lyrics to "Volk ans Gewehr" (People, to arms) were even submitted as evidence in the Nuremburg trials.

Armed with anti-Semitic songs and literature, the members of the Nordic Youth marched out against their ideological foes. Adverts also enticed them to purchase the society's own knife – the "Anti-Semite" – for 5.50 kronor.

It is not only the youth organisation that is fiercely anti-Semitic. The Jews are described in the parent party's newspaper with the same invective as in the youth society's writings. The NSAP does its utmost to *define* Jews and Judaism in accordance with the beliefs and methods of German Nazism. Fearmongering, myths, lies, rumour-spreading and dehumanisation are methods frequently used by the Swedish Nazis in their efforts to "awaken the Swedish people" to an alleged "Jewish-Bolshevik conspiracy". The party also put its anti-Semitism into practice. For as long as it existed, the NSAP registered Jews in Sweden. The endeavour was high priority and appeals published in its organ *Den Svenske Folksocialisten* urged people to send in lists of Jews. The 20 March 1941 issue contained, for example, the following announcement:

"Many formations have omitted to send lists of Jews living in the area. Send such a list to the party exec."

Between the years 1933 and 1950, the NSAP collected the names of tens of thousands of Jews and other political opponents. One such register was recovered in 1997 during renovations of Lisell Hall in Malung; it contains some 3,000 names.

We can read about the register in the 28 September 2015 issue of newspaper *Dala-Demokraten*:

"Nazi symbols and the content of the documents were indisputable proof that the Swedish Nazis of the 1930s had registered primarily Jews as well as political opponents, whom they referred to as 'Jews in spirit'... The register records their names and those of their wives, children and parents, what property and companies they owned, and often their declared income. Notes are also made of where they were born, in many cases when they died and any crimes of which they might have been convicted. Some of the records contain obituary notices, and in many cases newspaper clippings of crimes and trials, jubilee portraits and of reviews of the performances of famous

artists were registered. The register contains a large number of well-known names."

The register has since been traced back to leading NSAP member Erik Walles, the one-time deputy leader of the NSAP/SSS.

The anti-Semitic theses that characterised Nazism were not only promulgated in newspapers and pamphlets. In the 1930s, the NSAP imported its methods and organisation from the German Nazis. For example, the Swedish Nazis set up "propaganda teams" after a German Nazi model. There is absolutely no doubt that Gustaf Ekström, in his capacity as elected member, was actively involved in the Nazis' party operations. The NSAP was an elite party and was extremely selective as to whom it allowed in. Members were expected to give of their time, commitment and money. The NSAP's service regulations make the demands clear. A member of the NSAP was expected to participate in the party's propaganda campaigns, attend membership meetings and public rallies organised by the party, read the party's newspapers and act as a role model of ideological devotion. We may presume that Gustaf Ekström was an active propagandist and travelled with the propaganda team that followed Sven Olov Lindholm. Perhaps he was with Sven Olov Lindholm when he visited his (Ekström's) home tracts of Lindesberg and Örebro in 1938. Ekström describes in his own words what it was like to take part in a meeting with Sven Olov Lindholm:

"I realised that this man [Lindholm] was the equal of any speaker I could ever imagine appearing. The tension was already at a peak when he marched in with his young companions and he performed very well on the rostrum."

A propaganda team comprised one or two trucks, sometimes accompanied by a motorbike. Their method involved driving a couple of days in advance to the town where Lindholm or some other leading representative was due to speak. Once in place, they pitched tents and placed adverts in the local newspapers announcing in somewhat ostentatious terms that "Lindholm is coming". Paste patrols would then issue from the camp to put up posters ahead of the meeting. Some trucks, painted with swastikas and such slogans as *"Sweden awake!"* or "Lindholm's Liberation Movement" would drive around the town blaring out their message.

This is the movement's own version of its activities. However, if we read contemporary newspaper articles, a different picture of the Swedish Nazi movement's propaganda campaigns emerges. Journalist and author Armas Sastamoinen, who has written what is effectively a standard work on Swedish Nazism of the 1930s and 40s, describes how in its own documents the Lindholm Movement had guidelines and instructions for slander and whispering campaigns. The Nordic Youth had its own newspaper – *Makt* (Power) – intended solely for its executives, containing explicit guidelines on how to pursue such campaigns. If slander and whispering failed, there were staged acts of violence designed, as they themselves put it, to make the Swedish people wake up to exactly what is at stake. One such act is performed by SA man Gösta Wiklund in 1933, who, along with a couple of Nazi companions, shoots himself and then tries to dupe the police and journalists into believing that the Communists are the culprits. To Wiklund's great indignation, the ploy fails. And there is no awakening of the Swedish people.

Swedish Nazi rallies often degenerated into brawls. Physical assault, gun running and shooting outside the offices of newspapers published by rivals were not uncommon. Journalists were also threatened and hung out as Jewish lackeys. Those who wrote about the Lindholm Movement risked receiving threatening letters. In the same documentary that featured Gustaf Ekström, *Blågul Nazism* from 1993, journalist Carl-Adam Nycop recounts what it was like to cover and write about the NSAP:

"I was swiftly branded a Jewish lackey and after that I received a torrent of threats, anonymous letters, they were going to castrate

me and they were going to do everything and anything. As you can imagine, it wasn't that nice but it was typical of their methods back then."

In Germany, the Nazis start taking things further. Not satisfied with disseminating their definition of the Jew as their and the German people's enemy via propaganda and rallies, they enact the Nuremburg Laws on 15 September 1935, legally establishing the alleged racial differences and thus depriving Jews of their German citizenship. In Sweden, the NSAP welcomes the laws in its official party organ, *Den Svenske Nationalsocialisten*. With the Nuremburg Laws in place, the German Nazis could widen their attack from tormenting Jews through propaganda, defamation, intimidation and violence to legally expropriating their property.

In 1936 Ekström resigns as secretary of the Nordic Youth and moves back to Lindesberg. Ekström has managed to secure a job at an Örebro paper mill. But this in no way means that his political commitments cease.

In October of the same year, he adds his name to a Nazi appeal published in Stormfacklan announcing the founding of a new offshoot of the Swedish Nazi Party, *Sällskapet för Svensk Fostran* (roughly: the Society for Swedish breeding). It contains the following line:

"The society shall support movements that protect our national heritage, that seek to maintain a healthy martial spirit in our youth towards our dysfunctional democracy."

Adverts that Sällskapet för Svensk Fostran placed in the same newspaper trumpet the association's messages: "Be Swedish" and "For Fatherland and Swedishness".

In 1937 Ekström moves to Engelbrektsgatan in Örebro, where he is appointed block (i.e. district) leader. He purchases shares in NS-press, the Nazi's own printing firm, for 500 kronor. The sum might seem modest but converted into today's money it amounts to almost 15,000 kronor – a goodly sized sum to invest in a risky political printing company. He also sends Christmas greetings to the party organ *Den Svenske Nationalsocialisten*. In 1938 he climbs another rung up his political career and becomes the party's SA leader in Örebro. SA stands for *Stormavdelning* in direct emulation of the German Nazis' Sturmabteilung (literally Storm Detachment).

Gustaf Ekström and his Nazi party companions encountered fierce resistance in Swedish society. The SA home in Gothenburg and the Nazi press were subjected to boycotts imposed by, respectively, the Transport Workers' Union and the Typographical Association. The trade union movement in Sweden was quick to realise the threat posed by Nazism and the conflict between the organisations occasionally ended in tumult and uproar. Already during the 1930s, the police were dispatching stenographers to the party meetings, where they collected newspaper articles and registered the names of sympathisers and party members. In February 1935 the police raid the party's Gothenburg headquarters on suspicion of violating the Act concerning illegal military activity by forming a paramilitary group. The case is concluded in court in August 1935 with an acquittal, which the NSAP took as a great propaganda victory; but it is a victory without political impact. Swedish voters are less interested in what the Nazis call the Jewish Question than in the price of milk and cereals.

The Swedish Trade Union Confederation, LO, relentlessly attacks the Nazis, mounting a resistance that Sven Olov Lindholm devotes a great deal of space to in his 1943 book *Svensk frihetskamp*. Nazism is accused by the trade union movement of being anti-worker and for the remainder of the 1930s LO wages a campaign denouncing the Nazis as traitors. In 1938, the hard-pressed party executive decides to change its name from the National Socialist Workers' Party to Swedish Socialist Unity, SSS (for the sake of simplicity we use the abbreviation NSAP/SSS to emphasise that it is the same party under a new name). And while the swastika is exchanged for the more Swedish Vasa sheaf, it does not mean that it is completely replaced; indeed, it often appears in stylised fashion above the sheaf emblem.

In the mid-1930s, the Swedish Nazis are enjoying the wind in their sails; they have international support and a momentum in their propaganda campaigns, boosted perhaps as people's curiosity is piqued by the movement that has come to power in neighbouring Germany. That said, their results in Sweden are very modest, if not a complete fiasco. The tally of members is about 10,000, and despite what the Swedish Nazis try to pass off as a successful struggle against Jews and Bolsheviks, the NSAP/SSS never win more than a paltry 17,000 or so votes in the 1936 General Election to the Second Chamber of the Riksdag.

Gustaf Ekström moves to Sundsvall in April 1939. He takes rooms with a woman at Sjögatan 7 and works as a cartographer for his brother-in-law, surveyor Albin Edlund. Of interest in this context is that Albin Edlund also sympathised with Swedish Nazism. In 1935 and 1937 he sent Christmas greetings to the National Socialist Bloc's organ *Riksposten*. The National Socialist Bloc was a rival of the NSAP/SSS.

On 1 September 1939 Germany invades Poland and the Second World War begins. Ironically, Nazism's triumphs in Germany will be a problem for the Swedish Nazis, many of whose key personages are drafted into emergency military standby, which was a severe blow to a movement that was dependent on the primarily young male members of its travelling propaganda teams.

On the same day as the outbreak of war, Ekström moves back to Örebro from Sundsvall. He is now employed at Åkers gun factory. However, his time there is short-lived as the war creeps closer to Sweden in general and to Gustaf Ekström in particular.

On 1 February 1940 Gustaf Ekström is called up to emergency military service with I3 regiment. He spends 48 days with the Life Company and is demobbed on 19 March. But already on 13 April 1940 he and hundreds of thousands of Swedish men are called up on standby again when Germany invades Denmark and Norway.

This time, Ekström ended up not in the Life Company but in the regimental depot. The invasion of our neighbours came as a shock and emergency standby is Sweden's answer to the threat that Nazi Germany poses to the country. In the course of a few weeks, France, Belgium and Holland also capitulate.

In 1940 when the Security Police start to step up their registration of Nazis in Sweden, Gustaf Ekström is one of those on whom they have their eye. In his files in the Security Police archive he is described as a fanatical and zealous Nazi.

In the war archive, we find Ekström's enlistment card *(stamkort)*, the document on which the defence forces registered details of their conscripts. Brief annotations on the yellow card-index card provide details of Ekström's military service. Attached to the card is a discipline card *(straffkort)* on which we can read that Ekström was found guilty of insulting a superior, improper conduct and neglect of duty. For this he was sentenced to six days close arrest. While the discipline card contains only these indications of character, more is revealed from his Security Police file, from which we learn that the police and military authorities are happy that he is serving at the depot, and not with one of the companies. A memo from the file states briefly:

"Ekström, a conscripted officer cadet with recruitment number 104 41/27, is currently serving at the I.3 depot as an assistant to the barracks officer. One must thus consider him to be working at a very harmless place, which, given what is known of him, must be considered satisfactory."

Ekström recalls this time in the 1993 interview:

"Life for the supporters of the European Nazis became increasingly hard-pressed on all sides of the home front. I too was pressed at the military unit I belonged to, where many soldiers and recruits found out about my political convictions. So I decided to leave Sweden for a few years and to enlist as a volunteer in Germany in the Waffen-SS."

Yet again, a determined Ekström finds that Sweden holds no future for him. In March 1941, his military duties come to an end and by April he decides to take the plunge and investigate the possibility of volunteering for the forces he has only recently been called up to stand guard against. Throughout our researches we have naturally asked ourselves: Why?

We have found three reasons that Gustaf Ekström gives for applying to the Waffen-SS. Two are purely ideological and the third is a consequence of his ideological convictions. In 1993 Ekström says that during his time in the Waffen-SS, he felt he was waging war on international Jewry:

"We constantly felt that we were fighting the domination of international Jewry over Europe and other continents. This we believed wholeheartedly."

He continues:

"We, and I can also say Swedes in general, would have wanted to see a purely fascist or Nazi Europe from North to South, from West to East, with the point aimed at Russia, which was then our arch enemy.... We wanted victory for Nazism and its allies, Mussolini, and Franco in Spain."

The alleged conspiracy theory about the domination of international Jewry that Ekström mentions is an invented anti-Semitic notion that holds Jews guilty of consolidating power and money for themselves in order to cast other peoples into perdition. It is an idea spread by the Lindholm Nazis and one that can still be encountered in various anti-Semitic contexts. The war on world Jewry was thus one of the motives that Ekström had for joining the Waffen-SS. Gustaf Ekström also said that he fought for Hitler's Germany in order to benefit the Swedish Nazis, convinced that a victory for Hitler over Great Britain would benefit the national movement in Sweden. In other words, there is a domestic policy reason for his serving with the Waffen-SS. In a letter to the German author Hans Werner Neulen he writes:

"A German victory over England would help the national organisations in Sweden to gain the upper hand in the political struggle."

When Ekström was interrogated by Säpo (the Swedish Security Police) after the war, he gave yet another reason: that his commitment to the Nazi cause after his military service in Sweden in 1941 made it difficult for him to find work at home. The fact is, however, that he could not have been looking for work for very long. He was demobbed in March and by April he was visiting the German legation in Stockholm to investigate the possibility of working for the Germans. Here he was told by the German authorities at the legation that a door stood open for him in the Waffen-SS.

On Walpurgis Night on 30 April 1941, Ekström travelled legally to Norway via the border crossing in Charlottenberg, issued with passport no. A:7647 and a visa made out by the German legation. From there he made his way down to Oslo and on to the SS recruitment office on Drammensveien, where he enlists into the Waffen-SS on 1 May 1941.

Chapter 5
Racial theory on the agenda

Gustaf Ekström spent a couple of nights in Oslo, probably at the SS barracks in Voxenkollen, just outside the capital, or at the Majorstuen barracks in the centre. He was then dispatched by rail on 6 May back through Sweden to Germany with troops on leave – this *permittenttrafik*, or "German train" as it was popularly known, was a Swedish concession to Nazi Germany during the early years of the War. Ekström thus travelled from Oslo via Trelleborg-Sassnitz down to Sennheim in occupied France, where the SS had its own training camps for recruits in the Waffen-SS called the *SS-Schule*, later known as *SS-Ausbildungslager*.

Ekström had the company of at least two other Swedish volunteers in Sennheim, Stig Cederholm and Olof Sandström, both of whom were also members of a Swedish Nazi organisation – Cederholm in Swedish Opposition/The New Swedish Movement and Sandström a fellow member of the NSAP/SSS. However, after their stint in Sennheim they seem to have separated. We have found no evidence to suggest that they stayed together.

It is estimated that some 100 to 200 Swedes enlisted with the Waffen-SS to fight for Nazi Germany during the Second World

War. Historian Tobias Hübinette has tried to compile a statistic and has arrived at upward of 180 Swedish volunteers. Regardless of the exact figure, the number of Swedes who decided to volunteer for the SS was modest compared to Danes and Norwegians, the number of whom can be counted in their thousands. Volunteering for the Waffen-SS must thus be regarded as a marginal activity that never really took root in Sweden. On the other hand, the proportion of Nazis and party sympathisers in the NSAP/SSS is greatly over-represented in the group of Swedes who signed up for the Waffen-SS.

It is usually claimed, a little perfunctorily, that the men who went over to the Waffen-SS were wayward young adventure-seekers; not so the determined and resolute Gustaf Ekström. Many others had to make their way illegally over the border to Norway, while he was able to travel there legally. It was difficult for men of an arms-bearing age, who were needed in the Swedish emergency military service, to obtain a pass for travelling out of the country. It is truly remarkable that Ekström was given such a document, despite having only recently been demobbed from I3.

According to a memo from the Swedish Consulate-General in Oslo on 19 February 1943, in obtaining his pass Ekström had been abetted by a company commander at Skövde logistic training regiment. At the age of 33 when joining the Waffen-SS, Ekström was one of the oldest Swedes to sign up as a volunteer during the entire war. In the interview from 1993, Ekström claims, wrongly, that he was about 25. It is possible that his memory failed him, but it is also possible that his words were both a very subtle apology and an attempt to play down the severity of his decision to join the War. On at least two points, however – his age and his legal border-crossing – Ekström stands apart from the other SS volunteers.

The Norwegian historian Harry Ellingsen has presented statistics on the enlistment of Norwegian volunteers in his book *Regiment Norge*. If we compare the time when Ekström applied to join the Waffen-SS, already in May 1941, he is one and a half years ahead of the peak of the autumn/spring of 1942/43 for the Nor-

1. Gustaf Ekström, in the municipal school in Lindesberg, 1923–1924. Ekström is in the middle row on the far left. Photo: Alfred Michelson, Lindesberg archive of cultural history.

2. Gustaf Ekström, school photograph, Örebro Technological Gymnasium, 1928. Photo: Örebro municipal archive.

3. Gustaf Ekström, third person sitting to the right. Family photograph, c. 1928, Lindesberg. Photo: Alfred Michelson, Lindesberg archive of cultural history.

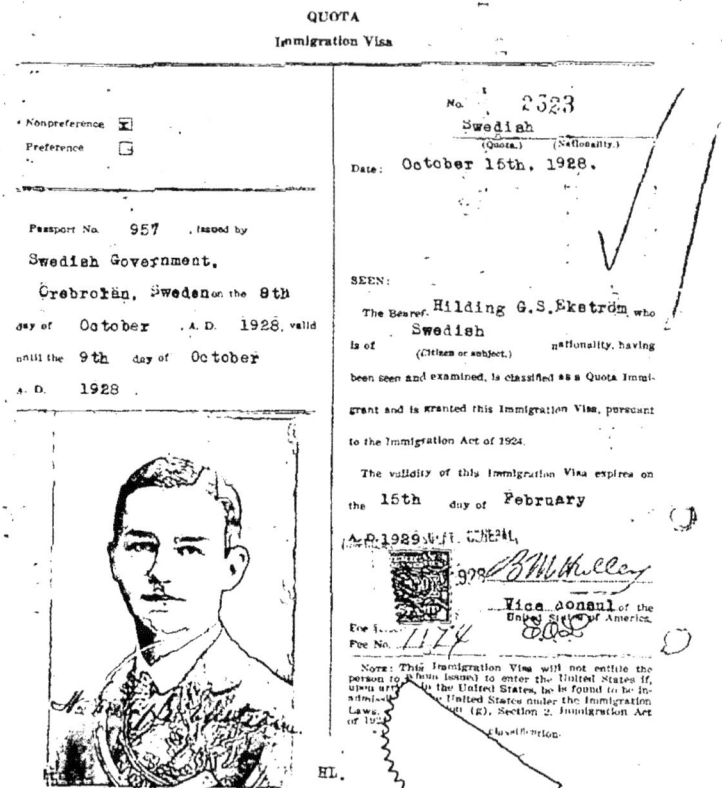

4. Gustaf Ekström. Photograph from his visa to the USA, 1928. U.S. Department of Homeland Security, U.S. Citizenship and Immigration Services.

5. Gustaf Ekström, SA uniform, NSAP/SSS, c. 1935. Ekström is sitting in the bottom row to the far right. Photo: The Bosse Schön archive.

6. Sven Olov Lindholm leader of the Swedish Nazi party (NSAP /SSS) holds speech from the pulpit at a meeting probably around 1942. Photo: Pressens Bild/TT

7. Swedish nazis on the march 1933. The flags were blue with yellow swastikas. Photo: TT.

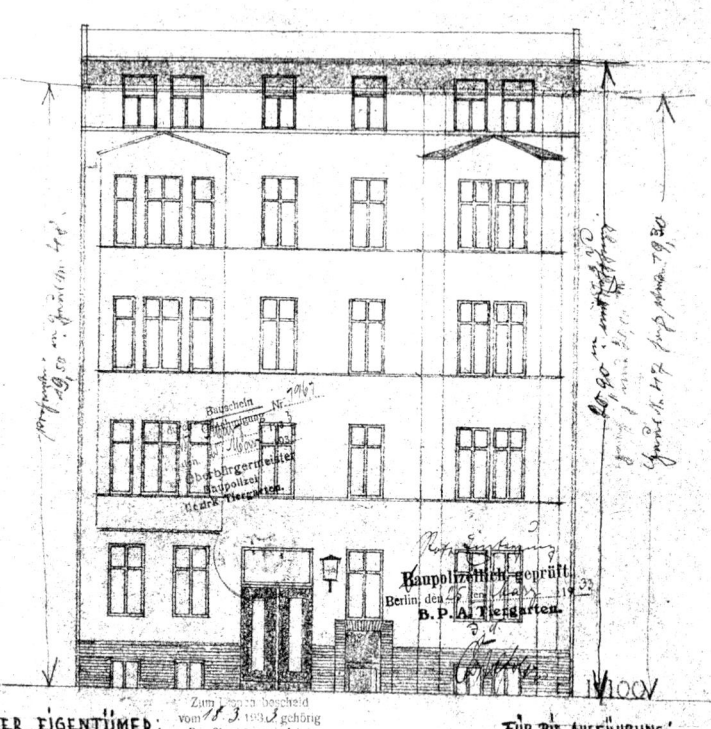

8. Plans of the Jewish nursing home at Lützowstrasse 48/49. The plans were drawn by architect Gustav Bauer and approved by Berlin's building inspectorate on 25 March 1933. To the left is the signature of Martin Salomonski, director of the nursing home. Landesarchiv Berlin.

Jüdisches Altersheim, Lützowstr. 48

9. Jüdisches Altersheim, Lützowstrasse 48, September 1933. Photo: Courtesy of the Leo Baeck Institute, New York.

Gedächtnistafel

10. Plaque commemorating the opening of the Jüdisches Altersheim, Lützowstrasse 48, September 1933. Photo: Courtesy of the Leo Baeck Institute, New York.

Kommerzienrat Adolf Jandorf s. A.

11. Painting of Adolf Jandorf (in whose memory the home was opened), Jüdisches Altersheim, Lützowstrasse 48, September 1933. Photo: Courtesy of the Leo Baeck Institute, New York.

12. Day-room (note the newspapers hanging on the wall), Jüdisches Altersheim, Lützowstrasse 48, September 1933. Photo: Courtesy of the Leo Baeck Institute, New York.

13. Dining room, Jüdisches Altersheim, Lützowstrasse 48, September 1933. Photo: Courtesy of the Leo Baeck Institute, New York.

14. Assembly room (note the leaded windows facing the street), Jüdisches Altersheim, Lützowstrasse 48, September 1933. Photo: Courtesy of the Leo Baeck Institute, New York.

Andachtsnische im Festsaal

15. Devotional niche in the assembly room, Jüdisches Altersheim, Lützowstrasse 48, September 1933. Photo: Courtesy of the Leo Baeck Institute, New York.

16. Single room, Jüdisches Altersheim, Lützowstrasse 48, September 1933. Photo: Courtesy of the Leo Baeck Institute, New York.

wegian volunteers. Age-wise, he is 10 years older than the vast majority of Norwegian SS volunteers, who were mostly between 18 and 26. He was also one of the first, not just from a Swedish perspective but from the Norwegian too.

Once in Sennheim, Ekström collected his equipment and lodged with other volunteers in the barracks. The camp, which largely still exists, lies in beautiful rolling countryside fringed by distant mountain peaks. For a few weeks that summer, Ekström was drilled in the basic Nazi racial ideas, texts and theories. Given his political engagement in Sweden, the content of these lessons would hardly have been alien to him. Other Swedish volunteers later reported that they felt uncomfortable with the theses drummed into the soldiers in Sennheim.

The training camp in Sennheim had opened on 17 November 1940, and during Ekström's time at the school, it was led by first commandant Rudolf Jacobsen. The school was set up to deal with the lack of familiarity that recruits from the occupied countries had for Teutonic discipline, which their German counterparts had already learnt through their mandatory membership of the *Hitlerjugend*. Films were also on the schedule. *Jud Süss* and *Der Ewige Jude*, two German anti-Semitic propaganda films that Joseph Goebbels had ordered for the German public, were part of the compulsory schedule. The recruits had to sit for hours studying the history of the German Nazi party and learning more about the "Great German and European Idea" and about the SS as the spearhead of Nazism. Part of the training was also adapted to the volunteers' home countries, so the Scandinavian recruits had to imbibe a vast quantity of teaching on the Jewish race and the alleged threat it was meant to pose to the Scandinavian countries.

All teaching was done in German, and while a problem for most recruits, for Gustaf Ekström – who had studied German at school in Sweden – it was probably something that set him apart from the rest of the barrack. He was presumably asked by non-German speaking volunteers to explain the news, the camp rules or sundry orders from the officers. A typical day for Gustaf Ekström at Sennheim might have looked like this:

07:30–08:30 Work as duty and honour
08:45–09:45 The history and basic tenets of the SS
09:45–10:45 Jewry
10:50–11:50 National socialist racial theory
14:00–15:00 Eastern policy
15:15–16:15 Nationalism
16.30–17:45 Film – Jud Süss

In addition to all this was, naturally, physical activity, drills and marching. On certain evenings, when off duty, Ekström might have visited one of the town's cafés with Cederholm and Sandström. The ideological education also included how SS soldiers were to conduct themselves as servants of the Führer. They also learned details of Adolf Hitler's early years and his struggle for the German people. Keywords on the agenda were lebensraum, blood affinity, and the necessity of marshalling all German energies into a Greater German Empire. The theories were presented as facts, despite their almost complete lack of anchoring in either science or the real world.

A decisive event occurs during Gustaf Ekström's time in Sennheim. On 22 June 1941 Germany invades the Soviet Union. Later, both in 1981 and 1993, Gustaf Ekström maintains that it was then that he realised that Germany was going to lose the War. In 1981, he is asked by the military historian Hans Werner Neulen to name the one most irreversible and critical event during his time with the Waffen-SS.

He answers thus:

"When Germany declared war on Soviet Russia on 22 June 1941: Now Germany and its supporters will lose the War."

In the 1993 interview, he says the following:

"It was the evening of 21 June 1941. The loudspeakers announced that Adolf Hitler had declared war on Soviet Russia. My first words to my companions were: Germany's going to lose the War."

Maybe Ekström did indeed know that Germany was going to lose the War; but given where we was just then, at a training camp for SS soldiers, and given that he was a devout and dedicated "anti-Bolshevik", he would have been unlikely to have made much of his defeatism, an attitude for which would almost certainly have been disciplined. It would be considered rather naive to think that there were no cheers and rejoicing – and singing too, no doubt – to be heard in the SS school when the announcement of the attack on the Soviet Union blared out. The situation in June 1941 also indicated that Germany was on the brink of complete victory, with much of continental Europe under its feet, Britain hard-pressed and the USA yet to enter the arena of conflict.

Ekström's observation that the War was lost has to be interpreted in light of his hindsight that the Soviet Union, and the war on the Eastern Front, was what sealed Nazi Germany's fate. Around four out of five German soldiers who were killed or reported missing were fighting the Soviet Union on the Eastern Front. He continues, in the 1993 interview, when asked why he carried on although he knew that the War was lost:

"We fully appreciated that in such circumstances we could not abandon these Germans who had been, I was about to say betrayed, by their leaders to the war on Russia which is and was Germany's destiny."

As already mentioned, Ekström learnt during his time in Sennheim that Germany's lebensraum and German destiny lay in the east, that the future for the "German race" was to stand victorious over the Jewish-Bolshevik conspiracy. But that fate was predicated on a German victory, not a German defeat, and who the victor would be was of course unknown to Ekström when he was in Sennheim. So all his talk of abandonment must be seen more as a post hoc rationalisation; instead, it was probably a matter of following those whom he was ideologically convinced would win.

After the attack on the Soviet Union, some elements of the SS education programme change to include more content on Nazism's illusory Jewish-Bolshevik conspiracy. According to this fabricated notion, the destiny of the German people and of Europe was to be decided in the east, with the SS having the self-appointed role as the critical ideological and racial elite that would secure a German victory in the struggle for lebensraum. All of this was woven into the race-ideological Nazi myths of the purity of German blood and the superiority of the German people.

Over and above this ideological schooling, soldiers were also given a proper dose of physical training and military drills, including day-long marches, with singing, to the First World War monument 956 metres up on Hartmannsweilerkopf peak. When after just over six weeks their studies at Sennheim drew to a close, it was time for Gustaf Ekström to swear an oath of loyalty to Adolf Hitler in Germany:

"*Ich schwöre Dir, Adolf Hitler, als germanischer Führer, Treue und Tapferkeit. Ich gelobe Dir und den von Dir bestimmten Vorgesetzten Gehorsam bis den Tod, so wahr mir Gott helfe.*"

Which translates as:

"*I swear to you, Adolf Hitler, leader of Germany, loyalty and courage. I promise you and those whom you have appointed to lead me, obedience unto death, so help me God.*"

There were several variations on this oath during the War, but the theme of loyalty to Hitler unto death was always the essence. Normally the oath was sworn at ceremonies with drumming, fanfares, flags and standards. Speeches were held and poems read. The oath itself was sworn by the troops in unison as they repeated line by line the prompt of an officer.

Gustaf Ekström promises to lay down his life for Hitler. It is this very ideological and political element of the Waffen-SS that will later weigh heavily in the judgement passed by the Nuremberg tribunal on the organisation after the War.

After the ideological schooling in Sennheim there was basic military training and then service with a Waffen-SS company. In July 1941, Gustaf Ekström arrives at the SS's Wetzelsdorf barracks in the now Austrian city of Graz. He has been transferred to the 2nd replacement battalion of the 4th SS regiment, known as "Der Führer". This Waffen-SS regiment is the first with which Ekström serves. Later, a special replacement battalion is established in Wetzelsdorf for Scandinavian volunteers, but that will not be until late 1941. Until 30 August 1941, the replacement battalion "Der Führer" remained in Wetzelsdorf. It is subsequently transferred to Stralsund in northern Germany, but by then Gustaf Ekström has already left Graz for his first Waffen-SS mission.

It might be worth mentioning that "Der Führer" would be the subject of much comment during the War. Soldiers from the first battalion in the regiment carried out the massacre in Oradour, the French village where over 500 men, women and children were slaughtered on 10 June 1944. The Wetzelsdorf barracks in Graz also have a dark history. At the end of the War, on 2 April 1945, long after Gustaf Ekström had left them, there was a massacre of 219 people, mostly resistance fighters, prisoners of war and Hungarian-Jewish forced labourers, who were shot and thrown into a bomb crater in the football pitch in the middle of the barracks grounds.

Ekström stays at the Wetzelsdorf barracks for about two months. Shooting, exercise and weapon drills are on the curriculum. The length of the training was adjusted according to the soldiers' previous knowledge and experience, and the type of deployment that awaited them. Gustaf Ekström's first posting is not, however, at the front. His skills are needed at the central administration of the SS in Berlin, who saw value in his age (he was, after all, relatively old) and his knowledge of German, Swedish and – following his three years in the USA – English. His long experience of propaganda campaigns from his time with the Swedish NSAP/SSS could also have determined his career in the SS. Ekström had also, as we have discussed, spent some time on standby duty in I3. As the SS's recruitment activities expand, it also needs people who can monitor the countries from which new enlistments to the Waffen-SS can be drawn. It is a job to which Ekström is eminently suited.

On 1 September 1941, Gustaf Ekström reports for duty at the SS-Hauptamt in Berlin, one of twelve SS headquarters.

Chapter 6
A telephone directory reveals its secrets

In the autumn of 2015 we travelled to Berlin. All we knew then was that Ekström had worked at the central office called SS-Hauptamt. We wanted to find out where Gustaf Ekström and the SS-Hauptamt were during the time he served there. The natural first step for us was to start looking at the place where we know the office was located until 1940, on the former Prinz Albrecht Strasse. Here, where the SS and Gestapo once had their offices, is now the large exhibition centre and museum called *Topographie des Terrors* (The Topography of Terror). The centre has a vast library of SS and German Nazi material. Outside, excavated parts of the Gestapo's notorious prison cells and other areas of the building's foundations have been opened to public view. The location is in the centre of Berlin, just next to Hermann Göring's former Ministry of Aviation.

The librarian at the Topographie des Terrors Foundation looks pensive. She has just shown us a map in a well-reputed standard German work on the SS by Tuchel and Schattenfroh. According to this book, in 1943 the SS-Hauptamt was at Lützowstrasse 48/49. But now we are standing perusing Berlin's address book for that year, where a Jewish nursing home for the elderly – Jüdische Altersheime e.V. – is registered at the same address. The librarian shakes her head. That can't be, she says, and opens another book containing copies of correspondence between different SS offices. There too, in the letterheads, the SS-Hauptamt address is given as Lützowstrasse 48/49. Surely a Jewish nursing home cannot be in the same building as one of the SS's central command offices?

We manage to get hold of the 1936 and 1941 Berlin telephone directories in a second-hand bookshop. The nursing home is registered in the 1936 directory but not the one for 1941, where the SS-Hauptamt is now registered at Lützowstrasse 48/49. This is when the penny drops. Our next stop is the *Bundesarchiv* in Berlin, the world's largest archive of documents from Nazi Germany. Here we find an important three-page document dated Berlin 7 January 1941, from which we learn that as of 15 January 1941, the SS-Hauptamt and its subsidiary authorities will be moving into their new offices on Lützowstrasse 48/49. This confirms what we understood from the Berlin telephone directories and address books. The SS confiscated the building from the Jewish nursing home and moved in its own command centre, the SS-Hauptamt, where Gustaf Ekström later served. As so often is the case when we trace Gustaf Ekström's life, every answer raises a new question. Who was living in the home and what happened to them? Who were the people that the SS evicted? And can they still be tracked down, 75 years later?

We start looking for people who could have resided there. Our inquiries at various archives lead nowhere. We find only a few books in German that make any mention at all of Lützowstrasse. Nothing, be it in German, Swedish or English, yields any information. This is a puzzle we will have to piece together ourselves. Finally, we find a lead that we can follow. Since the residents of the nursing home were Jews, we could assume that they had their property confiscated. This means that someone, either themselves or a relative, could have reported being dispossessed of their property after the War. These restitution demands were once registered in Germany in a gigantic card index of over 800,000 records. But we are in luck – the card index has recently been digitalised by the Berlin *Landesarchiv*. It is now much easier to look for appeals for reclaimed property from people who survived or the relatives of those who did not. This is where we score our first hit. We find a restitution demand concerning one Max Ascher, born 28 March 1869, whose last place of residence was Altersheim, Lützowstrasse, Berlin. Max Ascher has lost gold, silver, jewellery, a radio and household utensils. The submitter of the petition is Gertrud Ascher, daughter of Max Ascher. She was born in 1908, making her the same age as Ekström.

Max Ascher is our first find. When we have found him, we realise that it is fully possible, but probably extremely time consuming, to identify all the other residents of the Lützowstrasse nursing home. This means that we have a slight chance of finding out what happened to them. How many of them were there? Who was Max Ascher? Did he survive the War? Did he ever get his jewellery and radio back?

Gustaf Ekström steps through the door of Lützowstrasse 48/49 in Berlin. He settles down in his new uniform to commence his service at the SS-Hauptamt. Gustaf Ekström is working in the rooms that once belonged to a former Jewish nursing home. Maybe he was sitting in Max Ascher's old room, who knows? But what we do know is that Max Ascher and the other pensioners living there had to clear out.

Chapter 7
An organisation built for terror

Gustaf Ekström voluntarily joined a section of an organisation that was created to instil terror. Let us take a closer look at the SS. For most people, the letters SS probably conjure up images of war crimes, terror and concentration camps. And rightly so. The SS was a political and ideological organisation, and the heart of Nazi Germany's security complex. Eventually, the entire SS evolved into a myriad sub-organisations that changed continuously over the course of the War. The organisation is complex and in parts hard to describe.

The SS had two main branches, the *Allgemeine-SS* the *Waffen-SS*, but the line dividing these two branches becomes increasingly diffuse almost to the point of non-existence as the War progresses. The Waffen-SS can most simply be defined as the German Nazi party's own armed forces, and it was this part to which Gustaf Ekström belonged. The SS also had a central administration comprising 12 main offices, which were often staffed by personnel from the Allgemeine-SS, but also from the Waffen-SS. These offices dealt with logistics, administration and other matters for the Waffen-SS, matters of race and settlement, legal issues and intelligence and security activities. In addition to this, the SS managed concentration camp personnel, the mobile killer squads in the Einsatzgruppen, and the SS-Sonderkommandos who managed the extermination camps, such as SS-Sonderkommando Treblinka (not to be confused with the Sonderkommandos that consisted of Jews forced to aid in the incineration of corpses). There were also police units and volunteer activities in the occupied countries. All in all, there were hundreds of thousands of employees spread effectively the length and breadth of occupied Europe.

The SS has a strong position of power in German society. In many respects it would be correct to say that the SS actually operates Nazi Germany's terror machine, one that is trained on both its own population as well as those of the occupied areas. The German security service is controlled with an iron fist by the SS from its headquarters on Prinz Albrecht Strasse, where the Gestapo was also based.

During the SS's most influential era, its mere name could strike fear into anyone simply by virtue of the organisation's brutal reputation. The SS profiled itself as an ideological elite in the German Nazi party, the self-appointed interpreter and implementer of Nazism's political programme.

Heinrich Himmler and his right-hand man Reinhard Heydrich built up the position of power that the SS had in the party and later in the German state. The SS controlled the secret security police – the Gestapo – and had set up its own security service.

The organisation also had control of the power exercised by all other state bodies in every country occupied by Germany. The SS had played a critical part in the German Nazi state's efforts to exterminate and wipe out Europe's Jewish population. The SS planned, administrated and implemented the Holocaust, abetted by all of German society.

The Waffen-SS eventually came to comprise a force of hundreds of thousands of men who fought on all fronts or worked at the central SS administration in Berlin. The expansion of the Waffen-SS was also a way for Himmler to compete with the regular

Wehrmacht generals – a way, in other words, for his organisation to appropriate power in the Nazi state apparatus.

The Waffen-SS was also an organisation that accepted volunteers from other countries. Their recruitment activities were important for the SS and a means by which the Waffen-SS was able to grow. Recruitment was overseen by the SS-Hauptamt in Berlin, where Gustaf Ekström worked. The head of the SS-Hauptamt was SS-Obergruppenführer Gottlob Berger. In March 1941, Berger tasked the Swiss SS-Obersturmbannführer Franz Riedweg and SS-Oberführer Rudolf Jacobsen with establishing a network of recruitment offices through which the SS hoped to reach men who were willing to fight for Nazism. The offices were placed under the charge of the SS-Hauptamt and located in the occupied countries that were considered to qualify as "Germanic" in the SS's race-ideological worldview – Norway amongst them.

The SS and the rest of the Nazi bureaucratic apparatus expanded substantially in Berlin during the War, a process that had begun effectively when it came to power in 1933 but that gathered real momentum after the outbreak of war and before the invasion of the Soviet Union in June 1941. A spate of offices and branches of the Nazi party's countless organisations opened around Berlin at the time of Gustaf Ekström's arrival in the organisation, which is when the SS has developed into one of the most – if not the most – important instruments of power in Nazi Germany. Its power derived from the violence or intimidation that the organisation managed to spread, whether at the hands of the Gestapo, through the concentration or death camp executions, or as units at the front.

Chapter 8
There were 256 of them

We found them. We found the names of all the residents of the Jewish nursing home. Using data from the census that was taken in Germany on 17 May 1939, we were able to compile as complete a list as possible. The question we asked ourselves about how many who had survived the War had, however, a dismal answer.

The 1939 census was conducted in Germany and the annexed areas of Austria and the Sudetenland. According to the 1935 Nuremburg Laws a person with one or two Jewish grandparents was considered mixed-race Jewish, while someone with more than two was counted as fully Jewish. Consequently, every head of household had to fill in a supplementary card on the possible Jewish background of every family member's grandparents. Those who declared one or more Jewish grandparents were gathered in a "minority census". These cards were collected by the Reichssippenamt, the special authority in Nazi Germany assigned to identify people's origins and bloodline. The cards remained intact throughout the War.

Thanks in part to the efforts of the non-profit organisation "Tracing the past e.V.", much of the census has now been digitalised and rendered searchable. One of the card items to have been codified is place of residence.

When we studied the photographs of the nursing home on Lützowstrasse, we counted 42 seats in the dining room and figured that there were probably around 70 people living at the address, assuming that the residents ate in two shifts and that some of the rooms or apartments were possibly fitted with their own kitchenettes. But when we do a search on Lützowstrasse 48/49 we get hundreds of hits. Max Ascher is there. The names continue: Abraham, Arndt, Aronsohn, Auerbach, Baumgardt, Dawidowsky, Hagelberg, Hirsch, Hirschberg – all in all, 256 individuals comprising 184 women and 72 men. Even though the majority of the residents were elderly, it turns out that it was home to younger people too. We also find entire families living there. Some of the youngest in the building were only around 20 years old. The nursing home on Lützowstrasse was probably filled beyond its capacity in 1939. The persecutions have been going on since the Nazis came to power and the rules have gradually forced more and more Jews into cohabitation.

Now that we have all the names, birth dates and birth places of all the former residents of the building in which Ekström later worked, we can proceed to try to piece together the puzzle of what happened to them. We start by comparing the names on our list with those in *Gedenkbuch Berlins*, the book published as a memorial to the Jewish victims of National Socialism in Berlin. It is an enormous tome, as thick as a telephone directory, that weighs in at 3.5 kilos. Its 1,450 pages contain 56,969 names of Jews in Berlin who were murdered during the Second World War. In addition to standard personal details like birthday and birth place is information about deportation and about where and when each person died. After having studied memorial books and details from the Bundesarchiv, we find that 166 of those who lived on Lützowstrasse were murdered during the Holocaust, five of them having been driven to suicide by the persecutions. All in all we have been able to ascertain the fate of 237 of the 256 individuals we found in the census; regrettably, what became of 19 of these people we will probably never know. Eight people managed to emigrate, Agnes Keiler and Selma Bütow to the USA, Rose Kalenscher, Moritz and Doris Holzheim, Leopold and Regina Jablonowski to Brazil and Paula Rosenbaum to Cuba. Another two, Michael Jacubowski and Amalia Rosenthal were deported, but were amongst the 1,200 Jews whose freedom was bought from Theresienstadt and who were then taken to Switzerland on 5–7 February 1945. With the help of the International Tracing Service we can also confirm that Renate Golinski, one of the younger residents on Lützowstrasse, survived. In the memorial book she is incorrectly listed as murdered, but thanks to other registries, including the list of people liberated from Mauthausen concentration camp, we are able to follow her struggle to survive through various extermination and concentration camps. A total of eleven of the 256 Jews who once lived on Lützowstrasse survived the War; three of them survived the horrors of the camps, eight managed to escape by fleeing Germany.

We also find eyewitness accounts from the nursing home in Ester Golan's book *"Auf Wiedersehen in unserem Land"*. Ester Golan was rescued during the Holocaust by her parents, who had managed to secure a place for her on one of the *kindertransports* from Berlin to Scotland. The book contains letters that Ester's parents later wrote to her from Berlin.

In the letters, Ester's mother gives an account of what it was like to work at the nursing home on Lützowstrasse. In September 1939 she writes to her daughter the following:

"I have been working in the kitchen of the nursing home on Lützowstraße since 15 August. The work is very interesting and varied. In the first fortnight, I cleaned 6-8 rooms per floor, three toilets, a bathroom and two really long corridors every day. I must, and am happy to do all these chores. Right now I just work in the kitchen and distribute dinner on two floors with another woman. The dist-

ribution I will have to gradually learn. We distribute just short of 300 portions."

She continues in another letter:

"My job at the nursing home is going really well. Renate Golinski is good and hard-working, and she treats me with courtesy and affection."

On 15 December, she writes that she is working hard. She rises at 5:30 a.m. and goes to work; she is to have cleaned and heated up two ovens by the morning. The letter also reveals that she worked in the kitchen with one of the eight surviving people of the 256, Renate Golinski. Renate Golinski was 15 when this letter was written. It is also worth noting the number of portions: "just short of 300" – a figure that tallies with the information we found in the census on the number of residents.

Yad Vashem in Israel is a momentum a museum, an archive and a research centre devoted to the memory of the victims and heroes of the Holocaust. Its archive contains 62 million documents, testimonies, photographs and other such material, including a register of the victims of the Shoah – the Hebrew term for the Holocaust. Here we find more information on the hundreds of people who once lived in the nursing home. We find copies of transport lists drawn up for the deportation of Jews from Berlin, interrogation transcripts and testimonies recorded on both paper and film. Our picture of events clears.

After Hitler came to power in early 1933, the same year as the home on Lützowstrasse was opened, anti-Jewish propaganda and violence intensified. There were assaults in broad daylight by uniformed SA men and raids on shops and Jewish institutions. Jews were dragged off to local SA offices, beaten up and robbed of their possessions. In April 1933, the Nazi party called for a comprehensive boycott of Jewish shopkeepers, doctors, lawyers and other professionals. In the following June, Jews were forbidden to run market stalls in Berlin; Jewish doctors had their licences revoked and a great many Jewish civil servants lost their jobs. The Jewish community in Berlin, faced with the growing number of people excluded from their jobs, expanded its social welfare provision in an attempt to deal with the ever-worsening situation.

In 1933, 19,000 Jews in Berlin were dependent on the Jewish community's own welfare undertakings. Yet another 21,000 received the so-called "winter aid". In 1934, teachers who had married a Jew that year were prohibited from working in the city's schools. It became harder and harder for Jews to make a living in Berlin, and by the end of the year, over 22,000 of them had emigrated and fled. However, the number of emigrant Jews from Berlin then drops to 6,000 in 1935, to rise slightly again to an annual 10,000 or so from 1938 to 1938. The decline cannot be attributed, however, to any easing of the situation for Jews in Berlin; rather it is an indication of the opposite. In just two years, the Berlin authorities introduced 55 different regulations and a raft of other measures that strictly limited Jewish assets. They simply could not afford to leave. From 1938 to 1939, 32,000 Jews leave Berlin in what must be seen as a last ditch effort to flee. The laws are now so draconian that any Jew who chooses to emigrate is more or less destitute.

As mentioned above, September 1935 saw the enactment of the Nuremburg Laws, a collection of legislative measures that gave the Nazi authorities licence to define who was a Jew and to then deprive that person of their civil rights. When the laws were introduced, effectively all Jews in public service lost their jobs. As time passed, the laws were supplemented with other provisions, everything from declaring park benches "Not for Jews" to the barring of Jews from certain parts of the city, such as parks and bathing areas. In this way, all of society was included in the pogrom. And things grew worse. In 1938, kristallnacht sees a national campaign of persecution against synagogues and shops. Jews are forbidden to own a telephone, shops and firms are confiscated and forcibly sold to "Aryan" purchasers. In 1939, Jews in Berlin start to be subjected to forced labour. In June 1940, the first step is taken towards the large-scale mass-murder of the "insane" in Nazi Germany, when 200 Jewish patients, women, men and children are collected by bus from Sanatorium Berlin-Buch and transferred to Brandenburg asylum, where they are gassed to death.

In September 1941, the same month that Gustaf Ekström arrives in Berlin and starts working at the SS-Hauptamt on Lützowstrasse, a rule is implemented that compels all Jews in Berlin to wear the Star of David on their clothes.

German historian Akim Jah describes in his book on the deportations of Berlin's Jews what happened when another nursing home was sequestered, one at Berkaerstrasse 31–34. This was the flagship of the Jewish welfare institutions. Using Akim Jah's account, we can start to imagine the fate of the nursing home on Lützowstrasse. The Gestapo probably sent a seizure order for the nursing home to the Jewish community in Berlin at some point in 1940, stating that the building had to be evacuated and the residents re-housed in other, already over-full nursing homes in the city. The property at Lützowstrasse 48/49 was seized by the Gestapo and the Jewish nursing home was forced to cease operating. Some of their possessions the residents are possibly allowed to keep, but given that the homes that they are to be sent to are already overcrowded, there is not much they can take with them. The building is then renovated at the expense of the Jewish community. We may assume, for one, that the assembly room's leaded windows with their stained glass symbols of Judaism are summarily replaced.

For other seized properties, existing invoices show that the evicted Jews are made to pay for the repainting and renovation of the apartments and homes that the German authorities have stolen under the leadership of Albert Speer. The building is "Aryanised" by the German authorities, and on 15 January 1941 the SS-Hauptamt moves in.

By January 1941, all the residents at Lützowstrasse 48/49 had already been evicted to other addresses around Berlin, mostly to other nursing homes or Jewish properties. Some 20 Jews were moved a mere 100 metres down the street to a property at Lützowstrasse 77, close to Magdeburger Platz. Another two dozen or so were moved to Derfflingerstrasse 17, a street that crosses Lützowstrasse. About 40 Jews who had once been residents of the nursing home find themselves within a radius of 100 metres from the SS-Hauptamt.

This means that Gustaf Ekström works just a hundred or so metres from many of the former residents. It is not only in a figurative sense that his path was once trod by the Jews once living on Lützowstrasse; it is literally the case too. They have entered and exited using the same doors, they have walked the same pavements, looked out of the same windows, and boarded the same tram at the same stop. Ekström has sat in the same day-room, tripped on the same stairs as the 256 Jews we have found in the archives and memorial books.

After the residents have been evicted, AG Gesellschaft für automatische Telephonie continues to send invoices to the Jewish community for the telephone installation, and to the people responsible for its finances, it must have felt deeply unjust for the telephone company to kick up a fuss about a 37 riksmark bill when they have just been dispossessed of one of their finest nursing homes. The invoice also shows in a sense how the persecution of the Jews was ignored in the day-to-day life of the city. Everything continues as normal, as if the expropriation of their property, including the telephone installation, has never happened. What is important is that the bill gets paid.

Chapter 9
At the SS-Hauptamt

When Gustaf Ekström arrives in Berlin in late August-early September 1941, the SS-Hauptamt has been operating from Lützowstrasse for upwards of seven months, with some two score Jews from its premises living only a hundred or so metres away. They walked there with the obligatory yellow Star of David sewn in full view on their left breast, while Ekström went around in his new uniform with his SS-Hauptamt band sewn onto his left sleeve. Did they ever meet each other's eye? Did Gustaf Ekström even see them?

During these first months in Berlin, Ekström saw a city in a fairly undamaged state. To be sure, the British were dispatching bombers over Berlin, but still on a tiny scale compared with the later war.

The night between 2 and 3 September 1941, the RAF carries out a night-time raid on the city. It is probably the first bombardment that Gustaf Ekström has experienced since starting work at the SS-Hauptamt on 1 September 1941. Full-scale war has at last come to Berlin. 49 British bombers take part and pound nearby Friedrichshain, the cattle market and the railway stations in the eastern part of the city.

Unlike his time in Sennheim and Wetzelsdorf, out of range of the British bombers, the air raid sirens, the searchlights illuminating the dark Berlin night, the explosions and the returning flak must have been a novel experience for Gustaf Ekström that night. And it would not be the last bombing raid he would experience either.

Even though this raid alone had no major military consequence or destructive impact on Berlin, it is probably still a very special occasion during Ekström's time with the Waffen-SS.

One of the first things Gustaf Ekström does when he is settled in Berlin is to make contact with the NSAP/SSS's Ortsgrupp. Its offices are, as we have mentioned, at Immelmannstrasse 10. He reports there, as NSAP/SSS volunteers in Germany are instructed to. Here, he and the other volunteer Swedes have an opportunity to meet and presumably discuss the situation at home. The offices also operate a postal service. Maybe he sends a parcel to his mother, who is still in Lindesberg. He also probably meets Thorolf Hillblad, the journalist and correspondent who oversaw its activities, here too.

The SS-Hauptamt, like at all other SS authorities at this time, is buzzing with activity. The SS administration in Berlin has mushroomed into an enormous organisation employing thousands of people. Its recruitment activities, with which Gustaf Ekström is now occupied, are important.

We hoped we could find Ekström's SS file. So we turned again to the Bundesarchiv, which keeps the SS personnel archive. Just in case, we also contacted the National Archives and Records Administration in Maryland, USA, which holds copies of the entire collection of SS files that was confiscated by the Allies at the end of the War. Regrettably, it seems that Ekström's personal file was misplaced at some point during the War. Even though much of the SS archive has been preserved, parts of it have been lost, either actively destroyed when the Red Army entered Berlin or methodically, such as the files for the 96 individuals who were responsible for Operation Reinhard, of which there is no trace. We also take this opportunity, again to be on the safe side, to contact Deutsche Dienststelle (WASt), which has over 18 million files on people who served in the German army during the Second World War.

A couple of weeks later we receive a reply from the USA, but it is a disappointing one, as it also is from the WASt. We call the officer at the Bundesarchiv who is handling our request. He has at last found Gustaf Ekström in one of the card indices in the Bundesarchiv collection, but not his SS file. After a couple of weeks' further correspondence, we finally receive a copy of a card index entry. Sure enough, it confirms Ekström's enlistment into the Waffen-SS on 1 May 1941. There is also a good deal of other information on the card that we will return to later, but, unfortunately, no details of his official positions.

Many of the Security Police informants in Sweden have reported that Ekström was involved in the SS-Hauptamt's propaganda activities. He read and censored newspaper articles, worked as an interpreter and did translations. This is all very probably true. As we have mentioned, Ekström had a good command of German and English, and when interrogated on his return after the War he told the police himself that he was an SS-Hauptamt interpreter and translator from 1 September to 1 November 1941. His job in this capacity was to translate Swedish newspaper articles about Germany in general and national socialism in particular; as for which conversations and circumstances he acted as an interpreter we can only guess. But since increasing numbers of Swedes applied to the Waffen-SS and far from all spoke German, the organisation needed interpreters. In times of war and internal power struggles, information is crucial, and having someone who can handle foreign languages is, of course, vital for an official body like the SS-Hauptamt.

Ekström's position as an interpreter was part of the extensive recruitment infrastructure that had been put in place under Gottlob Berger and Franz Riedweg. Essentially, the primary function of the SS-Hauptamt was overseeing recruitments to the Waffen-SS in the occupied countries and ancillary responsibilities. Recruitment required the rooms, personnel, intelligence, propaganda and training facilities necessary to indoctrinate the volunteers into the SS worldview. The propaganda material produced by the SS-Hauptamt comprised books, pamphlets and other printed material intended to make the process run as smoothly as possible and to bring soldiers from other countries into line with Nazi ideology.

In October 1941, Hitler launches his attack on Moscow. The final triumph and the capitulation of the Soviet Union are, as the victory-intoxicated Nazis believe, within reach. Anyone who wants to take part in the historic course of events has to get a move on lest he miss the campaign. At some point during the month, Ekström decides, as he later puts it, to "do his bit on the Bolshevik front" and requests voluntary deployment in the east. It is at roughly this time that the deportation of the Jews who had once lived on Lützowstrasse commences.

Chapter 10
Irene Heim

Adolf Hitler approved the plans for the mass deportation of Jews in September 1941, a decision that must be considered in light of the initial military successes on the Eastern front. The war in the east was seen in terms of *Generalplan Ost*, the plans for a German colonisation of eastern Europe and the Soviet Union, whose citizens would be "reduced" and whose homes were to be claimed by Germans. A consequence of this was the genocide.

Intent particularly on exterminating Jews and communists, the SS Einsatzgruppen followed the front line east, murdering as it went. As more and more land was conquered by German forces, the slaughter grows more brutal and capacious, simply because there are more people to kill. Good railway communications in eastern Poland enabled the building of the ghettos, concentration camps and extermination camps. And the geographical distance to Western Europe made it easy to keep what was happening a secret.

The mass-expulsion decision had swift ramifications for Berlin's already hard-pressed Jews. The plans had been drawn up by several high-level Nazi officials in the Nazi administration, of which the SS and Heinrich Himmler was the hub. The Yad Vashem archive contains a letter dated 18 September 1941 that Himmler sent to a regional Nazi leader based in Warthegau in occupied Poland, with a copy to Reinhard Heydrich, head of the Reichssicherheitshauptamt, Nazi Germany's main security Office. He writes:

"It is the Führer's wish that the Third Reich and the protectorate shall be cleansed of Jews as soon as possible, from east to west. I will therefore begin the deportation of Jews this year, if possible...firstly to the areas in the east which fell under the Third Reich two years ago."

Between 15 October and 5 November 1941, the first 20 transports took place from Germany and annexed Austria, Luxemburg and Czechoslovakia. They comprised 19,593 Jews and were destined for the ghetto in Litzmannstadt – as the Polish city of Lodz was renamed after the occupation.

Irene Heim was amongst the expellees from Lützowstrasse 48/49. Born in 1911 and at the age of 30, she was one of the youngest residents. That even younger people also lived in a house for the elderly was due to the forced overcrowding of Berlin's Jews, who having been kicked out their apartments and houses had no choice but to move in with others who had met the same fate. Irene Heim was a bookkeeper by profession, as we learn from the handwritten note on the transport list drawn up ahead of her deportation.

The third transport from Berlin, named simply Transport 3 in the detailed register that the Nazis kept of their deportations, is where we find her. She has been assigned the number 360 in the long roll-call of 1,000 names.

At the same time as Gustaf Ekström receives word that he can start to pack his bags for his trip as a volunteer to the Eastern Front, Irene Heim receives word from the Jewish community. She is to make ready for her deportation. We do not know how Gustaf Ekström looked forward to his new posting. Maybe he saw it as an adventure, something that reminded him of the field excursions he would go on when secretary for the Nordic Youth. Or perhaps it was something more romantic – self-sacrifice at the alter of his ideology, perhaps. Of maybe it was simply a career move in the SS. Nor do we know how Irene Heim felt when she was given her deportation orders. She was probably terrified, or perhaps despondent or in shock.

In 1941 it was initially the Jewish community that was ordered to compile deportation lists for its members and ensure that those on the lists presented themselves at the designated assembly points. Irene Heim was told that she had to make her way to the synagogue on Levetzowstrasse, which had been converted into a transit camp. Here, in central Berlin, we start to see the first cogs in the logistical machine that would drive the Holocaust.

Irene Heim is one of the 1,000 of Jews crowded into the transit camp. Some of them die here, others take their own lives when they are given their deportation papers. When everyone has been counted and the paperwork has been done, they are made to walk the ten kilometres from Levetzowstrasse to Grunewald station in south-west Berlin. Right through the centre of the city the 1,000 Jews walk, before everyone else's eyes. On 27 October 1941 the train leaves the station. The destination is the ghetto in Litzmannstadt. Irene Heim is allocated a place in Reiterstrasse 13/19.

And as the deportation train rattles eastward, Gustaf Ekström flies to Helsinki to assume his new duties in the service of Nazism.

Chapter 11
Propaganda at the front

Gustaf Ekström travels to the Eastern Front to work as a Kriegsberichter, a kind of war reporter or correspondent, for the Waffen-SS 4th war correspondent platoon (Kriegsberichter-Zug), which has been tied to Waffen-SS "Nord" division.

After the First World War, the German armed forces had realised the importance of propaganda and how information can be effectively exploited. Adolf Hitler devotes many pages in *Mein Kampf* to the role of war propaganda and in 1938 ordered the establishment of propaganda companies within the Wehrmacht. At the time of the attack on the Soviet Union, several propaganda companies had been tied to the Eastern Front, including one (PK 680) in Finland. Not wishing to be outdone, the Waffen-SS sets up its own propaganda units in 1940. In August 1941, the 4th war correspondence platoon is transferred to the Waffen-SS "Nord" division, which has been assembled in Finland for the war on the Soviet Union. Finland has been a co-belligerent with Germany against the Soviet Union since 25 June 1941.

Gustaf Ekström arrives in Helsinki, before travelling further north through the country to the inaccessible forests of Karelia. Ekström's "Nord" division is based around the village of Kiestinki, or Kestenga as the Russians call it, and it is here that he starts work in November.

Together with the other soldiers in the war correspondent platoon, Gustaf Ekström reports on the war in Finland. They write texts, take photographs, draw sketches and produce radio broadcasts and films. It is also in the platoon's remit to provide entertainment for the troops.

Ekström's unit is also tasked with running propaganda campaigns against the enemy, such as distributing leaflets designed to undermine the Soviet army's morale, with calls to lay down their arms, surrender and so forth. Other functions are to shield its own soldiers from Soviet propaganda and to mislead and conceal military operations. Ekström's platoon collaborated with the Wehrmacht's propaganda company 680, which was stationed in Finland at the same time. Their propaganda was broadcast by the Lapplandsender radio station in Rovaniemi, and there were several newspapers, such as the *Lappland-Kurier*. Here, readers could learn about German successes, solve crosswords and, of course, immerse themselves in the Nazi worldview and its anti-Semitic doctrine. For here too, in the forests of the far north, Nazi loathing of Jews was prevalent in words and pictures. An article published in the *Lappland-Kurier* on 4 September 1941 carried the double-page headline "Jews set to help. Moscow radio calls for help from all Jews".

Another article refers to a claim made by *Svenska Dagbladet* that in England the general feeling is that if Hitler wins the war in the East within 10 weeks, his position on the continent will be unassailable. On 10 November 1941 the newspaper writes in reference to the Soviet ambassador in the USA, Maxim Litvinov, that the "Jewified USA press... is rejoicing at the career of the Jew Finkelstein (authors' note: although his real name was Litvinov, the Nazi press always wrote Finkelstein to emphasise the Jewish-Bolshevik conspiracy) from street robber to one of the world's leading diplomats". Such anti-Semitic hate writing can be found side-by-side with polished articles about the progress of the War. Headlines

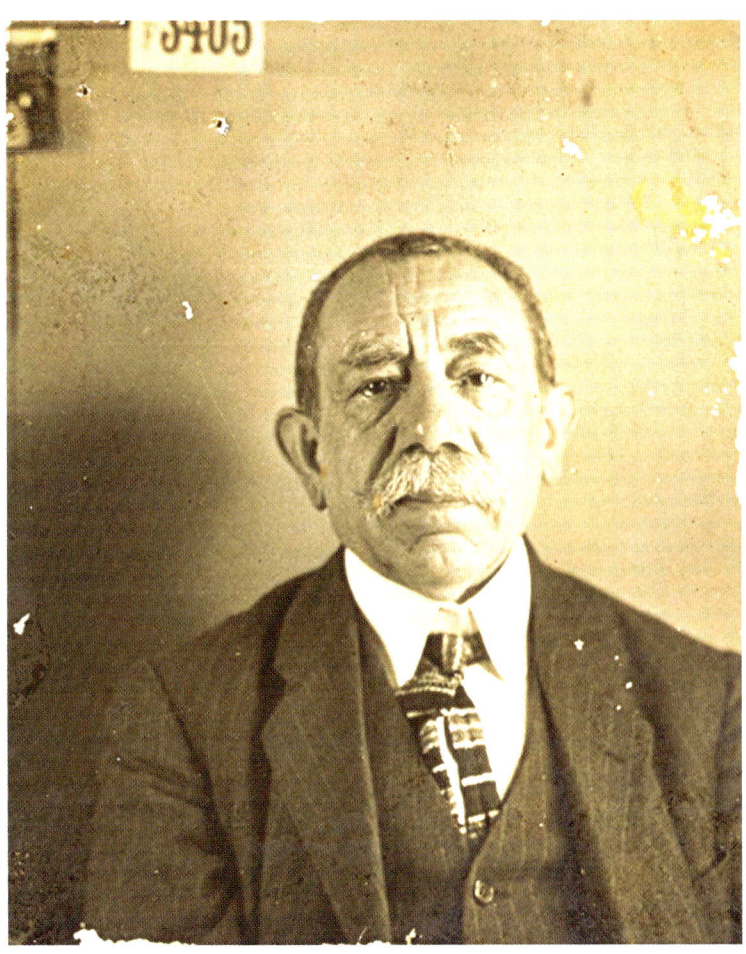

17. Nathan Baumgardt, one of the residents evicted from Lützowstrasse 48/49. Nathan Baumgardt was deported on Transport I/46 on 17 August 1942 to Theresienstadt, where he dies on 10 September 1942. Photo: Hall of Names, Page of Testimony for Nathan Baumgardt, Yad Vashem.

18. Doris and Moritz Holzheim, residents at Lützowstrasse 48/49, emigrated to Brazil on 19 August 1940. Photo: Immigration Cards, National Archives in Rio de Janeiro, Brazil.

19. Leopold and Regina Jablonowski, residents at Lützowstrasse 48/49, emigrated to Brazil on 7 June 1939. Photo: Immigration Cards, National Archives in Rio de Janeiro, Brazil.

20. Rosa Kalenscher, resident at Lützowstrasse 48/49, emigrated to Brazil on 25 December 1939. Photo: Immigration Cards, National Archives in Rio de Janeiro, Brazil.

21. Agnes Keiler, resident at Lützowstrasse 48/49, emigrated to the USA on 20 March 1940. Photo: U.S Citizenship and Immigration Services, USA.

22. Regina Abraham, one of the residents evicted from Lützowstrasse 48/49. Regina Abraham was deported first to Theresienstadt on 7 September 1942 on Transport I/60, and again to Auschwitz on 18 April 1944 on Transport Eb. Regina Abraham was murdered in Auschwitz. Photo: Hall of Names, Page of Testimony for Regina Abraham, Yad Vashem.

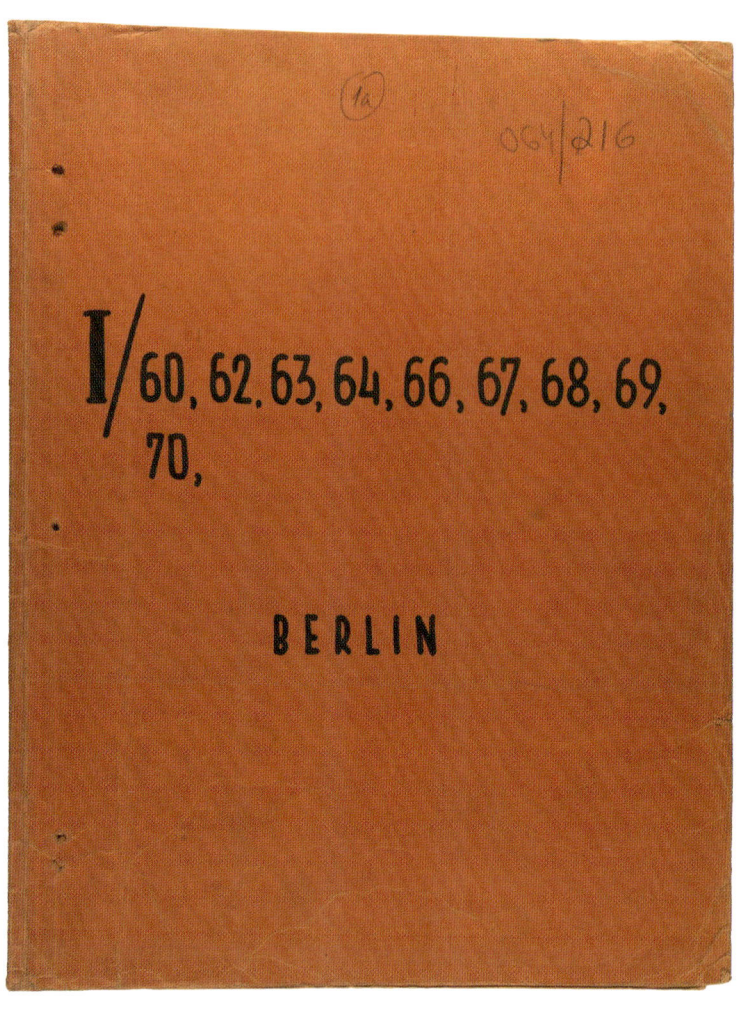

23. File and lists of the names of the 1,000 Jews deported from Berlin to Theresienstadt on transports I/60-I/64 and I/66-I/70 between 7 and 25 September 1942. Regina Abraham was deported on Transport I/60. Record/file YVA O.64/218, Yad Vashem.

```
60. Berliner Transport                          7.9.1942
   I/60

Lfd.  Name              Beruf    Geb.    Letzte              Kennkar-   Kennzei-
Nr.   Vorname                    Dat.    Adresse             tennr.     chennr.

6228  Klug              ohne     28.9.   Bln.N.54,Grena-     A039391    09229
      Abraham Chaim I.           1874    dierstr.9

6229  Kohn              ohne     7.2.    NO.55,Jablons-      A152009    09230
      Therese Sara               1875    kistr.25

6230  Lewin             ohne     19.7.   N.Joachimstr.9      A145525    09232
      Rosa Sara                  1876

6231  Montag            ohne     3.12.   NO.55,Pasteur-      A769402    09245
      Ernestine Sara             1871    str.32

6232  Seelig            ohne     28.6.   N.54,Lothrin-       A195249    09257
      Berthold Israel            1868    gerstr.11

6233  Seelig            ohne     22.4.          "                       09256
      Hannah Sara                1863

6234  Gross             ohne     17.5.   C.2,Georgen-        A240803    09263
      Jenny Sara                 1858    kirchstr.27

6235  Weichbrodt        ohne     25.4.   SO.16,Joseph-       A026588    09264
      Wolf Israel                1857    str.14

6236  Weichbrodt        ohne     22.3.          "                       09265
      Therese Sara               1867

6237  Wiener            ohne     18.12.  NO.55,Christbur-    A152396    09266
      Ernestine Sara             1873    gerstr.3

6238  Wind              ohne     12.12.  NO.55,Chode-        A177388    09267
      Bertha Sara                1867    wieckistr.41

6239  Wolffenstein      ohne     21.3.   NO.55,Greifs-       A177942    09268
      Röschen Sara               1874    walderstr.160

6240  Teller            ohne     25.16.  NO55,Winsstr.14                09274
      Wolf Israel                1873

6241  Teller            ohne     29.10.         "            A188149    09275
      Betty Sara                 1887

6242  Mannheim          ohne     9.4.           "                       09276
      Gertrud Sara               1871

6243  Hammer            ohne     20.9.          "                       09277
      Rosalie Sara               1865

6244  Verschleisser     ohne     2.7.           "            A373965    09277a
      Lilli Sara                 1885

6245  Abraham           ohne     19.8.   N,Schönhauser                  09479
      Regina Sara                1887    Allee 23/25

6246  Heymann           ohne     4.12.   C,Heiliggeist-      A01778     09480
      Klara Sara                 1866    str.38

6247  Samter            ohne     8.1.    Radinkendorf        B00025     09478
      Lina Sara                  1872
```

24. Regina Abraham is number 6234 (third from last) on the list of the deported. The list states that she was unemployed (Beruf: Ohne) and residing at N. Schönhauser Allee 23/25 in Berlin at the time of her deportation on 7 September 1942. Record/file YVA O.64/218, Yad Vashem.

```
Der Chef des ϟϟ-Hauptamtes        Berlin, den 7. Januar 1941
C.A. Ia - 22
                                     0012

Betr.: Verlegung der Dienststellen des ϟϟ-Hauptamtes von
       Berlin SW 11, Prinz Albrecht Straße 9 nach Berlin W 35,
       Lützowstr. 48/49.
Bezug: Ohne
Anlg.: Ohne


Verteiler IV
------------


Das ϟϟ-Hauptamt und die zum ϟϟ-Hauptamt gehörenden ϟϟ-Ämter und
ϟϟ-Dienststellen werden ab 15. Januar 1941 in das neue Dienstge-
bäude des ϟϟ-Hauptamtes

                    Berlin W 35, Lützowstr. 48/49

verlegt. Der Umzug der einzelnen Ämter und Dienststellen erfolgt
nach folgenden Terminen:

                    zum 15. Januar 1941: Chef des ϟϟ-Hauptamtes
                                         Postein- und Ausgangsstelle
                                         des ϟϟ-Hauptamtes
                                         Verwaltung ϟϟ-Hauptamt
                                         Ergänzungsamt der Waffen-ϟϟ
                    ab 15. Februar 1941: Erfassungsamt
                                         Amt für Leibesübungen
                                         Hpt.Abt. Weltanschauliche
                                         Erziehung d.germ.ϟϟ-Freiw.
                                         in ϟϟ-Nordland und in ϟϟ-West-
                                         land
                                         Hpt.Abt. Statistik

Das Schulungsamt und das Fürsorge- und Versorgungsamt (Berlin -
München) verbleiben in ihren alten Dienststellen:
                    Schulungsamt:
                    Berlin SW 68, Hedemannstr. 24, Fernruf: 19 5251
                    Fürsorge- und Versorgungsamt:
                    Berlin W 15, Kurfürstendamm 217, Fernruf: 91 8691

                                                              -2-
```

25. The SS-Hauptamt sets up at Lützowstrasse 48/49, 7 January 1941. NS 33 Bundesarchiv.

26. Address and telephone number of the Jüdische Altersheim. 1936 Berlin telephone directory. Authors' private archive.

27. Address and telephone number of the SS-Hauptamt at Lützowstrasse 48/49. 1941 Berlin telephone directory. Authors' private archive.

28. Address and telephone number of the SS-Hauptamt at Lützowstrasse 48/49, department Amt VI at Hagenstrasse 39–47, Grunewald. Supplement to the 1943 Berlin telephone directory. Authors' private archive.

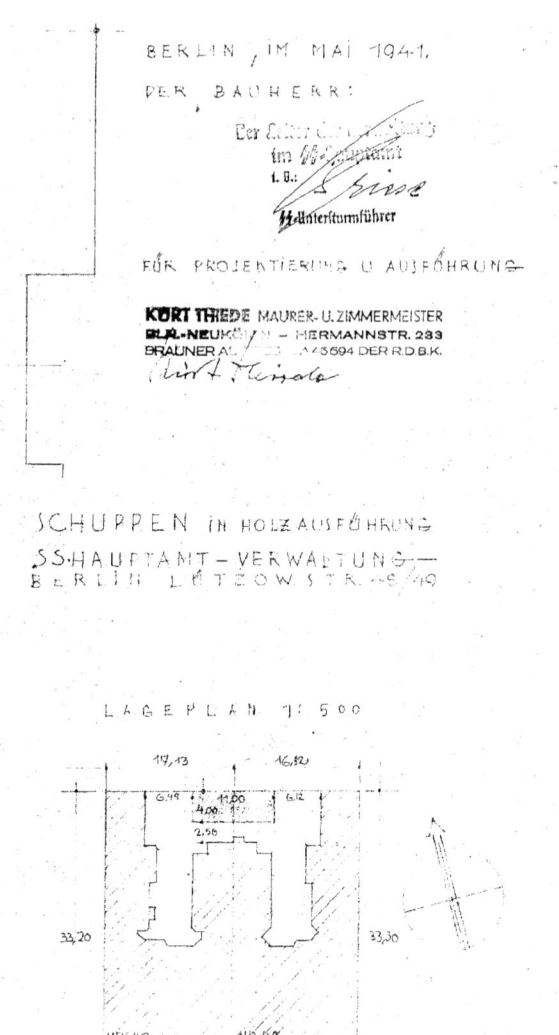

29. May 1941. SS-Hauptamt instructs building contractor Kurt Thiede to rebuild parts of the nursing home. Landesarchiv Berlin.

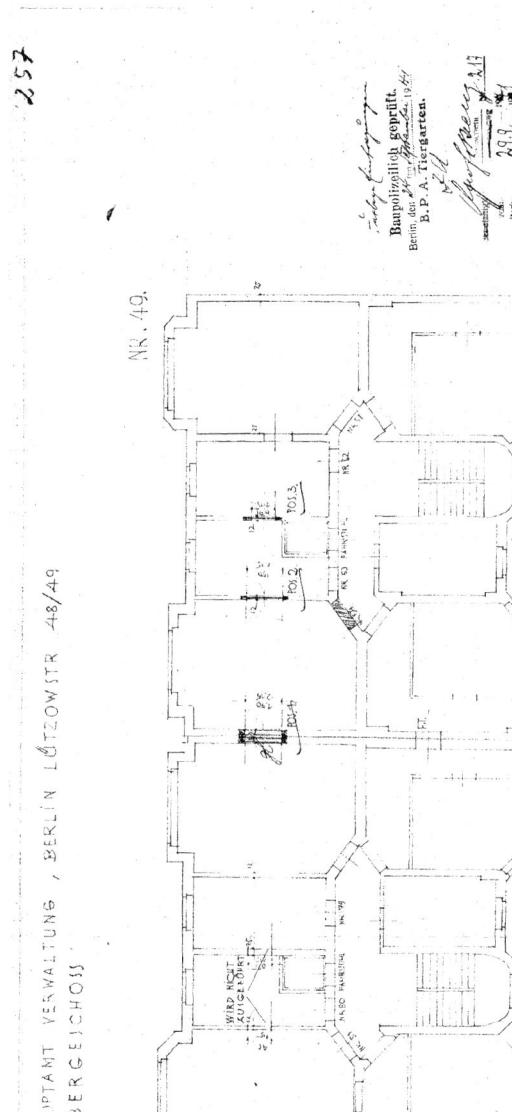

30. September 1941. Cutaway view showing the rebuilding work and other changes to be made to the property by the SS-Hauptamt. Landesarchiv Berlin.

31. Hagenstrasse 39–47, Grunewald, 1940. At the time the photograph is taken, the building is a Catholic girls' home. One of the girls has marked the room she stayed in with an X and the words "Mein Zimmer" (my room). The buildings, which had made up the Jewish-run Sanatorium Grunewald (owned by the Behrendt Meyer family) were expropriated by the Nazi authorities around 1938. Gustaf Ekström served in the building after it had been seized by the SS-Hauptamt. Photo: Authors' private archive.

32. Kiestinki, ruins by the lake, 8 August 1941. Photo: SA-Kuva.

33. Kiestinki, German vehicles bogged down in mud, 16 April 1942. Photo: SA-Kuva.

blare out "Soviet transport sunk", "Yalta taken", "Two years of war, two years of victories".

The war correspondent platoon received continual reports from the nearby front. Once the censor had cast an eye over the material it was turned into draft press releases for further distribution to, say, the office of the Reich Press Chief at the Ministry of Propaganda in Berlin. Here, the texts might undergo further revision before being circulated to newspapers around Germany. It is estimated that some 80,000 such reports and source texts and over two million photographs were produced by the German propaganda troops during the War. Ekström might well have recognised some of his duties at his correspondent platoon from the patrols and propaganda teams he worked with during his time with the Lindholm Movement in Sweden a few years previously.

Ekström's division, Waffen-SS "Nord", was not suited to war in an Arctic environment, and it soon transpired that the soldiers were poorly trained and equipped for the harsh terrain of the Karelian forests and mires. In July 1941, a single day's battle at the town of Salla led to serious losses, with over 600 dead and missing. The head of the division was compelled to report that the unit was no longer fit for war. The division was then removed from the action at the Salla front and transferred the Finnish 3rd army corps. Instead of being grouped with its own field of responsibility, the SS division's units were distributed amongst other Finnish units in the hope that they would fare better in the forest war against the Russians. Along with a few Finnish units, they were tasked with cutting off the railway from Murmansk. The attack force would head towards Kiestinki and then on to the railway that passes through the village of Louhi.

The terrain around Kiestinki is, even by Finnish standards, the worst imaginable for soldiers. With only one accessible route along which to advance, the German and Finnish troops had its work cut out repelling the defence mounted by the 88th Soviet rifle division.

Despite the tremendous difficulties, the Finnish-German forces manage to break through the Soviet defences at the Sohjana river on 31 July 1941. A few days later, the troops enter the deserted village of Kiestinki. But east of Kiestinki is as far as they get. They never reach the railway that they intend to cut off, and neither side has the energy or resources to conduct any more major offensives. The fighting comes to a standstill apart from some bouts of aggressive reconnaissance. The German and Finnish troops devote their time instead to building up infrastructure in the area. They build barracks, recreation centres, a hospital and a jetty so that transport planes can land on the local lake.

When Ekström arrives in Kiestinki, the fighting and the German-Finnish offensive has already lost momentum.

Even though the German-Finnish offensive has been thwarted, the Soviet supreme command judges the Murmansk railway to still be under threat east of Kiestinki. On 25 April 1942 Soviet forces attack the German-Finnish positions but are beaten back, and a month later a Finnish counter-offensive retakes some of the territory lost. After that, nothing much happens on this front until 1944.

Gustaf Ekström never experiences these battles, however. He leaves Kiestinki in early March 1942 and returns to Berlin after four months' service on the Eastern Front.

He travels back to Germany on the "German train" through northern Sweden. Between Haparanda and Östersund, the railway carriage in which Ekström's luggage has been stashed is broken into. According to his own account, his trunk is forced open and plundered. His passport is one of the items stolen. This is a problem for Ekström. Even though it expired in April 1942, it would be hard for him to travel again to Sweden and back to Germany.

After a few days' ride via Haparanda, Trondheim and Oslo, Gustaf Ekström arrives back in Berlin. Like all those over two million men who served for 60 days in a warzone or 14 consecutive days in active fighting at the Eastern Front, Ekström is awarded an Eastern Front Medal. The obverse face shows the Nazi imperial symbol of an eagle clasping a swastika in its claws; on the reverse is the text "Winterschlacht im Osten 1941/42" (Winter battle in the East 1941/42). Ekström is now also promoted to Rottenführer, or section leader.

Irene Heim, the young woman who was deported to the ghetto in Litzmannstadt as Ekström travelled to Finland, is selected for a new transport on 5 May 1942. This time she is sent to the Kulmhof extermination camp, as the former Chelmno has now been renamed by the German occupation forces. There she is crammed into a gas truck with other Jews and gassed to death. Gas trucks were regular lorries that the Nazis had converted into instruments of mass-murder by simply running a tube from the exhaust pipe into the sealed container at the back; the people packed inside soon died from carbon monoxide poisoning.

Ekström rises up in the SS hierarchy during the winter of 1942, the same year that the elderly former residents of Lützowstrasse begin a completely different journey. One that heads eastward.

Chapter 12
The transports east

At the same time as Gustaf Ekström is in the war correspondent platoon with the Waffen-SS "Nord" division, the transport programme from Berlin to the Riga, Warsaw and Minsk ghettos intensifies. On 20 January 1942, top Nazi officials and bureaucrats gather for a conference in Wannsee, a suburb of Berlin. Under the leadership of SS-Obergruppenführer Reinhard Heydrich, they make sure that all government agencies are on board with the "final solution to the Jewish question" – to deport and exterminate Europe's Jewish population.

It is now, at the turn of 1941/42, that many of the elderly residents of the Lützowstrasse nursing home are forcibly deported to the east. The expulsion was organised as follows: about a fortnight prior to departure, the expellee received notification of his or her imminent deportation. The message contained the necessary instructions, such the maximum luggage allowance (50 kilos). The expellee was then required to detail all his or her possessions on a special form.

A few days before the train departed, the Gestapo rounded up the Jews at their various addresses around Berlin. Often they only had a couple of minutes to bid farewell to the homes they would never see again. A lorry would be waiting on the street outside, onto which the Jews would be loaded, usually screaming and struggling, to be driven away to the assembly points. There are few extant photographs from these incidents, but in a collection from the little town of Lörrach there is some preserved photographic material that gives some indication of how these deportations from Germany's towns and cities were effected. They were done in front of everyone's eyes. On stairwells and doorways, people stood witnessing how the Gestapo herded away the Jews. The tumult drew hordes of bystanders and people would line the streets watching the lorries cart the Jews off to the assembly points. These places were called *Sammellager* or transit camps, and demonstrate how the concentration camp system extended all the way in to the heart of Berlin. At the time of the first deportations, one of these camps was the synagogue at Levetzowstrasse 7–8.

The transit camps provided something of a foretaste of the terror that awaited at the final destinations. On arrival at the camp, the Jews were registered and ordered to hand over their valuables lists and the keys to their homes. They also had to sign a document transferring all their property, with the exception of their 50 kilo luggage, to the German state. All cash and personal effects that they might have packed also had to be surrendered. This process was often violent and the camps were surrounded by police; it could also take a long time. The deportees had to manage as best they could under the terrible conditions in the overcrowded camp. People collapsed and suicide was not unknown. The elderly died from exhaustion. Through these camps, right under the noses of the citizens of Berlin, tens of thousands of Jews were shunted off to the ghettos, concentration camps and extermination camps. When the registration and assembly process was complete, the Jews had to cover the ten kilometres or so to Grunewald railway station on foot. Straight through Berlin they had to walk, surrounded by guards. These transports took place several times a week.

Grunewald station still exists. If it was not for platform 17, it would look like any other city railway station. Today, just as it was in the 1940s, Grunewald is one of Berlin's most attractive residential areas with its grand patrician villas set in their lush gardens. It was from platform 17 that the transports headed east. When we visited the place while writing this book, we were struck by how close the deportation trains were to the regular trains and the surrounding residential idyll. The screams and cries of fear as thousands of humans were herded on board must have seared through the affluent area as the clattering of thousands of shod feet trudging along the streets echoed amongst the houses. The residents could simply not have missed the horror taking place maybe 100 metres from their kitchen windows, or on the platform beside the one from where they themselves would catch their train to work in the city. What conversations were held at the breakfast table as the caravan of terrified people shuffled past? What did the people living nearby think when they witnessed all this?

One of the residents of Grunewald who witnessed the deportations was interviewed for a book titled *Die Grunewald-Rampe*. Here she describes how they would just stand watching as the deportations proceeded. She particularly remembers a day when a column of women and children were led through their streets. The children were weeping silently beside their mothers, and the sight horrified her.

As the rate of deportation increased, more transit camps opened in Berlin, and more stations started to be requisitioned for the purpose. Once the Jews had been deported, all their confiscated property was sold. Their apartments were transferred to the state and to the authority under the charge of Berlin's General Building Inspector, Albert Speer.

When tracking down the Jews who lived at Lützowstrasse 48/49, we found 24 individuals who were sent to Riga. One of them was Elisabeth Borchardt. She was deported on Transport 9 on 19 January 1942 at the age of 62. We can imagine that the Gestapo came for her at W62 Derflingenstrasse 72, to where she had been evicted when the nursing home on Lützowstrasse was closed down and taken over by the Gestapo and the SS.

In freezing winter temperatures, she and the others were forced on board the Deutsche Reichsbahn train, destination the Riga ghetto. Not that any of them knew that. When the transports from Berlin to the Riga ghetto began, the ghetto was already packed with Jews from the occupied areas in the east. To solve the problems that arose when some 10,000 extra people arrived to be crammed into this already overcrowded space, the local SS organisation and Einsatzgruppen A carried out mass-executions of the Latvian Jews already living there. On 30 November and 8 December 1941 between 20,000 and 30,000 Jews were massacred in Rumbula forest, a stone's throw from Riga, to make way for the new arrivals.

Jews from Berlin were also murdered in the same forest, including former Lützowstrasse resident Edith Scheidemann, who had been deported from Berlin to Riga on 27 November 1941 along with at least 1,048 other Jews. After a three-day long train journey, she and her fellow deportees were gunned down as soon as they arrived in Riga. Edith Scheidemann was young, only 20, with her whole life ahead of her, when she was forced to strip and run the gauntlet through two lines of guards, who beat and whipped her to spur her on towards the forest. Once there she was made to lie face down on top of the corpses of the recently executed in one of the pits that had been dug. This part of the mass-murder process was in keeping with a method developed by SS-Obergruppenführer Friedrich Jeckeln during similar circumstances in Ukraine and that he himself dubbed Sardinenpackung, or sardine packing. The Einsatzgruppen strove to be effective in their endeavours and kill as many people as possible. Jeckeln was the officer in command at the Rumbula massacre and the men in Einsatzgruppen A obeyed his orders and followed his method. When Edith Scheidemann had lain down in the mass grave she was killed with a single shot to the neck. She was then buried under the next victim.

The killing was still going on inside and outside the ghetto when the next transports to Riga arrived. In places, the snow was stained red with blood, and the hastily discarded clothes and personal belonging lay in heaps. Survivors recall seeing food still on tables, frozen in the winter air. Babies' bottles were found outside the houses.

According to Yad Vashem, Transport 9 – the transport on which Elisabeth Borchardt from Lützowstrasse 48/49 travelled – consisted of between 995 and 1,002 Jews, of whom between 9 and 19 apparently survived. Most of them were elderly and infirm, the average age being 55. At least 40 of them were, however, younger than 15. None of them had received any information at all about where they were headed. After about three days' train ride they arrived at Skirotava, the station in Riga, on 23 January 1942. Apart from the hardships brought by the deportation, many of them are likely to have died of hypothermia. The winter of 1941–1942 was mercilessly cold, with temperatures of -40 not uncommon around the Baltic in the first months of 1942.

Also on the train was Salo Stransky. He was one of those from Transport 9 who survived the Riga ghetto. In 1969 he testified in the trial against SS-Standartenführer Otto Bovensiepen, former head of the Gestapo in Berlin (1941–1943) and therefore one of those responsible for the deportations from the city. In Stransky's words:

"Early in the morning of 17 or 18 January 1942, I was unexpectedly snatched from my apartment by two people from the Gestapo and taken by bus to the synagogue on Levetzowstrasse, where 200-300 women and man of all ages had been gathered. ... I can't remember if I had to sign a piece of paper or if I was told that all my belongings and assets were confiscated. ... I'd brought with me a large rucksack full of personal belongings, such as underclothes and shoes, that I was allowed to keep. But the rucksack was searched for valuables by the Gestapo.... None of us knew where we were being sent. Around lunchtime on 19 January, we were made to walk from Levetzowstrasse to Grunewald railway station. I couldn't see if any of the elderly, children or others who had trouble walking were driven there. As I recall, we were all made to walk. ... At Grunewald station we were

made to board a long train made up of goods wagons. About 40 or 50 people had to share a wagon and were given no supplies. In my current estimation, the journey took two and a half days. ... Some of my suffering friends died along the way. Three elderly people died in my wagon. I don't know what of, but maybe the poor victims were in a state of shock that led to heart failure. We were terrified and no one knew what fate awaited us. It was only when we arrived at Skirotava that their intentions became clear. We were met by Latvian SS men, who ordered us out of the wagons as quickly as possible. If you weren't quick enough you were beaten. The guards that had accompanied us from Berlin witnessed everything. As soon as we arrived at Skirotava we were separated – older men from younger, and women and women with children were taken to one side. All our luggage was loaded onto trucks and was never seen again. The elderly who were unable to walk were instructed to board the trucks. As long as we could walk, we younger ones, including the women and children, were marched into the ghetto in Riga. The ones who'd been loaded onto trucks were never heard from again. They were probably shot shortly afterwards."

Wolfgang Josef Vogel was also on Transport 9 and would survive the Riga ghetto. He also testified against SS-Standartenführer Otto Bovensiepen at his trial in 1969. His opening testimony also sheds light on how Berlin's Jews were manhandled as their property was stolen:

"I was living at first with my mother on Grosse Frankfurter Strasse. As a result of orders that the Nazis had given, we had to move to an apartment on Prinzenalle 87, which was being shared by other Jews. My mother, Selma Vogel, her sister and I were taken from the apartment by two Gestapo men in civilian clothes onto a tram that took us to the synagogue on Levetzowstrasse. I remember from my schooldays at Kaiserstrasse that more and more children went missing by the day. The teachers told us that our classmates had been interned by didn't go into any further detail. ... As soon as we arrived

at the synagogue on Levetzowstrasse we were led into a large room where long rows of tables had been set up. We had to go up to the tables and hand over our cases, which we never saw again. As I recall, we had to give up our watches, pens, even rings. ... I remember numbers being called out over loudspeakers and that these people could leave the synagogue. ... I think our transport took three or four days before we arrived at Skirotava. That was when I realised why we were being deported. When we were unloaded, my friends and I were beaten and humiliated by the SS. I can still remember the following incident: An SS man ordered a younger deportee to pick up a piece of paper that was lying close to the railway tracks. When he refused he was shot, just like that, with a carbine. It was a bitterly cold day in Skirotava. I remember that our hands froze to the rails of the wagon if we used them for support when getting off the train. The snow was in piles metres deep. As soon as we'd left the train, the SS went along our ranks picking out the older men, little children and the sick and frail. If I'm not mistaken, they were driven to Salaspils. At least that was the rumour. My mother, aunt and I had to march from Skirotava to the ghetto in Riga."

In an interview with the Shoah Foundation, Walter Lachman, another Transport 9 survivor, gave the following testimony of his arrival at the Riga ghetto:

"Those who can't walk, get onto the trucks, they told us. For some reason we decided to walk, maybe because we'd been cooped up for so long and didn't want to get back into another vehicle. Others probably didn't even make it to the ghetto. They told us to leave our cases, that was the last we saw of them, they disappeared. After that we had to walk for two or three hours.... What we didn't know then was that just before we arrived... the Germans had shot...Latvian Jews who'd been living in the ghetto. ... We were taken to the houses that the Latvian Jews had been living in before getting shot. Their clothes were still there and there was still food on the table. We were hungry so we ate it."

We do not know what happened to Elisabeth Borchardt in the ghetto other than that she did not survive. Was she one of the ones who had the energy to walk, did she make it all the way there? Or was she one of the ones who were loaded onto a truck and murdered shortly after arrival? Maybe she was one of the ones who suffocated in the gas trucks that the SS used? Or perhaps she was murdered during the Dünamunde Action, when the SS shot 4,400 prisoners in cold blood between February and April 1942. If she managed to avoid this, she would have lived and been put to forced labour under terrible conditions.

In the autumn of 1913, the order is given to liquidate the ghetto. Thousands of prisoners are dispatched to Auschwitz, where they are immediately murdered in the gas chambers. The few Jews who remain after the transports to Auschwitz are transferred to Stutthof concentration camp.

On 25 January 1942, a few days after Elisabeth Borchardt leaves Berlin, another 1,000-plus Jews are deported on Transport 10, which departs from the same platform at Grunewald station. On the train are Margarete Cohn, Clara Falk, Jette and Joseph Hirschberg, Pauline Holzheim, Helene Jacoby, Johanna Lewy, Regina Manasse, Helene and Martin Oppenheim, Felix and Ida Rosenthal, Willy Stern, Amelie Wagner and Selma Westenberg. All of them were once residents of the Lützowstrasse nursing home and are now being deported to the Riga ghetto. None of them survive.

The average age on Transport 10 was 58, but there were 23 children under 15. As with the earlier transports, the final destination was kept from the deportees. They were first seized by the Gestapo and taken to the transit camp on Levetzowstrasse. They were then marched to Grunewald station and made to board the train that the Gestapo had requisitioned from Deutsche Reichsbahn. The train arrived at Skirotava on 30 January 1942. This time, it took an estimated five days, during which time the severe cold claimed many lives in the uninsulated goods wagons. Unfortunately we have not found any testimonies from this transport. However, a report from the Einzatskommando dated 2 February 1942 reproduced at Yad Vashem gives a general description of what happened to the Riga deportees at this time:

"All in all, 19,000 Jews have arrived at Riga from the Third Reich and protectorate. ... Of the Jews that have arrived from the Third Reich only a few are fit for labour. 70–80 per cent are children and elderly men who are unable to work. The death rate is particularly high amongst these Jews, who have neither the health nor physical stamina to survive the severe winter."

Riga was not the only ghetto that Berlin's Jews were sent to. The Warsaw ghetto also received many transports from Berlin containing thousands of Jews. On 2 April 1942, some 1,000 Jews are taken from the transit camp on Levetzowstrasse to Grunewald station, where they are herded onto Transport 12, destination Warsaw. Amongst them are Johanna and Richard Lewy and Selma Wulff from the Lützowstrasse nursing home. Three days later on 5 April, the transport arrives at Umschlagsplatz on Stawski Street in the Warsaw ghetto. Again, there are no first-hand accounts from this transport, although one diary has survived. It was written by Adam Czerniakow, who was chairman of the Jewish Council in the Warsaw ghetto. On 5 April 1942, the same day as this deportation arrived from Berlin, he writes:

"The Umschlagplatz, 4 am. At 8 am, 1,025 expellees from Berlin came in. All together there will be 2,019 persons in the quarantine. We cleared the way and led them to the 109/111 Leszno street facility. The Order Service in front, the German police on the sides. Trailing behind a dozen carts with baggage and a few more with the sick. One of the sick has his leg in a cast (he was taken from a hospital). Mainly older people, partly intelligentsia. Many women."

The Warsaw ghetto was the largest in all of Nazi-occupied Europe and was at least as horrific as Riga. From October to November 1940, at least 400,000 Jews who lived in German-occupied Poland were forced into the ghetto, an area of about 3.4 sq. km. The ghetto was already overcrowded by the time of Transport 12's arrival. People were starving and there was a lack of every kind of necessity. The Germans who controlled the ghetto had deliberately cut off all food supplies.

In May 1942 more transports are sent from Berlin to Minsk, although not to the Minsk ghetto. Transport 16 leaves Grunewald station on about 24 June 1942. On board is Johanna Calvary from the Lützowstrasse nursing home. Her profession is given on one of the transport cards as *"Hausangestellte"* or housemaid. When the deported Jews are forced off the train, they are made to march to the forest at Blagovshchina close to the Maly Trostenets extermination camp, roughly 15 kilometres outside Minsk – where they are promptly shot by the SS and dumped into freshly dug mass graves. According to Yad Vashem a number of Jews from this transport were loaded onto trucks and gassed to death.

The memorial book of murdered Jews in Berlin gives the number of Jews deported on this transport as 201. While no survivors have been found, Yad Vashem has an eye-witness account from one of the perpetrators – SS-Unterscharführer Johann Arlt, who describes the slaughter with terse indifference in a report dated 3 August 1942:

"The work being done by the remaining men here in Minsk has continued along the same lines. The Jewish transports arrive regularly and we deal with them. That is why we were already busy again on 18 and 19 June 1942, digging pits near the camp. ... On 26 June the expected transport arrives with Jews from the Reich."

Johanna Calvary is the last person from the nursing home at Lützowstrasse 48/49 to be sent to the ghettos or killing grounds in the east. In total, 30 of the 256 people from the nursing home are murdered during this first phase of the deportations. The transports are now assigned a new destination: Theresienstadt.

Chapter 13
Amongst the houses in Grunewald

Ekström returns to Berlin in early March 1942 to do propaganda work at the SS-Hauptamt as an interpreter and translator. However, he is no longer at Lützowstrasse 48/49. The SS-Hauptamt is still at that address, but it has expanded – so much so, that the SS has to claim more property around Berlin. So Ekström's new office is at Hagenstrasse 39–47 in the Grunewald district.

The premises on Hagenstrasse actually comprise a number of large conjoined villas with a spacious, tranquil garden bordering on Grunewald forest. Grunewald was, and still is, one of Berlin's most affluent residential areas. It is home to the uppermost echelons of Berlin – and German – society: actors, scientists, bankers and top military. Amongst the titles from the 1940s, we find Excellency, Professor and Director-General. The sumptuous dwellings are also coveted by Nazi leaders, many of whom manage to appropriate properties here for themselves for next to nothing through the so-called "Aryanisation process" - a euphemism for the theft, often through forced sale, of Jewish property. This property was then sold on via banks to people whom the regime wished to reward or who were seen as suitable new owners. SS Reichsführer Heinrich

Himmler acquired a house here on the same street as and just a short walk away from Gustaf Ekström's new office.

The buildings at Hagenstrasse 39–47 had once been a sanatorium for pneumonia called Sanatorium Grunewald. Like the offices at Lützowstrasse 48/49, this was a confiscated Jewish property. To understand how this came about, we have to rewind a few years.

***

1928. The twenty-year-old Jew Cecilie Behrendt has been working at Sanatorium Grunewald with her aunt, Helene Behrendt Meyer since 7 April. Maybe today, 1 October she is sorting out the bills in the office. Cecilie in now a fairly experienced member of the sanatorium staff, but is quitting in order to move back to her family home in Frankfurt. Aunt Helene writes out her employment certificate on a sheet of paper bearing the sanatorium's green letterhead, testifying to her diligence. She also writes that she is sad that Cecilie has to travel back to Frankfurt, the implication being that she would rather Cecilie stayed to learn all about every aspect of the sanatorium.

Sanatorium Grunewald is owned and run by Cecilie Behrendt's relatives, the Behrendt Meyer family – her aunt Helene and her uncle Max Meyer, and will also be run by Cecilie's other aunt, Adele Behrendt. The Jewish family has owned and run the sanatorium in Grunewald since the turn of the century, when it was first built.

Back in Frankfurt, Cecilie soon meets her husband-to-be, Helmut Sieverts, a gentile. They wed and Cecilie takes his surname: Sieverts. They have three children together, one of whom dies in infancy.

Life for the Sieverts becomes increasingly strained in Germany in the 1930s. The Nuremberg Laws, which the Nazis enact in 1935, have rendered their marriage illegal. The laws are constantly being sharpened so that even people living with Jews are affected. Helmut finds it harder to find work. Being married to a Jew is reason enough for an employer to sack someone.

To the family's great horror, Helmut's brother Rudolf Sieverts joins the Nazis.

After the War, one particularly portentous memory that the family shares was when Rudolf came to visit them in their home. It was with terror that they regarded him in his new Nazi uniform. Rudolf Sieverts made a career for himself in the Nazi party apparatus. He takes his seat as a member of the Kolonialärztlichen Akadamie der NSDAP and is made HJ-Bannfuhrer in the Hitler Jugend. When Rudolf Sieverts visits a concentration camp at the end of the 1930s, he witnesses how the Nazis treat the Jews. He subsequently urges his brother, Helmut, to leave the country with his Jewish wife Cecilie and the children. But the warning was not given out of fraternal love. The main thing on Rudolf's mind, as the family later realised, was protecting his career and removing the problem of his Jewish relatives. Relations between the brothers were soured for ever more.

In the end, the Sieverts decide to flee Germany. Cecilie travels to the city of her birth, Danzig, which these days is called Gdańsk and is situated in Poland. Here she obtains the necessary papers for a visa to the USA. She makes the journey to Danzig alone, shortly after the death of her baby. She will later describe it as a very arduous experience.

The draconian laws introduced in Nazi Germany upset the Sieverts' escape plans. The Reich Flight Tax, or *Reichsfluchtsteuer*, effectively prevented Jews leaving the country from taking any cash at all. For its part, the USA demands that people entering the country have to be able to support themselves and their family. So the Sieverts purchase furniture and other valuable items to avoid having their money stolen by the Nazis in flight tax. Their shopping list includes a Swedish piano, an antique Dutch organ and carpets. But despite having done all they can to secure their assets, the family is faced with one last major problem. Cecilie Sieverts's mother, Elise Behrendt Hochstaedter, is sick, probably with cancer, and is unable to travel with them, as the family has to prove it has sufficient liquidity to pay for her care in the USA. The family therefore has to leave the country without Cecilie's mother, who remains in Germany. It is a heartbreaking decision to make and one that plagues the family with guilt for long afterwards. The German authorities refuse to give Cecilie's mother adequate care and she is declared dead at a clinic in Frankfurt on Christmas day 1940, having either been murdered with poison or gas through the euthanasia programme or taken her own life.

One of Cecilie's children tells us:

"Our mother was always anxious about how Grandma died. She felt guilty about having to leave her behind in Germany when the rest of the family emigrated in 1938. My parents tried to get her over to the USA, but it was impossible."

One of the family's most cherished photographs is from their very last Easter stroll in "Paradies", a park in the German town of Jena on 17 April 1938. The snapshot, which Cecilie Sieverts kept by her bed her whole life, shows her mother Elise and their two sons, Henning and Arne, whom she took with her; it was the last time they were together. Henning Sieverts, who was with the family when they escaped from Germany, tells us:

"I remember we were happy about fleeing. Because fleeing was what it was, albeit under more civilised conditions. We left Germany on the passenger ship the SS Manhattan from Hamburg on 4 May 1938. It was just before my fourth birthday and my big brother Arne was about to turn five. We ran and played in the ship's long corridors and I have a vivid memory of the dining room. It was where I tasted Cornflakes for the first time in my life.

We arrived in Newark harbour on 10 May 1938, where Dad was waiting for us. He'd travelled on ahead. After a few days' travel by train we arrived in Milwaukee. I've not given our flight much thought since then, after all I wasn't even four years old. But my brother and I were very aware of our background and that we'd fled."

In the family album are photographs of the boys playing on the deck, seemingly unaware of how lucky the family is and what would have been at stake if they had not been able to leave. Their fate could, however, have been very different. For as they were about to board the ship they found that their tickets were missing, probably stolen. Panicking, Cecilie Sieverts searched in vain through her possessions. Fortunately, she eventually managed to persuade the shipping company to issue them with new ones, for had she not succeeded in doing so there on the Hamburg quayside in early May 1938, they would have been stuck in Germany for good; the tickets were the difference between life and death.

Henning Sieverts continues:

"After the War, we were, in spite of everything, content. We must remember that we never experienced the War and the worst of the persecution of Jews. Nor did we experience the post-war hardships – the hunger, cold and massive migrations."

What happened to the Sieverts happened to many others. Families were divided and scattered by the Nazi's horrendous persecutions. Friends, brothers and sisters were pitted against each other, as families were pulled up by the roots. Chance often decided who was to survive.

Jewish newspapers frequently carry adverts for Sanatorium Grunewald in the 1930s. On 17 April 1935 the sanatorium advertises in *Jüdische Rundschau* and again, as late as 6 May 1937, in *Central-Verein-Zeitung*. Such adverts are for many Jewish companies a final effort to bring in a little revenue. The laws have gradually pushed the Jews out of Germany's business sector, just like they have from society in general. The number of Jewish companies in Berlin has been halved since 1933. After 1937 we find no such advertisements.

In the 1937 address book a new owner for the property suddenly appears: Deutsche Hypothekenbank. It is one of the many banks that handled confiscated Jewish real estate and other property for selling on in the Aryanisation process. In May 1938, the Catholic Gesellschaft Heiligen Herz Jesu (the Society of the Sacred Heart) purchases the property from the bank and uses it to start a students' home for young Catholic girls. However, the girls will only be able to stay there for a few years as the property changes hands again. In June 1941, the Gestapo violently evacuates the Catholic home and evicts the girls staying there. The sisters and 40 of their girls take refuge in the convent of St Gabriel at Bayernallee in Charlottenburg, a district a few kilometres to the north.

If Cecilie Sieverts's family had not been forced to flee, they would have been able to continue running the sanatorium and take it over from their relatives. When Helene Behrendt Meyer and her closest family died in 1933–1936, the property would have passed to Cecilie Sieverts. But this was not to be. The Nazi laws and persecutions precluded this possibility. On 11 July 1938 Jews are forbidden to visit sanatoriums, bathing houses and spas. The SS-Hauptamt, the office at which Ekström worked, finally takes over the Sieverts family's property.

In Berlin's restitution-demand register we find six documents drawn up by Cecilie Sieverts, née Behrendt, then living in the USA, concerning the sanatorium on Hagenstrasse. The demand is directed at Paula Werhahn and concerns the properties at Hagenstrasse 39–47. In the same register we also find out that Paula Werhahn was one of the sisters of the Society of the Sacred Heart and the one who bought the building on Hagenstrasse from Deutsche Hypothekenbank in 1938 on behalf of her society. The Society of the Sacred Heart also submits a restitution demand, but it is directed at the German Third Reich and thus relates to the Gestapo's takeover.

The expansion of SS bureaucracy was made possible by the forced confiscation of Jewish homes and property. The Behrendt-Sieverts family's sanatorium was swallowed up by the expanding SS, just like the Jewish nursing home on Lützowstrasse.

***

April 1942. Gustaf Ekström is sitting in one of the rooms that Cecilie Sieverts once worked in. He and his SS colleagues are churning out propaganda legitimising and encouraging the hatred, persecution and mass-slaughter of Jews. The SS office in Grunewald has some 100 to 150 people working for it. In addition to its propaganda activities, it also liaises with other SS offices in the occupied countries. The office is therefore called SS-Hauptamt Germanische Leitstelle (Germanic Liason Office) and utilises Waffen-SS volunteers from the occupied countries to expand the Third Reich into north-west Europe.

The archive material and correspondence that concerns the office was largely lost during the closing phase of the war, which in itself is remarkable since the buildings in Grunewald are still standing; however, much of the propaganda material that the SS-Hauptamt turned out has, thanks to the sheer size of its print runs and extent of its circulation, been preserved.

In April 1942 the SS-Hauptamt publishes the book *Aufbruch*, a collection of letters from SS volunteers around the world – edited and censored, naturally, and selected with a propagandist's eyes. Some of the letters in the book are allegedly from Swedish SS volunteers and one is a letter that claims to be from a Swedish volunteer in the Waffen-SS: "As a German SS officer I have much, much greater opportunities in life than I could have in Sweden, where so many Jews and other junk can carry on as they please". Anti-Semitism, race ideology and hatred of the Jews is endemic in all propaganda produced by the authority which Gustaf Ekström serves.

Another item printed by the SS-Hauptamt is the pamphlet *Rassenpolitik* (Racial Policy), which elevates the race issue to a matter of German life and death and touts the SS's role and race-policy mission as being to defend both ideology and "race" as an elite sector of National Socialist society.

The SS-Hauptamt also published newspapers. One of them is

SS-Leitheft, which was published in translation in many of the occupied countries. The newspaper is packed with racism, Nazi ideology and, sometimes, articles that more less resemble pulp literature, with scantily clad women. The content is also combined with aspects of the culture that the SS and the Nazi regime considered de rigueur, such as the music dramas of Richard Wagner, the myth of the Viking stereotype and the legends, invented or rewritten, of the Norsemen.

In 1942 the SS-Hauptamt publishes one the most infamous racist and anti-Semitic publications from Nazi Germany – an illustrated propaganda tract titled *Der Untermensch* (The Subhuman): It is translated into several languages and spread across the whole of Nazi Europe. The 52-page book is published at the same time as the SS Einsatzguppen are murdering the millions of Jews, Soviet soldiers and civilians who cross their path on the Eastern Front. The text has one purpose and one purpose only: to dehumanise Jews, Russians and other "inferior" peoples in the east, whom the book portrays as a destructive force bent on destroying the world for the Aryans, the Germans, the pure-blooded.

Given that this tract is often used to exemplify the brutal race-ideological element of Nazism, it is worth staying with it for a little longer. The book is laid out as a series of double-page spreads, with poor and destitute Eastern Europeans dressed in rags and living in dilapidated hovels on the left, and their antitheses – grand churches, the finest homes in Western Europe and uniformed SS men – on the right. Thus is the concept of *Untermensch* promulgated throughout the pages of this book, which is nothing but a crude attempt to defend and justify the slaughter and barbarity of which the Einsatzgruppen and other units in Eastern Europe are guilty. Ekström was working at the SS-Hauptamt at the same time as the book was being produced in 1942.

All this propaganda radiating from the SS-Hauptamt drove the idea that the War was a war about worldviews and race. Above all, this war was being fought on the Eastern Front, which Hitler had called a war of extermination in both an ideological and racial sense. The propaganda was an important driver of the Holocaust, and in bonding all parts of German society made them receptive to Nazism's political innovation – the idea that a race can be totally eradicated from the surface of the Earth. The SS-Hauptamt played a key role in the formulation and definition of Nazi racial ideology throughout the War. In Denmark the local office of the SS-Hauptamt on A. F. Kriegersvej in Copenhagen also played a role beyond propaganda and recruitment. A meeting was apparently held by Danish Nazis in the canteen in late August 1943 to discuss and plan the wholesale expulsion of the country's Jews.

The ideas expounded in the propaganda are put into literal effect when the residents of the nursing home on Lützowstrasse are first evicted and then concentrated in the ghettos, robbed of their property, deported and finally murdered. They are made manifest when the Behrendt-Sieverts are forced out of their property, the Grunewald Sanatorium, and have their possessions, cash and other valuables confiscated as they are forced to flee. They are also made manifest when Cecilie Sieverts's mother is denied the care she needs and is left with no choice but to commit suicide or face the mortal consequences of the Nazi euthanasia programme.

One of the cardinal components of the holocaust ideology, the transports to the ghettos, the concentration and extermination camps, took place just a few blocks from Ekström and the SS men at the offices of the SS-Hauptamt on Hagenstrasse. If Gustaf Ekström so wished, it would have taken a little under 15 minutes to walk through the villa estate in the spring weather to Grunewald station, which was one of the three stations in Berlin from where the city's 50,000 Jews were deported to the east. If he had been in the vicinity of the station on 2 April 1942, he might have watched the 1,025 Jews being deported to the Warsaw ghetto that day. Johanna and Richard Lewy and Selma Wulff were amongst those forced onto the train. All three had previously lived on Lützowstrasse. Who knows, maybe Ekström heard the tumult, spoke to his SS colleagues and went there to have a look?

After a few months in Berlin, Ekström is granted leave. At the beginning of May 1942, he leaves the villas in Grunewald and makes his way to Norway.

Chapter 14
Towards Theresienstadt

Max Ascher was a merchant by trade. He was born on 28 March 1869 in Naugard, which today lies in north-east Poland. On 11 October 1905 he marries Else Gabriele Gumpert, born 18 January 1880 in Brooklyn, New York. They settle in Berlin and have three children: Arthur, Getrude and Lotte. Arthur dies in 1927, only 20 years old. The following year, Else Gabriele herself dies, aged 48. Max Ascher moves as a retired widower into the nursing home on Lützowstrasse, while Gertrude and Lotte probably manage to escape from Germany. At least we know they survive the War, the persecutions and the Holocaust. Max Ascher is one of the 130 people from the nursing home at Lützowstrasse 48/49 who is deported to Theresienstadt.

Theresienstadt, the old fortress town north of Prague in German-occupied Czechoslovakia, was fitted out as a concentration-cum-transit camp at the end of November 1941. Much of the area was taken up with old military barracks, which were used to house thousands of deported Jews from Germany and other parts of Europe that had been occupied by the German forces. Conditions in the ghetto were appalling. Many of the Jews deported there were elderly and died from starvation, disease, malnourishment and a complete absence of medical care. While the propaganda of the SS-led deportation apparatus portrayed Theresienstadt as a model ghetto for all Jewish settlements, it was in fact a camp where Jewish prisoners were corralled before being sent on to extermination camps.

Starting in June 1942, there were 123 elderly transports from Berlin to Theresienstadt, "elderly" because in most cases they were full of Jews from the city's nursing homes. Most of these transports were made in a simple wagon coupled to normal train traffic from Berlin via Dresden to Prague. The trains stopped en route at Bohusovice, where the deportees were dropped off. These smaller transports could count between 50 and 100 Jews each and departed daily from one of Berlin's three stations used by the Gestapo. There were, however, larger transports; these *Grosse Altertransport* (large elderly transports) carried up to 1,000 people each. The Gestapo, under the leadership of the SS, had to requisition entire trains from Deutsche Reichsbahn for the purpose.

Just like the Jews who were deported to the ghettos in Riga, Warsaw and Minsk, those sent to Theresienstadt were told to first assemble at a transit camp. Before, the synagogue on Levetzowstrasse was the main place for this, but now another transit camp has been established in Berlin in an old nursing home on Grosse Hamburger Strasse.

In accordance with the customary instruction, the deportees were to leave their homes clean and tidy and with all taxes and fees paid. They were allowed one suitcase, 50 Reichsmark, a change of clothes, shoes, bedclothes, household utensils and food for just over a week. Once at the transit camp, the Jews had to sign a declaration consenting to the appropriation of their property by the German state. The Gestapo confiscated everything of value, such as homes, jewellery, money, securities, art and whatever else could generate revenues. The money was either used to finance the deportation itself or spent by the SS. Many of the confiscated valuables disappeared in the corruption that followed in the wake of the deportations.

On 15 May 1942, the department of Jewish affairs at the Reichssicherheitshauptamt (Reich Security Main Office) issued guidelines for prioritising the evacuation of Berlin's Jewish nursing homes. In the morning of 2 June 1942, Transport I/1 departs from Berlin's Anhalter Bahnhof. The letter I stands for Berlin and 1 for the first "Altertransport". One of the deportees on this train is Laura Fabian, a previous resident of the nursing home on Lützowstrasse. Laura Fabian was born in 1861 and so was 81 years old when she was forced to leave Berlin. She is one of 50 Jews on Transport I/1 – 37 women and 13 men. She is not the oldest. That honour goes to a lady who is 95.

The elderly had been collected from the transit camp on Grosse Hamburger Strasse, from where they had to walk a few hundred metres to the tram stop at Monbijouplatz, where a tram from BVG, Berlin public transport company, awaited them. At around five in the morning, the tram trundled away to platform 1 at Anhalter Bahnhof. Here, the 50 Jews who were to be deported were ordered on board a third-class wagon that was then coupled to the regular train that departed for Dresden at 6 a.m. In Dresden, it was re-coupled to another regular train to Prague. Later that evening, the train stopped at Bohusovice station a few kilometres south of Theresienstadt.

In an eye-witness account preserved in the Yad Vashem archive, Hildegard Henschel, wife of the last chairman of Berlin's Jewish community, describes the elderly transport to Theresienstadt:

"The transports to Theresienstadt began on 1 June 1942. ... The nursing home on Grosse Hamburger Strasse was converted into a transit camp for the people being deported on these transports. Initially they took 50 people at a time, and later 100 such 'evacuees'. At five a.m. they were loaded onto a special tram, which then took them to Anhalter Bahnhof. There, one or two carriages were connected to [a train] ... and they were sent to Theresienstadt under quite unbearable circumstances. But no one in Berlin knew what awaited them

there. The staff [from the Jewish community] that went on the train never returned to work, so no one received any information."

When the train arrived at Bohusovice, the Jews were received by men from the SS and the local gendarmerie, who marched them off to the camp. Only those who were unable to walk were allowed to travel by truck. Laura Fabian dies on 15 September 1942, a matter of months after her arrival at Theresienstadt. There are no sources that mention any survivors from Transport I/1, the train that took her to Theresienstadt.

Transport I/2, the other elderly transport, departs from Berlin to Theresienstadt two days after Transport I/1, on 4 June. On board is another former resident of Lützowstrasse, Sara Sternberg. She was born in 1854 and is 88 years old. Just over two months later on 7 August 1942 she too dies in Theresienstadt.

With no access to healthcare, medicine and hygiene articles many of the elderly died of disease. In the order of the day from the Jewish council of elders in Theresienstadt from 10 August 1942, we find Sara Sternberg on the list of those who have died in the past few days. We can also read instructions that everyone is to make sure to wash their hands properly to reduce the spread of infection, and to keep the shared well clean. Many diseases are caused by the appalling sanitary conditions of the camp. Starvation, malnutrition, diarrhoea, typhoid and spotted fever were rife. There is no information about any survivors from this second elderly transport either.

Already the next day, 5 June 1942, Transport I/3 departs from Berlin. This one is designated a "Sondertransport" (Special transport). The reason is that this transport contains relatives of the members of a resistance group – the Baum Group – which on 18 May 1942 had tried to set fire to Joseph Goebbels's anti-Semitic and anti-Communist exhibition "Das Sowjetparadies" in Berlin's Lustgarten. The sabotage failed and the fire was extinguished. The Gestapo acted with ruthless efficiency and before long hundreds of people had been captured and imprisoned. Herbert Baum, the group's leader, was tortured to death in the prison. Hundreds of people who were suspected of complicity were executed in concentration camps around Berlin, and their relatives were sent on Transport I/3 to Berlin.

On this transport on 5 June is also one Laura Ring, who has lived at the nursing home on Lützowstrasse. She is 76. The youngest is a two-year-old boy. Eighty of the deportees are women, 20 are men. Just like the others, they are rounded up in the early morning and put on the tram to Anhalter Bahnhof. From there they are taken by train to Leitmeritz station, north of Theresienstadt and made to march the rest of the way to the camp. The oldest are driven there by truck. An estimated 26 people survived this transport, of which some gave a first-hand account. Testifying in court against the Berlin Chief of Gestapo, Otto Bovensiepen, in the 1960s, Frieda Steinhagen described the transport as follows:

"On 4 or 5 June 1942, a representative of the Jewish community on Oranienburgerstrasse comes to my apartment to tell me that my son and I are to be collected in a few days' time and taken to a camp. He added that we were to be sent to Theresienstadt and that we had a luggage allowance of 50 kilos suitcase. ... On 5 or 6 June, one or two men from the Gestapo arrived at my door and took my son and me to the transit camp on Grosse Hamburger Strasse. ... I travelled there on the tram escorted by the Gestapo. We stayed at Grosse Hamburger Strasse for one day. The next morning we were taken to the railway station. ... It was Anhalter Bahnhof. ... I still recall that before we left we were frisked by women [from the Gestapo]... and I was made to hand over my watch and my fountain pen. ... We travelled in a covered wagon and arrived at Leitmeritz in the evening. On the way, the train stopped at a station in Dresden and a member of the Jewish community came and remarked that our transport was made up of widows. That evening we went on foot from Leitmeritz to Theresienstadt."

Henry Schindler was also on this transport. His father was one of

34. Der Untermensch. One of the SS-Hauptamt's best known anti-Semitic and racist publications. From 1942. Authors' private archive.

35. Max and Helene Behrendt Meyer, aunt of Cecilie Behrendt Sieverts and owner of Sanatorium Grunewald. C. 1928, Salinenpromenade in Bad Kissingen. Photo: The Sieverts Family private collection.

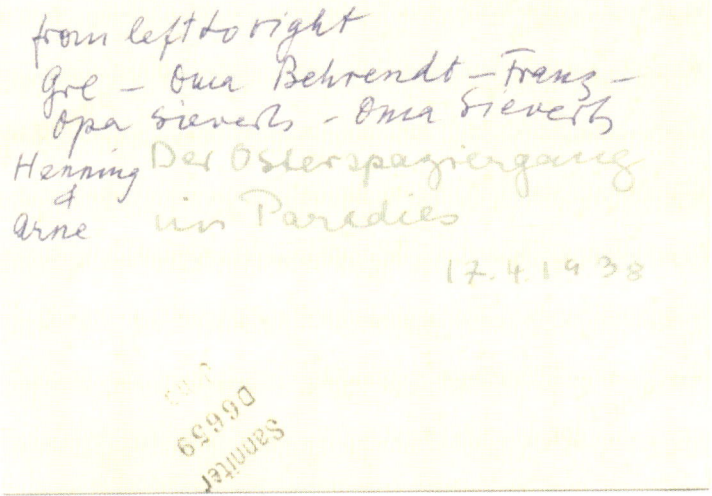

36. The Behrendts Sieverts family's last walk on 17 April 1938 before emigrating to the USA. From the left: Mrs Jaening, "Oma" Elise Behrendt (who later died in a Frankfurt clinic in 1940), Franz Behrendt (who also fled in 1939), "Oma" and "Opa" Sieverts, plus the children Henning and Arne. Photo: The Sieverts Family private collection.

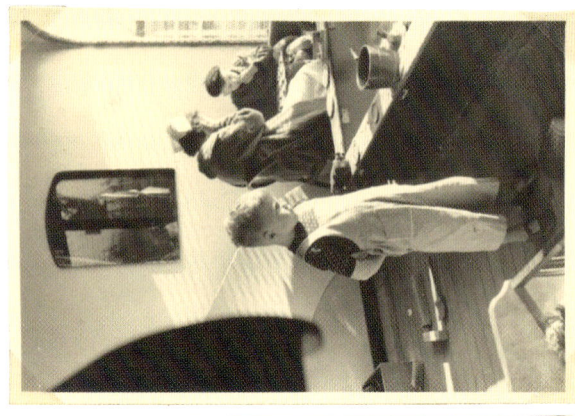

37. Henning and Arne Sieverts playing on board SS Manhattan on 5 May 1938 en route to the security of the USA. Photo: The Sieverts Family private collection.

38. The Sieverts family in the USA c. 1945/1946. From the left: Cecilie, Laurie, Henning, Arne and Helmut. Photo: The Sieverts Family private collection.

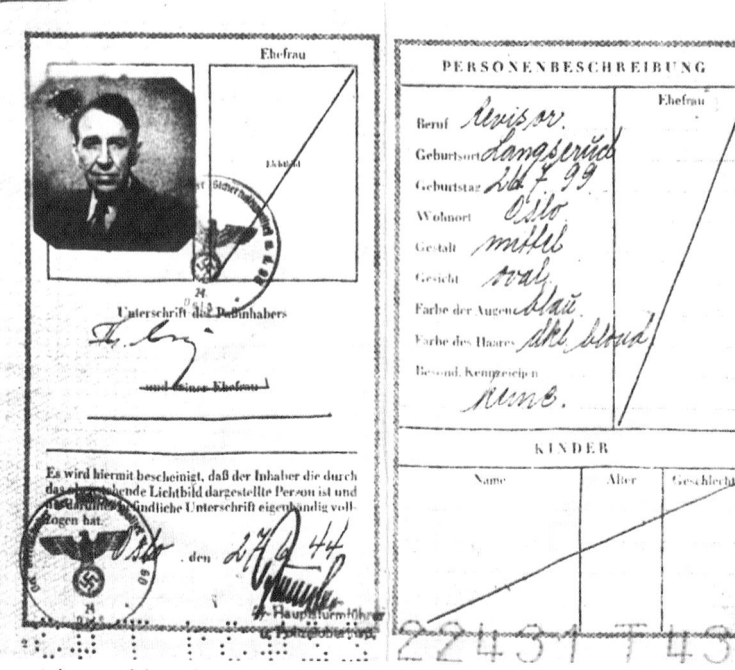

39. Thorwald Calais's German passport. Photo: Authors' private archive.

40. Olof Sandström enlisted with the Waffen-SS at the same time as Gustaf Ekström and they were together during their first months of training. Olof Sandström was a die-hard Nazi and member of the NSAP, and worked for the Germans in the SS and as a civilian official at the SS-Hauptamt. In April 1945, as Ekström was fleeing the Americans, they met in Berlin. While Ekström was able to make his way back to Sweden on the white buses, Sandström had to flee by foot. Detail of Sandström's passport application, 10 August, 1942. Photo: Authors' private archive.

41. Ekström, Gustaf, Karteikarte des NSDStB, Bundesarchiv, Berlin.

42. Theresienstadt, doorway in the Small Fortress, concentration camp east, May 1945. Theresienstadt also used the slogan "Arbeit macht Frei" (work sets you free). Photo: Authors' private archive.

43. Auschwitz, May/June 1944. The photograph shows selection at the ramp in Auschwitz shortly after the arrival of a train containing Hungarian Jews. It is part of the famous Auschwitz album, which was found by Holocaust survivor Lili Jacob in Mittelbau-Dora concentration camp in 1945. Photo: Yad Vashem/United States Holocaust Museum.

44. Ruins, Lützowstrasse 1944. Photo: Authors' private archive.

45. Ruins, Nuremberg, April 1945. Photo: NARA.

46. Party membership books of the "Sozialistische Reichspartei Deutschlands - SRP-, which translates as the Socialist Reich Party of Germany, of which General Otto Ernst Remer, is vice-chairman, is distributed during an illegal party meeting in a forest near Nuremberg, Federal German Republic, 8 September, 1951. A black, white and red striped flag is hanging from the trees, the old flag of the German Empire. Gustaf Ekström was active in the SRP in the Nuremberg region. Photo: Associated Press.

47. Munich, Germany - Otto Ernst Remer gives a speech to his fellow Socialist Reich Party members at a rally 5 February 1951. Photo: Keystone Pictures/zumapress.com.

48. The party conference of the Neo-Nazi National Democratic Party Germany (NPD) on 14 November, 1976, Frankfurt am Main. Party leader Martin Mussgnug sits in the middle. In August 1977 Gustaf Ekström pays a visit to the NPD executive and the circle surrounding Mussgnug. Photo: TT.

49. Former members of the Waffen-SS have a look at pictures and information about members of the Waffen-SS who are missing since the end of World War II during a meeting of the "Hilfsgemeinschaft auf Gegenseitigkeit der Angehörigen der ehemaligen Waffen-SS e.V." (short: HIAG, translates as: "Mutual Help Association of Former Waffen-SS Members") in Gelsenkirchen, on the 16 November, 1952. HIAG was a lobby group and a denialist veterans' organisation founded by former high-ranking Waffen-SS personnel in West Germany in 1951. Its main objective was to achieve legal, economic and historical rehabilitation of the Waffen-SS. Photo: TT.

the people to have been executed for trying to set fire to Goebbels's propaganda exhibition. In an interview with the Shoa Foundation from after the War, he recalls arriving at Theresienstadt and receiving the news of his father's execution:

"We were placed in very old army barracks called Kavalierkaserne, one of the oldest buildings in the Theresienstadt concentration camp. An SS officer came riding up. He ordered all the other prisoners who were already there to evacuate the yard, to not look out of the windows and to not listen to what he had to say. ... And he started to read out 154 names, my father's amongst them. These men had been executed on the orders of Heinrich Himmler."

The Yad Vashem archive contains a diary that Egon Gonda Redlich kept during her time at Theresienstadt. She writes of the same event as Henry Schindler:

"5 June 1942. ... Young women arrive from Germany. Their husbands have been imprisoned and they've been sent here. ... 6 June 1942. Sabbath. ... A dreadful appel was held for them. They ordered us to stay out of the yard under threat of the firing squad."

On 12 June another two of the former residents of Lützowstrasse 48/49 are deported. Dorothea Lack and Emelie Sternberg are on this transport, I/6. The procedure is the same as before. Heinrich Stahl, chairman of the Jewish community until 1940, is on board with them. He was also the owner of the album containing the only extant photographs of the nursing home at Lützowstrasse 48/49 that we found in Leo Beck's archive in New York. Heinrich Stahl had tried to emigrate from Germany, but the authorities refused to issue him a passport. The Gestapo kept a watch on him and he was forbidden to act on behalf of the Jewish cause. In Theresienstadt, Stahl was given a place on the Council of Elders and he continued to work until his death from pneumonia on 4 November 1942.

Emelie Sternberg dies on 18 August 1942 in Theresienstadt, shortly followed by Dorothea Lack, according to her death certificate at 3.10 p.m. on 30 August 1942 in block E VII, room 64. Like many others, she succumbs to intestinal infection caused by the extraordinarily poor sanitary conditions in the camp.

The transports from Berlin continue throughout the summer. One or two of those who once lived in the nursing home on Lützowstrasse disappear every week. On 23 June 1942 Luise Kirstein is deported on Transport I/10, as one of 50 people. There is only one survivor from this transport – Abraham Isaak Coffield. His testimony can be found in the Yad Vashem archive:

"At 9.30 a.m. on 21 June 1942 I was summoned to the Gestapo office at Bürgstrasse 26, as they had some questions to ask me. When I duly arrived, they informed me that my wife and I were to be deported to Theresienstadt. I was not allowed to return home but was taken immediately to the transit camp on Grosse Hamburger Strasse. My wife was told to pack the necessary clothes and to prepare for the transport. We weren't allowed to take any documents or money. Everything was taken from us. Before departure we had to sign a declaration of consent to having all our property confiscated on account of my anti-state, Communist attitude. A bailiff gave me the declaration form. At 5 a.m. on 23 June, around 50 of us were taken to Anhalter Bahnhof, were two carriages had been prepared for us. They let us write letters and the officer in charge of the transport placed the letters himself in the letterbox in Dresden. ... We were housed in a barn in the Magdeburg barracks and lay in the straw without blankets."

Coffield also provides a glimpse of the daily life at Theresienstadt. After a couple of days he is transferred to Badhausgasse 15 in the camp, where he is put in charge of sanitation – toilets, water, etc. His testimony continues:

"I sleep with 20 people in a tin room. Lice and insects are our hou-

semates. The bread we get is too little and mouldy, and all we were given in the morning was coffee substitute. Lunch was some slimy broth with the odd potato in it. The worst thing for me was the rapidly rising mortality rate and I had to lay the poor wives, who'd been snatched from their loved ones, dressed only in a short shirt, so many there were, in a washhouse on a meagre layer of straw. There were no horse-drawn hearses, only a wheelbarrow that two men went from house to house with collecting the bodies, which were initially buried but then later cremated. The ashes were placed in urns and tagged. It was a model of order. One day, at the end of 1944 I guess, all the urns were dumped in the Eger river."

On 17 August 1942, 997 Jews were gathered together on a "Grosse Altertransport" in Berlin, Transport I/46. It is the first of its kind from Berlin to Theresienstadt, as it differs from the earlier "small" elderly transports, which have been carrying 50 or 100 Jews. On board is Nathan Baumgardt, one of the few residents from Lützowstrasse of whom we have a photograph. Max Ascher, the first person we found in our search for the former residents, was also there, along with another 38 people who had once lived on Lützowstrasse.

After processing at the transit camp, all 997 Jews were transported to Berlin-Moabits station for freight traffic. Here Max Ascher, Nathan Baumgardt and all the others had to wait hours for train Da 502, placed by Deutsche Reichsbahn at the Gestapo's disposal against payment, to depart. The youngest on board was a 15-year-old boy and the eldest an 86-year-old woman. Only between 13 and 16 individuals of the 997 who were on board when the train left Berlin are reported to have survived the Holocaust.

Up until early 1943, upwards of 15,000 Jews or people with a Jewish background in Berlin were exempted from deportation. To be exempt from deportation, you had to be recognised by the German authorities as working in an industry vital to the German war effort. Many of the elderly who had so far been exempted from deportation were war veterans from the First World War or their relatives. This was probably the case for the Golinski family, who had so far managed to avoid deportation. On 20 February 1943, however, the department of Jewish affairs at the Reichssicherheitshauptamt under Adolf Eichmann decided to revoke the exemption. Now, even Jews working at essential factories and Jewish war veterans were also to be deported.

A mere week after the decision was taken, soldiers from the SS-Liebstandarte Adolf Hitler unit carried out the so-termed "Fabrikaktion" (Factory Action), during which Jews were roughly snatched from their workplaces around Berlin. Allowed only the possessions they had with them at work, they were loaded onto lorries and driven straight to the different transit camps that were now dotted around Berlin. As this was going on, the Berlin Gestapo swooped down on all those wearing the obligatory yellow Star of David on their coats. When this extensive operation was over, Berlin had been effectively emptied of Jews, with the exception of those who had managed to go into hiding or the few that were married to Gentiles.

Shortly after the Fabrikaktion, the Gestapo emptied the transit camps, despatching most of their occupants by the "East transport" straight to Auschwitz. Only one of the transports from Berlin in March 1943 went to Theresienstadt, the fourth and last of the elderly transports, named I/90 or the 4th Grosse Altertransport. On board was the entire Golinski family.

The deportation train, ordered by the Gestapo and supplied by Deutsche Reichsbahn, departed on 17 March 1943 from Berlin-Moabits goods station, although one eye-witness account has it leaving from Grunewald. According to Yad Vashem there was anything from 1,285 to 1,342 people on board. At least 1,000 of them were from Berlin, the rest from different parts of Germany. The youngest was a baby of only a few months, and the oldest a 92-year-old. The records vary, but only between 170 and 221 individuals survived this transport.

The Golinski family and all the others were gathered at the Grosse Hamburger Strasse transit camp. They were then driven in the early morning by lorry to the station, where they had to wait for hours until everyone had been ticked off the deportation lists. By late evening, the Gestapo were done with the paperwork and the train, this time made up of cattle trucks, could set off towards its destination. Conditions on board were appalling, with just a few straw mattresses and a plastic bucket to cater for the needs of over 50 adults. The doors were kept locked for the entire journey.

They arrived early the following morning, when a three-kilometre march from the station to the Theresienstadt concentration camp awaited them. Ruth Baldwin Rosenblatt, one of the few survivors of this transport, gives her own account of the march:

"We walked for about two hours, at least that's as long as it felt to me. We were all carrying our cases – it wasn't so bad for me as I was 14 and my parents could cope, but many of the elderly dumped theirs pretty quickly. They were simply too old and too weak to carry them."

The Golinskis were amongst the last of the Jews living at Lützowstrasse 48/49 to be deported from Berlin to Theresienstadt. For those who survived Theresienstadt, there were even more horrific destinations ahead.

Chapter 15
Encounter with a traitor

Gustaf Ekström re-packs his bag and heads off to Oslo on the "German train". This is the third time he has travelled through Sweden during the War as a soldier in the Waffen-SS. Once in Oslo he makes for the Swedish consulate-general, where he applies for a new travel pass for Sweden. In a memo from 11 May 1942, secretary Kronvall at the Foreign Ministry notes that:

"A person purporting to be Swedish citizen Hilding Gustaf Sigvard Ekström ... has contacted the Swedish consulate-general in Oslo to apply for a Swedish passport."

Ekström used his driving licence and his gymnasium grades and claimed to have arrived on a direct flight from Germany to Norway and lost his Swedish passport in Germany, where he claimed to have been studying at university. In another conversation, Ekström said that he had lost his passport in Oslo. On all these points Ekström is being economical with the truth. He did not fly to Oslo, and is known to have lost his passport on a "German Train" after serving at the Eastern Front on his way back to Germany.

There is no record of what Gustaf Ekström was wearing when he visited the consulate-general, but we presume he was in civilian clothes; and he no doubt deliberately omitted to mention that he was serving as Rottenführer at the SS-Hauptamt in Berlin. A very different occupation indeed to the studies he told the Foreign Ministry he was pursuing.

Secretary Kronvall nevertheless smelt a rat. He requested information from the sixth department's register and even notified the Foreign Ministry. Magnus Hallenborg, head of the ministry's legal office sets the bureaucratic machinery in motion and orders a thorough investigation into how Ekström's passport has gone missing. If Ekström is unable to provide a satisfactory account of how he misplaced it, he will be issued with a provisional passport that he can only use for his return to Sweden. It is clear from another memo that the consulate-general did not buy Ekström's story:

"The applicant has given particularly dubious and sometimes mendacious replies to questions about what his passport looked like, the stamps in it etc., in addition to which it has been established that his story about having arrived by aeroplane on 4 May was false."

Ekström eventually receives a temporary passport. This means that he cannot travel back to Norway or Germany and his desk at the office of the Waffen-SS if he passes through Sweden first. Presumably disappointed, he travels to Lillehammer, where he spends most of his leave. He chooses not to use the temporary passport to travel home to Sweden, as doing so would force him to leave the SS.

Ekström had told the consulate-general that he wanted to visit his mother in Lindesberg, and it could well be the case that he was feeling homesick. He had been away from his family for over a year and had had little opportunity to write home.

But there is another side to his desire to travel home. With a new passport, Gustaf Ekström would be able to travel freely between

Germany or German-occupied Norway and Sweden. This would certainly be an asset for the SS, as he would be able to help in the recruitment effort as he travelled. The time Gustaf Ekström spends in Norway from his first period of leave in May 1942 to the late winter of 1943 is the time that is shrouded in the greatest obscurity and to which he gave the most evasive answers when questioned about it on returning after the War. In certain respects, Ekström's own account wholly contradicts those given independently by other SS volunteers. We do not know for sure if he returns to Berlin after his period of leave or if he is actually relocated to the Waffen-SS Ersatzkommando Norwegen recruitment office in Oslo immediately after his Norwegian leave. He offers no answer to this when questioned about it after the War.

At some time during the spring or early summer of 1942, Gustaf Ekström gets in touch with another Swede working for the Germans, one Thorwald Calais. Calais was a Swedish Nazi and a fellow party member of Ekström's, who was in charge of the activities of the Lindholm Movement in and around Arvika. From the 400-plus-page security police file on Calais, we learn that he was a person who was regarded as a serious problem. He was classified as a Group A Swedish Nazi, a category that was judged to pose the greatest threat to national security.

Calais made his way illegally over the border to Norway on 18 April 1942, just two weeks before Ekström travelled to Oslo on leave. According to Olof Einar Andersson, who accompanied Calais to Norway, the aim was to pay a visit to the Norwegian Nazi Orvar Säter in order to collect 200,000 kronor on behalf of the NSAP/SSS. Other accounts have it that Calais fled to Norway to escape the police, who had a warrant out for his arrest.

Calais and Andersson's funding mission does not go as planned, so Calais places himself at the Germans' disposal and becomes an agent for the German security police. SÄPO's file on Calais places him with the Gestapo, but it is more likely that he served with the regular SiPO or the intelligence service, Abwehr. We contacted the Bundesarchiv and several Norwegian archives to find out more about Thorwald Calais but with little success. We will probably never know of his doings unless more documents are unearthed or made public.

Thorwald Calais eventually built up an extensive network of Swedish, Norwegian and German spies, all operating on behalf of the Germans. A dozen or so of them were sentenced to lengthy prison terms in Sweden and Norway. Judging by SÄPO's interrogations and investigations, it seems that, amongst other things, Calais was trying to map out the positions of the Swedish troops deployed along the Värmland border. His modus operandi has all the trappings of a classic spy movie: false identities, coded letters, bribes, alcohol, secret locations on the Norwegian border where people would meet and exchange classified information, manhunts and gunfire.

Already during the War, Calais was known to the Swedish press, and a great many articles were written about him – which is where the gravity of the situation becomes clear. The newspaper *Arbetet* describes Calais as the "Recruiter-Saboteur" and *Expressen* identifies him as the leader of "German underground work". Calais is suspected by the media of complicity in the Hårsfjärd Disaster of 17 September 1941, when an explosion caused the sinking of three destroyers in the Stockholm archipelago with the loss of 33 lives.

Regardless of the truth of these details, is had been proved beyond doubt that Calais establishes himself as an intermediary in Oslo and the active head of a spy network in Sweden. Several SS volunteers mention Calais when questioned by SÄPO after the War, describing him as the one who issued orders at the Waffen-SS recruitment office on Drammensveien and whom Swedish volunteers were to contact on enlisting with the Waffen-SS. These volunteers he would apparently then invite back to his rooms, first at Mareidalsveijen 225, entrance A, and later at Björn Stallare vei 11, in an attempt to elicit information about the Swedish defences – an act, in other words, of high treason. His method involved offering alcohol, tobacco and anything else that was considered a luxury item during the War. What had the newly arrived volunteers seen along the border? What troops had they encountered? Men who had recently been called up for standby duty were, naturally, of particular interest, since they had fresh information to give Calais about Swedish troops.

On numerous occasions during the War, SÄPO tried in vain to get their hands on Calais by enticing him over the border to Sweden; they also endeavoured to interrogate all those whom they suspected of being in contact with him.

While Gustaf Ekström himself makes no mention of Thorwald Calais in the account he gives of his time in Norway, his extensive cooperation with the traitor is brought to light by other, mutually independent interviews – most importantly that with Calais's wife, Linnea, who was questioned while in quarantine in Älmhult in May 1945. There she described how her husband met her at Oslo railway station on 10 July in the company of Gustaf Ekström.

Ekström himself claims that he was in Berlin at this time and that he started working in Oslo much later, namely 1 September 1942. Another individual – a Swedish SS volunteer by the name of Gerhard Stolpe – places Ekström in Oslo around 10 July 1942. In Stolpe's account, when he reported at the recruitment office on Drammensveien in mid-July 1942, a Swedish Rottenführer called Gustaf Ekström told him to contact Swedish citizen Thorwald Calais, which Stolpe duly did.

It is easy to deduce that Ekström was both a personal friend of Thorwald Calais's and that he actively and on his own initiative supported him in his intelligence efforts by collecting information that the German security service and German armed forces could use in their planning of a possible attack on Sweden. In addition to this, Ekström worked as an interpreter and a translator at the SS recruitment office in Oslo. Ekström's giving the wrong date for his stay in Oslo seems more like an attempt to reduce the danger of his being too closely associated with Thorwald Calais. We may assume that with his central position in the Oslo recruitment office and formerly at the SS-Hauptamt, Ekström was well informed about how the Swedish papers were covering Thorwald Calais. To give detailed replies to police questions about this would naturally have risked putting him in a very sticky situation.

Ekström states himself that he left the Ersatzkommando and the recruitment office in Oslo on 1 November 1942 and returned to Berlin to continue his work at the SS-Hauptamt. Other Swedish SS volunteers place him, however, still in Oslo during this time. Another reason why Ekström was evasive about this time is that the police suspected Calais of operating a recruitment route for the Waffen-SS via Arvika, particularly for the SS "Wiking" division. It is likely that their suspicions were correct.

Thorwald Calais and his family leave Oslo in 1944, having applied for and been granted German citizenship. Calais has secured a job at a department of the German propaganda ministry – "Antikomintern, Abteilung Nord" – and is selected to accompany an international delegation, assembled by the Germans in the interests of propaganda, sent to view the mass graves left by Soviet security service atrocities during the country's occupation of the eastern parts of Poland.

Thorwald Calais and Gustaf Ekström will never see each other again. The last time they met was probably when they celebrated New Year 1943 in Oslo together. However, Calais's wife Linnea will see Ekström once more, although under very different circumstances than when they were standing toasting in the new year in the Norwegian capital.

And at the same time as Ekström is celebrating the new year with the Calaises, the situation for the remaining deportees from Lützowstrasse has seriously worsened. They are now in or on their way to Theresienstadt; some have already left Theresienstadt.

Chapter 16
From Lützowstrasse to the Holocaust

The deportations from all over Europe had flooded the Theresienstadt concentration camp throughout the summer of 1942. By September the camp is overflowing and the problems mount. Disease, starvation and unbearable sanitation claim many lives. The body count rises by the day. To complete the "final solution to the Jewish question", as the Nazis called their genocide, the number of transports from Theresienstadt to the various extermination camps in Poland increase. The weak, elderly and sick are selected first.

The three extermination camps at Treblinka, Sobibór and Belzec are without parallel in world history in their brutal, mechanical and industrial capacity to kill. The camps were set up by staff from the SS's former euthanasia programme, which was named the "T-4 programme" after the War, as the office that administrated the murders was at Tiergartenstrasse 4 in Berlin.

Individuals such as SS-Sturmbannführer Christian Wirth, SS-Hauptscharführer Lorenz Hackenholt and SS-Hauptsturmführer Franz Stangl had worked for many years at different facilities around the Third Reich killing the people whom the Nazis considered inferior. Under the T-4 programme, different methods of mass-slaughter were experimented with and tested. Gassing was a method that was carried out in gas chambers and gas trucks at a number of establishments disguised as convalescent homes. Despite all the secrecy, there were actually some critical voices raised. The church protested and relatives wrote letters to Hitler's Reich Chancellery. The T-4 programme was discontinued in 1941 when the German invasion of the Soviet Union opened up opportunities for an intensive expansion of the concentration/extermination camp operations in the occupied areas. It also dawned on the SS that the wholesale murder of Western Europe's Jews was not possible to achieve using the Einsatzgruppen model that was common in the east. Western European Jews needed to be relocated to Eastern Europe for the "final solution" to be realised.

The Treblinka extermination camp is established in the spring of 1942 by order of SS Reichsführer Heinrich Himmler as part of what would later be dubbed Operation Reinhard – the mass-murder of Polish Jews. Himmler appoints SS-Gruppenführer Odilo Globocnik to be in charge of the action. The extermination camps differ from the ghettos, transit camps and concentration camps. They had one purpose and one purpose only: genocide. When building Treblinka, the SS draws on its experience from the already established extermination camps at Belzec and Sobibór.

On 23 July 1942, the first gassings take place in the camp's three gas chambers. After the first transports of Jews arrive from the Warsaw ghetto, the numbers quickly rise to inconceivable levels; over a quarter of a million people are murdered in Treblinka in the summer of 1942 alone.

At the end of August, it becomes obvious to Himmler and Globocnik that Treblinka's killing capacity is too small for the arriving transports. The machine running the gas chamber, an old Russian tank engine, kept breaking down. The mass graves were constantly filling up and piles of corpses started to rise around the camp. The SS temporarily suspends the transports to Treblinka and replaces the commandant, SS-Obersturmführer Irmfried Eberl with SS-Hauptsturmführer Franz Stangl, who had previously served at Sobibór. Stangl expands the camp's capacity from three to ten gas chambers, and it is not long before the mass slaughter recommences.

Franz Stangl states in his testimony and in interviews with author Gitta Sereny that between 12,000 and 15,000 people could be killed at Treblinka during a single day. "The operation", as Stangl called the killing, went on from early morning to late evening. Other testimonies, such as SS-Obersturmführer Kurt Gerstein's, indicate that as many as 25,000 people could be murdered during a single day. Kurt Gerstein was exonerated and rehabilitated in 1965.

Covering an area of about 600 by 400 metres, Treblinka was not a large camp. During its brief life, from July 1942 to August 1943, it is estimated that at least 900,000 Jews were killed in this small space. The station master at Treblinka, Franciszek Zabecki, was a Polish resistance fighter; he places the number at 1.2 million, based on his observations and the meticulous records he kept of the number of transports and wagons that arrived at the camp. Fewer than 70 of the 900,000 to 1.2 million people who ended up here are thought to have survived.

For virtually everyone transportation to Treblinka meant certain death, often with just a few hours of leaving the train, sometimes directly. The trains to Treblinka cannot be compared to the transports from Berlin to Theresienstadt, where individual wagons were coupled with regular passenger trains. To Treblinka, people were conveyed in overcrowded goods and cattle wagons. Guards had no compunction about beating children or shooting those who did not make the trains in time. There was neither food nor water, and it was not uncommon for the trains to stand idle for hours, sometimes days, at nearby Malkinia station, forcing the Jews to wait in the baking heat or the freezing cold until the extermination camp could accommodate them.

On 19, 21, 23 and 26 September 1942, transports Bo, Bp, Bq and Br were sent to Treblinka from Theresienstadt. On board were 19 of those who once lived on Lützowstrasse. It is here, amongst these doomed souls, that we find Max Ascher. With him or shortly after him come many of the former nursing home residents: Auguste Behrendt, Jenny Davidowsky, Marie Feige, Jenny Hagelberg, Mathilde Levy, Siegfried Casparius, Louis Levin, Anna and Gustav Lewinson, Natalie Neuthal, Salomon Ordower, Scheindel Ordower, Sophie Rosenbaum, Rosa Rosenthal, Sally Herzog, Luise Kirstein, Paula and Sophie Michaelis, and Martha and Minna Salinger. They were all murdered at Treblinka. The numbers are hair-raising; on these four trains alone, 8,018 people were sent to their deaths. Only three people who travelled on these four transports are believed to have survived. All in all, 38 of the 256 Jews who lived on Lützowstrasse are sent to Treblinka, where they are murdered.

The horrific butchery that went on at Treblinka has been described many times. One of the most disturbing depictions comes from the Soviet war correspondent and author Vasily Grossman, who interviews the local population not long after the Red Army takes the area in August 1944. Those who have lived around Treblinka have been fully aware of what has been going on there and can therefore give Grossman detailed eye-witness accounts. He also interviews the 40 or so survivors who have gone into hiding into the surrounding pine forests. His account is also cited at the Nuremberg trials. Grossman writes the following about the arrivals at Treblinka:

"An SS Unteroffizier instructs the newcomers in a loud, clear voice to leave their things in the square and make their way to the bathhouse, taking with them only identity documents, valuables, and toiletries. ... And everyone is overwhelmed by a sense of helplessness, a sense of doom. There is no way to escape, no way to turn back, no way to fight back. ... The things that the new arrivals have just been made to abandon are now sorted out and valued."

Grossman continues to describe how they were then broken down mentally:

"The main thing in the next stage of processing the new arrivals was to break their will. There was a never-ending sequence of abrupt commands ... "Men are to remain where they are. Women and children must go to the barracks on the left and undress." This, according to the accounts of eyewitnesses, marked the start of heartrending scenes. Love – maternal, conjugal, or filial love – told people that they were seeing one another for the last time. Handshakes, kisses, blessings, tears, brief hurried words into which people put all their love, all their pain, all their tenderness, all their despair. ... Inside the women's barrack was a hairdresser. The hair of the naked women was cut by machine, old women had to take off their wigs... The men undressed outside in the yard. ... Everyone was feeling more and more anxious."

When the doomed Jews had been shorn and stripped naked, the next phase of the industrial extermination process began. The element of violence becomes more tangible:

"A new procedure would then begin. Naked people were led to the cash office and made to submit their documents and valuables. ... Here, at the cash office, came the turning point. ... They tore things off their victims' fingers, tore earrings out of their earlobes. ... Faster, faster, faster! Quick, hurry up! Run into the non-existence! ... They marched into a straight alley, with flowers and fir trees planted along it. It was 120 metres long and two metres wide and led to the place of execution. ... The road was sprinkled with white sand, and those who were walking in front with their hands up could see the fresh prints of bare feet in this loose sand: small women's feet, very small children's ones, those left by old people's feet. ... The Germans called this alley 'The Road of No Return'. ... Children had to run to keep up with the adults. ... The journey from the 'cash office' to the place of execution took sixty to seventy seconds."

Then came the actual killing:

"In front of them was a beautiful stone building decorated with wood, looking like an ancient temple. ... There were flowers growing by the entrance, and flowerpots stood there. But all around there was chaos, one could see piles of freshly dug earth everywhere. A vast excavator was throwing out tons of sandy yellow soil, grinding its steel jaws. ... The rattling of the machine digging from morning till evening, the enormous trench graves, mixed with a mad barking of dozens of Alsatian guard dogs. ... The wide door of the death house opened slowly. ... The SS men were beating people with sub-machine gun butts, urging on petrified women ... through the open doors into the gas chambers. ... The people of Wólka, the village closest to Treblinka, say that the screams of the women as they were being murdered were sometimes so horrible that the entire village went mad and ran into the forest to avoid having to hear these piercing screams that penetrated the trunks of trees, heaven and earth. They would then suddenly fall silent only to start up again, just as terrible and piercing as before, drilling into the skulls, bones and souls of anyone who heard them. This was repeated three or four times a day."

All this was experienced by Max Ascher when he was finally murdered in Treblinka one or two days after having been deported from Theresienstadt on 19 September 1942.

In 1943 hundreds of thousands of corpses were incinerated, on Himmler's orders, in enormous open ovens fitted with railway tracks to serve as racks. There were three such ovens at Treblinka, each 250 to 300 metres long, 20 to 25 metres wide and five metres deep. Each oven was filled with around 3,400 to 4,000 bodies at a time before being lit. The monstrous labour of burning all the dead bodies Grossman describes as follows:

"People who helped to burn the bodies say that the ovens looked like a huge volcano. A terrible heat blistered the faces of the workers, the flames rose 8–10 metres into the air and thick columns of greasy black smoke billowed up into the sky and hung like a heavy, *motionless blanket. At night, the local villagers could see these flames from 30–40 kilometres away. They were higher than the pine forests surrounding the camp. The smell of brunt human flesh filled the entire area."*

The killing in Treblinka goes on until 19 October 1943, when Operation Reinhard is brought to a close and Treblinka mothballed. The following day, the remaining Jews are sent to Sobibór and gassed to death there. The buildings and gas chambers are destroyed, and the bricks from the gas chambers are used to build a farm on the site. The ground was ploughed up and trees and lupins planted in the hope that the horrific crimes would remain hidden. But the soil speaks, and to this day, bones are pushed up out of the ground whenever it rains.

When Treblinka was closed down, the transports from Theresienstadt went to Auschwitz instead. This is where 14 of the Jews who lived on Lützowstrasse, and who were now at Theresienstadt, were sent. There were eight people on transports Ea, EI, En, Ev and Et: George and Helen Siegmann, Regine Lippmann, Erich Nathan, Renate and Paula Golinski and Lina Bernhard. Six of them were probably murdered in the gas chamber as soon as they arrived. Two of them, Erich and Renate Golinski, managed to survive Auschwitz. Erich was killed later in Gross-Rosen while Renate was deported to the concentration camp in Flossenbürg. All in all, there were 9,249 Jews on these five transports to Auschwitz. According to Yad Vashem, only 722 of them survived the War.

Auschwitz was an extermination-cum-labour camp that combined opportunistic industrial interests and systematic genocide. This meant that, unlike Treblinka and the other out-and-out extermination camps, there was a small, albeit extremely marginal, chance of survival for those deported there. The healthy and the young were picked out to do slave work under appalling conditions at chemical and pharmaceutical company IG Farben's facility at Auschwitz – "Buna".

Ada Levy, one of the survivors of the aforementioned transports, gives the following account of the trains to Auschwitz in her testimony:

"28 October 1944. My husband and I were also thrown into a freight truck that can hardly contain us all and that was immediately sealed up. ... The terrible conditions during this transport persisted for days and drove us to absolute desperation and almost to our deaths. ... After this journey to the unknown, without air, without water, without light, standing crushed against each other, sometimes against standing corpses, we were unloaded during the night. We had no idea where we were and were put in the hands of silent SS men wielding batons. Men and women were immediately separated, and even though I still hoped to see my husband again the next day I tried to give him another secret look in this horror-filled atmosphere without being aware that this was the last time! We then heard commands being barked: women marched ahead in pairs and in the bright beam of a spotlight stood an SS man sorting us out by pointing: left, right, left, right. ... Those of us on the left were made to march through the night along a country road. Lorries full of friends edged passed us on the way. ... We would have gladly changed places with them as we could hardly stand on our own two feet due to pain and exhaustion, without knowing that those on board the lorries were being driven to their deaths. No one has seen or heard from them since."

The course of events related by Ada Levy is probably what Regina Abraham also goes through when she is sent to Auschwitz from Theresienstadt on 18 April 1944. All trace of her vanishes at the unloading ramp in Auschwitz.

A year earlier, in March 1943, Nazism's claws had reached another of the former nursing home residents – Frieda Orbach. She was also murdered at Auschwitz. One of the few survivors from the transport on which Frieda Orbach was deported, Hans Peter Messerschmidt, describes the transports in his 60-page testimony as largely comprising Jewish community personnel. Frieda

Orbach was picked up from Auguststrasse 14/16, which means that she was probably working at the Jewish hospital. The deportees were taken from the transit camp to Moabits goods station and herded into cattle wagons by Gestapo guards with whips. The transport took at least a full day and night, and when the train finally arrived at Auschwitz Frieda Orbach, Hans Peter Messerschmidt and everyone else on board were hounded out of the wagons. Hans Peter Messerschmidt describes in brief yet poignant sentences their arrival: "Hurry out, put all your cases here... men to the left, women to the right. ... This was the unloading ramp in Auschwitz."

On arrival at Auschwitz, David Salz, who was also on board this transport, started searching for his mother, who had arrived on an earlier transport. He had even inquired about her at the Gestapo office in Berlin. He was beaten up and sent to Auschwitz:

"There was only room to stand. It was jam-packed. No air, but very cold. ... I can't remember how long we travelled for. ... I didn't know anyone. ... People were screaming. There was no lavatory. It was horrific. ... under these conditions, with the cruelty, brutality and the abominable plan that they had for transporting Jews to Auschwitz. We arrived at Auschwitz, again a lot of screaming, punching and pushing, the process began at once with canes and whips with rubber knots. They started to sort us out.... I knew I had to get put in the group selected for labour. I was 13 years old ... so I stood on tiptoe when it came to my turn. He asked – How old are you – 17; Profession? – Electrician. ... We saw women in the distance being forced to strip. We saw all that. They gave them towels and soap and they went off to wherever it was they went."

Orbach, Salz and Messerschmidt were completely surrounded by SS guards and prisoners in striped clothes stacked their luggage as they stepped onto the ramp. They were ordered to line up in rows of five for selection. Strong people, often between 16 and 50, were sent to one side, while all the others, including the elderly, women, children and babies were sent to the other, which meant that they were immediately sent to their deaths in the gas chambers. Frieda Orbach was 46 when she arrived at Auschwitz. If she was judged healthy and strong, she might have held out for a time and, like Hans Peter Messerschmidt and David Salz, been sent as a slave to the IG Farben industrial complex in Auschwitz Monowitz (Buna). However, all traces of her disappear, just like Regina Abraham, at the ramp. A total of 559 Jews from this transport from Berlin were murdered in the gas chambers that night, 13 March 1943. Only 13 from this transport survive the Holocaust. By the end of 1944, 162 of the 256 Jews who once lived in the nursing home have been deported from Berlin or fallen victim to the Holocaust.

Renate Golinski, who was deported on to Flossenbürg, finally ends up as a slave in the arms industry. Some of the time she spends in Freiberg working at the Max Hildebrandt factory, which manufactured lenses and sights for German missile weapons. In April 1945 she is dispatched on a death march to the concentration camp in Mauthausen, where she is liberated by US troops a month later. After spending some time in care, she manages to make her way back to Berlin before finally emigrating to Israel, where she works at Kibbutz Ma'ayan Zvi.

Six million Jews were exterminated during the Second World War. From Berlin alone, over 50,000 Jews were deported and killed. The Nazi violence that was visited upon the 256 former residents of the Lützowstrasse nursing home was by no means unique.

While working on this book, we came across a chilling map of the Deutsche Reichsbahn railway network from 1942. On it, we find the stations of Malkinia (the one closest to Treblinka), Sobibór, Belzec and Auschwitz marked just like any other, and this while the genocide was at its peak. The map also shows that the trains carrying their doomed human cargo passed though several countries and numerous stations, many of which they no doubt stopped at en route to their destination, revealing in stark clarity the true continental scale of the Holocaust.

However, maybe the Holocaust as a phenomenon cannot be

fully grasped from a general perspective and perhaps must be understood from the specifics, event by event, every deportation, every eviction, every photograph, every document, every personal fate. And only once these specifics are slotted into the greater context can we begin to understand.

Chapter 17
Nuremberg

Gustaf Ekström leaves Oslo in the new year of 1942–1943, and returns to the job of interpreter and translator at the SS-Hauptamt on Hagenstrasse 39–47 in Grunewald. In early February 1943, at the same time as the German forces capitulate at Stalingrad, Gustaf Ekström hands in his resignation to the Waffen-SS. He leaves the SS and Berlin to study applied chemistry at the Institute of Technology in Nuremberg. His resignation is accepted after about two years' service, and he commences his studies after a period of factory work at the Fresenius laboratories in Wiesbaden. Ekström's choice to continue his studies is no doubt welcomed by both the faculty and the SS, as in 1943 Germany was in desperate need of chemists and engineers.

It is from this time that Gustaf Ekström's card from the NSDStB, the German National Socialist Student Organisation, can be found in the Bundesarchiv catalogues. Ekström continued to be an organised Nazi, this time as a member of yet another body under the German Nazi party, one that devoted much of its time to book burning and the ideological monitoring of fellow students.

Nuremberg was the site of the vast Nazi rallies in the 1930s and can therefore be described as something of an ideological heartland for the Nazi movement. It was here that the famous filmmaker Leni Riefenstahl recorded the notorious propaganda film *Triumph of the Will*.

Nuremberg was also known for its narrow alleyways and charming mediaeval buildings. But the German cities will soon no longer look as they did when Ekström arrived in Germany in the spring of 1941. The War is going from bad to worse, and already in August 1943, just a couple of months after Ekström starts studying, the RAF have dropped around 1,500 tonnes of bombs on the city. On 27 August 1943, another 1,500 tonnes are dropped, resulting in the loss of thousands of lives. Nuremberg was a rich military target, possessing as it did key parts of the arms industry; the symbolic and propagandistic value of bombing the city where the great Nazi rallies were held either cannot be overestimated.

Teaching at the Institute of Technology continued during the War, although its buildings were not spared the bombing raids. Gustaf Ekström probably spent much of his time in the city's bomb shelters, one of which, right next to the university, has been preserved in the apartment block at Hirsvogelstrasse 14. Here there was room for 678 people; if Ekström had been close by when the air-raid sirens sounded, it might have been to this very room that he had to run.

The Allies are advancing on all fronts towards Germany's borders. On 6 June 1944 the Normandy landings leave Germany facing attack on three fronts: France in the west, the Soviet Union in the East and Italy in the south. Within a few months, Paris is liberated. The Red Army marches on Warsaw. Finland pulls out of the War and kicks out the German troops. The division that Ekström served with, Waffen-SS "Nord" Division, takes part in the rearguard fighting back to German-occupied Norway. During the battles, the division lays waste to the Finnish town of Rovaniemi in revenge for Finland's withdrawing from the War.

Countless thousand tonnes of bombs drop on Berlin, turning the city into a smoking pile of rubble. The NSAP/SSS offices at Immelmannstrasse 10 are totally destroyed during an air raid on 30

January 1944, followed by the SS-Hauptamt offices on Lützowstrasse later that same year. A contemporary photograph shows people hurrying away from the burned out ruins of the quarter.

On Monday 26 February 1945, some 1,200 US bombers are scrambled for Berlin, their aim to knock out communication lines and the Germany army infrastructure. That same morning, the Calais family wake up in their flat at Maikowskistrasse 16. Thorwald Calais leaves home for work at the Anti-Comintern. He makes it to his office in the large Rathaus in Schöneberg shortly before the air raid sirens sound. Thorwald Calais and hundreds of others make their way down to the shelter in the basement. The US planes drop almost 1,700 tonnes of anti-personnel bombs and over 1,200 tonnes of incendiary bombs. One of the heavier bombs hits the Rathaus and penetrates the shelter, killing Calais and hundreds of the others there with him. Thousands of people are killed and over 80,000 are made homeless by the bombardment. Calais is buried on 7 March in a mass grave at Wilmersdorfer Waldfreidhof Stahnsdorf. Linnea Calais decides to try to flee back to Sweden to escape the bombs and the approaching Red Army, which leaves widespread destruction in its wake as it advances on Germany.

As the Allies and the Red Army draw near, the Nazi regime's crimes against humanity become ever more obvious to a shocked world. In the east, the Majdanek concentration camp is liberated on 23 July 1944. On 27 January 1945, Auschwitz is liberated by Soviet troops. In the winter of 1945, the Red Army musters its forces one last time to begin the battle for Berlin in April. It is now beyond all doubt that the War for Germany is over. The bombs fall with increasing intensity in Ekström's Nuremberg too, and on 2 January 1945 the entire mediaeval city centre is reduced to rubble, killing 1,800 people and making some 100,000 homeless.

The American troops close in on Ekström. On 7 March 1945 they take the last intact bridge over the Rhine at Remagen. After that, things go quickly and within the space of a few weeks, the US troops are within spitting distance from Nuremberg.

On 5 April, the situation becomes untenable. Many of the city's historical buildings lie in ruins and the population has been halved. The university cancels all teaching and Gustaf Ekström deems it best to flee the approaching Americans. Furious Allied troops search frantically for SS soldiers; after having liberated the German concentration camps they hunt down those linked to the organisation responsible for carrying out the horrors that have been discovered. The east can offer no sanctuary for Ekström, nor the south. His only option is to try to make his way to Sweden. The question, though, is how? He still does not have a valid Swedish passport.

Help arrives in the body of another Swedish Nazi with a position high up in the Swedish civic administration and in the academic world. In 1933, a group of well-known German professors sign a pledge of allegiance to Adolf Hitler. One of them is the Swedish professor Sven Helander at the School of Economics in Nuremberg, who, according to the Christian Albrecht University in Kiel, was a member of the Nazi party between 1933 and 1945. He is also a regular writer for *Sverige-Tyskland*, a Swedish newspaper published by the pro-Nazi cultural association of the same name that carries, alongside interviews with Adolf Hitler, articles bearing such headlines as "The Global Jewish Problem" or written by the likes of Per Engdahl, leader of the New Swedish Movement.

In 1945 Sven Helander is at the Swedish Foreign Ministry's consulate in Nuremberg. Gustaf Ekström contacts him and with his help obtains special attestation of his Swedish citizenship and a personal recommendation to the Swedish legation in Berlin. Thus furnished with a new temporary passport, Ekström makes his way through a country in tatters up to Lübeck, where Helander has informed him that expat Swedes have gathered to ride home on the White Buses, the Red Cross' rescue action led by Folke Bernadotte.

So Ekström flees from the Americans with the assistance of another Swedish Nazi, and secures a seat on one of the busses that Sweden has sent to help former concentration camp prisoners from Theresienstadt, to where over a hundred of those once living on Lützowstrasse were deported. Many of them have described what it was like to arrive in Sweden after having survived the Holocaust. One of them is Hédi Fried, who survived both Bergen Belsen and Auschwitz. This is how she describes arriving in Sweden on the White Buses, the same rescue mission that Gustaf Ekström also returned home on:

"It was like coming to Paradise. We were welcomed with open arms, with milk chocolate and sandwiches..."

While Ekström heads towards Sweden, Sven Helander is still living around Nuremberg; on 9 December 1945, Dagens Nyheter writes that he has been taken by the US military police in West Germany. His detention drags out, and he is still in police custody by 27 March 1946. He is eventually released, however, and there is no record of his being convicted of any crime. In 1948, Sven Helander starts work at the Ministry of Finance at home in Sweden.

Once in Lübeck, Ekström meets Thorwald Calais's widow, Linnea, amongst the other expat Swedes waiting to be shipped home by the Red Cross. He asks her to make sure that his luggage is taken on her transport to Sweden, as Ekström himself will be travelling with the White Buses to Copenhagen, where he intends to exchange his 300 German *Reichsmark*. While the local branch of the German national bank cannot help him, a colleague from his time at the SS-Hauptamt in Berlin helps him to buy around 200 Danish kronor at the Waffen-SS service office in Copenhagen. Some of this money he spends in Copenhagen before arriving by air in Malmö on Saturday 21 April 1945.

Ekström now makes his way to the Red Cross quarantine centre for German former Swedish citizens in Älmhult, where he hopes to find Linnea Calais and his luggage. He roams around outside the area and finally locates Linnea Calais. This is when the police arrest him. A Malmö police detective hears the conversation and infers, quite rightly, that Ekström and Calais are known to each other. In the report that detective constable Knut G Nilsson writes about the incident, the conversation that drew his attention concerned Ekström's luggage, which had somehow been misplaced, much to Ekström's presumably very audible annoyance.

The Malmö police are aware that Thorwald Calais is wanted for espionage against Sweden. They have also been informed that he is believed to have died during the air raids of two months previously, on 26 February, although his fate has not been confirmed. So the police go searching for him amongst the inmates of the quarantine, and grow curious about Gustaf Ekström, who they think could be Thorwald Calais, and it is only once they have access to a description of Calais and compared photographs that their suspicions are dispelled.

It is also now that the more probing interrogations are held with Ekström. The records unfortunately do not include the more incisive police questions; for example, his dealings with Calais is never fully investigated. Afterwards, Ekström is also placed in quarantine, where he remains for a couple of weeks before finally returning home to his mother in Lindesberg.

On 30 April, a week after Ekström returned to Sweden, Hitler takes his own life, leading a little later to an unconditional German surrender. Millions upon millions of people have died, and yet more have been displaced. The newspapers are full of reports on concentration camps, the Holocaust, the killings – everything that Nazism has done in the German people's name. These accounts incite many SS veterans to eventually dissociate themselves from the organisation that had so much terror and death on its conscience. Not so Gustaf Ekström. He continues to be a member of the Swedish Nazi party, NSAP/SSS.

Just a month or so after the end of the War, Ekström is called up for refresher exercises at his former I3 in Örebro, his recent interrogation by the police about his connections with the wanted and suspected traitor Calais clearly being no deterrent to the Swedish armed forces. On 8 June 1945 Ekström completes his refresher course. Ekström admits to having no remorse after the War, and replying to author Hans Werner Neulen's question of how Swedish society treated him on his return, writes:

"Completely normally. In April 1946 I found myself a good job as a cartographer in Stockholm."

The de-Nazification process now begins in Germany. The civil population are made to visit the concentration camps and to bury the corpses. Films are recorded documenting the crimes and outrages and then screened at cinemas. Archives, correspondence and membership lists are confiscated, and the Nazi party and all its subordinate organisations are banned. Their symbols are banned, their greetings are banned, their expressions are banned. The first verse of the German national anthem is judged offensive and that too is banned, and rewritten. The old Nazi battle songs are banned from public performance.

Hearings are conducted and many leading Nazis are arrested and held to account at the Nuremberg trials. Amongst them is Gottlob Berger, head of the SS-Hauptamt and Ekström's former employer, who is sentenced to 25 years. Franz Riedweg, who was one of Ekström's superiors and who organised the recruitment operations in the occupied countries, is sentenced in his absence in 1947 to 16 years imprisonment in Switzerland.

The Nuremberg tribunal declares the SS in its entirety to be a criminal organisation. The tribunal writes in its judgement the following about the SS:

"The SS played a particularly significant role in the persecution of the Jews. ... It is impossible to single out any one branch of the SS which was not involved in these criminal activities. The Allgemeine SS was an active participant in the persecution of the Jews and was used as a source of concentration camp guards. Units of the Waffen SS were directly involved in the killing of prisoners of war and the atrocities in occupied countries. It supplied personnel for the Einsatzgruppen, and had command over the concentration camp guards after its ab-

sorption of the Totenkopf SS, which originally controlled the system. Various SS police units were also widely used in the atrocities in occupied countries and the extermination of the Jews there. The SS central organization supervised the activities of these various formations and was responsible for such special projects as the human experiments and "final solution" of the Jewish question. ... CONCLUSION: The SS was utilized for purposes which were criminal under the Charter, involving the persecution and extermination of the Jews, brutalities and killings in concentration camps, excesses in the administration of occupied territories, the administration of the slave labour programme and the mistreatment and murder of prisoners of war. ... In dealing with the SS the Tribunal includes all persons who had been officially accepted as members of the SS, including the members of the Allgemeine SS, members of the Waffen SS, members of the SS Totenkopf Verbände and the members of any of the different police forces who were members of the SS."

There were additional trials held in Eastern Europe after the War – of Auschwitz commandant Rudolf Höss, who was sentenced to death by Poland's Supreme National Tribunal and hanged on a gallows next to the crematoria in Auschwitz on 16 April 1947. SS-Obergruppenführer Friedrich Jeckeln, who was responsible for the Rumbula forest massacre (amongst other atrocities), was sentenced to death by a Russian military tribunal in Riga on 3 February 1946, and was hanged at the Square of Victory in Riga in front of a 4,000-strong crowd. SS-Standartenführer Otto Bovensiepen, head of the security service and the security police in Berlin in 1941–1943 and thus implicated in the deportation of the Jews from Berlin, was sentenced to death by a Danish court in 1948. He was freed, however, on 1 December 1953.

Despite many convictions and legal processes, the de-Nazification process in West Germany abates. All sectors of German society have been involved in the War and a new bogeyman has risen up against the nation in the shape of the Soviet Union. Slowly but surely, more Nazi officials regain their former positions with the police and other authorities. A number of the leading figures are convicted, but many of the murders and war criminals walk free.

Several lengthy trials are held in the 1960s. In 1963, a new case is brought against Otto Bovensiepen concerning the deportation of Jews from Berlin, but he suffers a heart attack in 1971. His state of health is deemed too poor and the trial is abandoned. 1963 sees the start of "Der Auschwitzprocess", in which 17 former staff of Auschwitz are given lengthy prison sentences. The Treblinka trials begin in 1964, and the Sobibór tribunal two years later. Several leading officials and many of their lower-ranking colleagues are convicted and sent to prison. Franz Stangl, the commandant at Treblinka, is sentenced on 22 December 1970 to life for the murder of at least 400,000 people. He dies in prison in 1971.

On 17 June 2016, 94-year-old camp guard Reinhold Hanning is sentenced to five years for complicity in the murder of 170,000 people in Auschwitz. Time will tell if this was the last trial of its kind.

Chapter 18
Nazis old and new

After the War, Ekström works as a cartographer and has at least two different home addresses in Stockholm up until 1947. He remains an active member of the Swedish Nazi party NSAP/SSS, which is now languishing as membership numbers wane. The party coffers are now empty. In 1950, the party executive decides to call it a day. Its remaining members seek refuge in other companion and veteran societies, such as Sveriges Nationella Förbund (SNF, the National League of Sweden). The Social Democrat "folkhem" programme begins in earnest during the postwar period, and the party will go on to govern the country until 1976. Sweden's various extremist movements descend into a more sect-like existence compared their prewar heyday.

A couple of years after the War, Gustaf Ekström, like so many other Nazis, turned his gaze to South America. This we know from the two occasions, 8 August 1947 and 27 April 1948, that he applies for a certificate of impunity to travel there. This information is in SÄPO's file on him in the National Archives. Unfortunately, it does not say which country he went to, but the fact is that at this time, Sweden was included in one of the so-called "rat lines"

```
                PROTOKOLL.
        Fäst vid Sverigedemokraterna-Malmö's årsmöte den 21/2-88 på S:t gertrud
        Kl.15.00-16.00.Antalet närvarande: 23 personer.
        § 1  Vice ordförande,Ulf Ranshede,öppnar mötet.
             Mötet godkänner stadge ändring, Ordförande och vice ordförande bytes
             till "Talesmän".
        § 2  Till mötes ordförande väljes Ulf Ranshede.
        § 3  Till mötes sekreterare väljes Gösta Bergquist
        § 4  Till justeringsmän,tillika rösträknare, väljes
             Marie Sandström.
             Micael Jonasson.
        § 5  Mötet godkänner presenterad röstlängd.
        § 6  Verksamhets berättelsen för 1987 uppläses och godkännes av mötesdel-
             tagarna.
        § 7  Säges att revisions berättelsen 1987 uppskjutes till årsmötet 1989.
        § 8  Styrelsen beviljas ansvarsfrihet för verksamhets året 1987.
        § 9  Till styrels för 1988 väljes:
             Talesman Ulf Ranshede
             Talesman Tillsätts senare av styrelsen
             Ledamot Marie Sandström
             Ledamot Micael Jonasson
             Ledamot Mats Tullberg
             Suppleant Ulf Gregow
             Suppleant Fritz Håkansson
             Suppleant Tommy Christianson
             Mötet fastslår att partiets firma, som hittills tecknats av Marie
             Sandström och Micael Jonasson, fortsätter teckna firman.
        §10  Till revision väljes: Gustav Ekstroem (Lund) och Mikael Jönsson
             (Staffanstorp).
        §11  Ulf Ranshede väljes som ombud till partiets förbundsstämma.
        §12  Till valkandidater 1988 väljes Ulf Ranshede,Marie Sandström,Micael
             Jonasson,Fritz Håkansson och Tommy Christianson.Det beslutas att styr-
             elsen bemyndigas att tillsätta ytterligare valkandidater när sådana
             finnes.
        §13  Allmän debatt
             Beslut; a)Styrelsen skall ommöjligt ordna parti lokal,närradio och
             parti kansli.
             b)Månadsbidrag skall sökas hos villiga medlemar och andra.
             c)Möjlignet till talarmöten i södra Skåne skall studeras.
                                                              forts.följer
```

50. The Sweden Democrats in Malmö, minutes of the annual meeting of 21 February 1988. §10 mentions Gustaf Ekström. Copy in the authors' private archive.

51. At a rally with the Sweden Democrats, august 1994, the square of St: Knut, Malmö. 150 or so member of the Sweden Democrats chant "Sieg Heil" and perform the Hitler salute. There is also men in uniform present in the crowd. Several of the members who attended this rally will later join Gustaf Ekström during the 30 November manifestations the same year. Photo: Martin Olson/Bilder i Syd.

52. Lund on 30 November 1994. Gustaf Ekström is standing by the base of the statue. He has doffed his hat for the laying of the wreath. Gösta Bergqvist dressed in a cap is seen to the left of Ekström. Photo: Jonn Leffmann.

53. Gustaf Ekström, passport photograph. Photo: Copy in the authors' private archive.

54. Lützowstrasse 48/49, 2015. Photo: Matti Palm.

55. Grunewald station, 2015. Röschen Silbermann lived on Lützowstrasse and was one of the thousands of Jews deported from Berlin. She was sent on Transport I/2 on 4 June 1942 to Theresienstadt concentration camp. The train departed from Grunewald, where a memorial has since been laid on platform 17. Photo: Matti Palm.

56. The Turkish motor vessel Asya, carrying 733 Jewish survivors arrives at Haifa, Palestine 3 April 1946, after being intercepted by a British destroyer near the coast. The Jews, who were attempting to enter Palestine illegally, were detained by immigration officials. The Hebrew name "Tel Hai" can be seen painted in Hebrew above the name "Asya". Renate Golinski were among the passengers. Photo: Dr Ernst Aschner/Keystone/Getty Images.

57. Renate Golinski and her son at the Kibbutz Ma'ayan Zvi in the town of Zikhron Ya'akov. Photo: Private.

Gustaf Ekström
* 9. 10. 07   ✝ 16. 7. 95
Unterscharführer der ehem. Waffen-SS
5. SS-Panzerdivision „Wiking"
Seine Kameraden in Schweden

ᛉ Ihre Ehre hieß Treue! ᛣ

58. The Obituray of Gustaf Ekström in Der Freiwillige, a journal for former members of the Waffen-SS. He is mistakenly said to have belonged to 5. SS-Panzerdivision "Wiking". At the bottom of the page a version of the SS motto is printed, "Ihre Ehre heiß True". (their honour is loyalty). The loyalty is linked to the oath the members of the SS took when swearing their allegiance to Adolf Hitler. The motto is today banned in Germany according to the German Strafgesetzbuch (Criminal Code) in section § 86a. Photo: Antifaschistische Pressearchiv, Berlin.

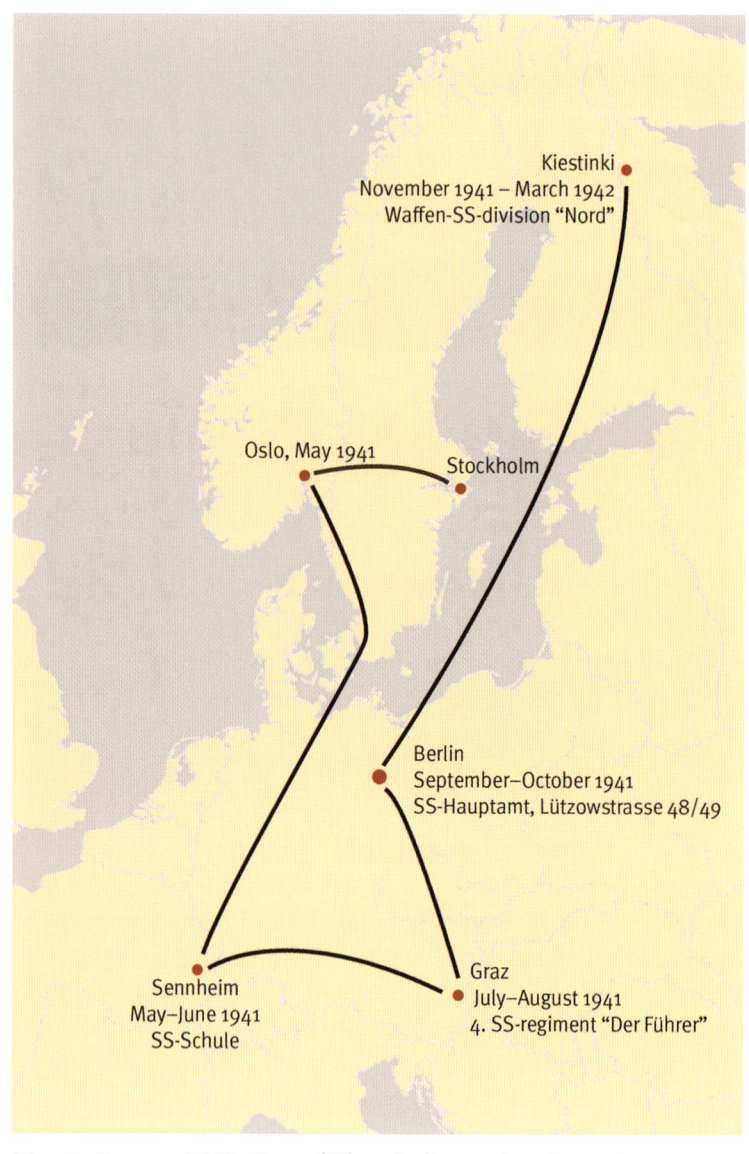

Map 1. Europe 1942, Gustaf Ekström's travels, 1941–1942.

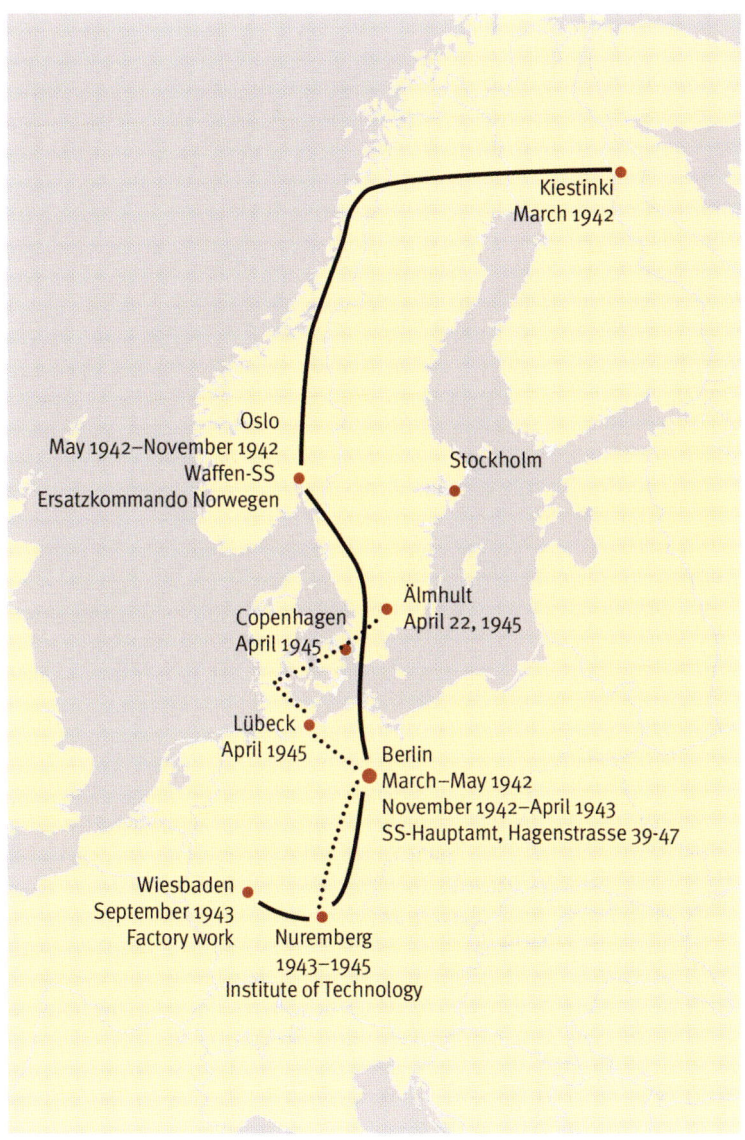

Map 2. Europe 1942, Gustaf Ekström's travels, 1942–1945.

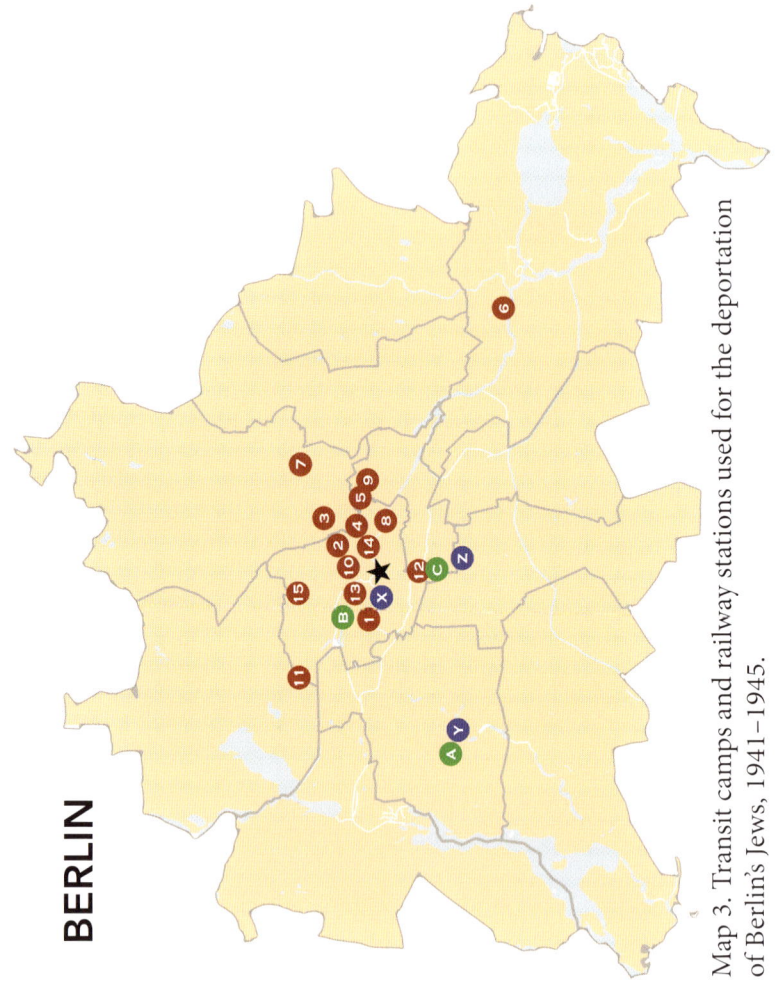

Map 3. Transit camps and railway stations used for the deportation of Berlin's Jews, 1941–1945.

Transit camps in Berlin 1941–1945
1. Levetzowstrasse 7/8
2. Grosse Hamburger Strasse 26
3. Schönhauser Allee 22
4. Artilleriestrasse 31 (today Tucholskystrasse)
5. Friedenstrasse 3
6. Mahlsdorfer Strasse 94
7. Parkstrasse 22
8. Brunnenstrasse 41
9. Gerlachstrasse 18/21 and 19/21 (today Mollstrasse)
10. Gormannstrasse 3
11. Hermann-Göring-Kaserne (Reinickendorf) (today Julius-Leber-Kaserne)
12. Mauerstraße (Mitte) (corner Zimmerstraße)
13. Feldzeugmeisterstrasse (Moabit)
14. Rosenstrasse 2-4
15. Schulstrasse 78

Train stations from where the deportation trains departed
A. Grunewald Bahnhof
B. Putlitzstrasse/Moabit freight train station
C. Anhalter Bahnhof

Important adresses for Gustaf Ekström
X. SS-Hauptamt/Lützowstrasse 48/49
Y. SS-Hauptamt/Hagenstrasse 39-47
Z. NSAP/SSS Ortsgrupp Berlin, Immelmannstrasse 10 (today Dudenstrasse)

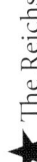 The Reichstag

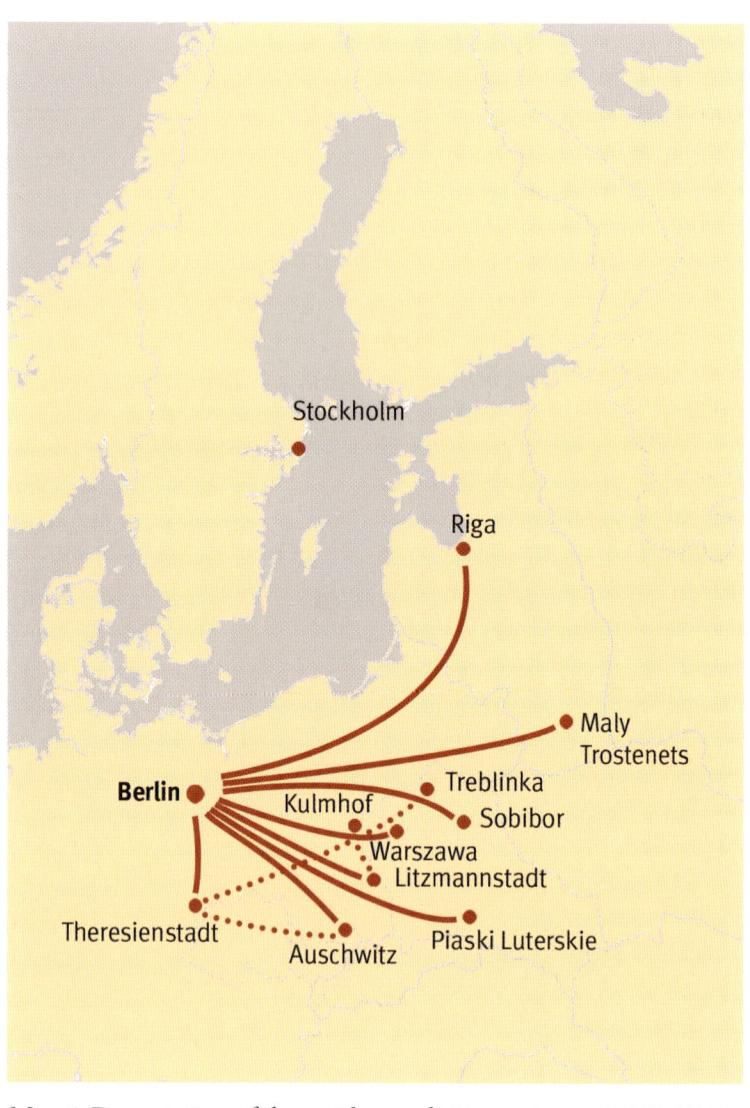

Map 4. Deportation of the residents of Lützowstrasse 48/49, 1941–1944.

for Nazis and war criminals fleeing from Germany to, above all, Argentina.

One thing that the many fleeing Nazis had in common was that they were dependent on someone helping them with financial and with practical matters, such as a place to hide while fleeing.

In South America were Swedes who were particularly active in helping Nazis escape from Europe. Swedish SS veteran Hans Caspar Kreuger, a fellow-member of the NSAP/SSS, is said to have been one of the key organisers of the mass Nazi flight to South America. Kreuger and another former SS soldier, Thorolf Hillblad, ran a travel agency with the rather telling name *Via Nord*. Hillblad was also the correspondent whom the NSAP/SSS had had on Immelmannstrasse in Berlin, which means that Ekström had met him when he visited the Swedish Nazis' Ortsgrupp in Berlin. Via Nord not only arranged visas and tickets, but also met the passengers and helped them find somewhere to live and a job in Argentina. The Argentinean author Uki Goñi describes Hans Caspar Kreuger and his travel agency as an important cog in Perón's machinery for helping Nazis into Argentina. Amongst other discoveries, Goñi has found that Via Nord arranged entry permits for SS-Oberscharführer Josef Schwammberger, the commandant of the Przemyśl ghetto between 1942 and 1945, and one of the most heinous of the SS war criminals who fled to Argentina. He obtained his visa to Argentina in 1948 and arrived by boat in March 1949. Schwammberger was eventually extradited and sentenced in Germany in 1991 to life for murder and complicity to murder.

The material we have access to does not say if Ekström had contact with Hillblad or Kreuger or any role in their activities in 1947 or 48, and our contacts with the Argentinean authorities were fruitless. To be sure, he could have travelled to South America as a tourist or to look for work, but it is also possible that he applied for an exit permit because he was part of the northern route for fleeing Nazis. But despite our assiduous efforts, we had come to a dead end with this. The South American chapter of Ekström's life will probably remain unwritten.

After Gustaf Ekström's trips to South America in 1947 and 48 he returns to Nuremberg and the American-occupied zone of what is now becoming West Germany. He resumes his studies in applied Chemistry at the Institute of Technology, where many of the professors who had once worked there have had to leave their chairs owing to their Nazi associations. But one professor remains from Ekström's wartime studies, Josef Röll. Professor Röll will, as we shall see, play a decisive role in Ekström's stay in Nuremberg.

In 1949, Germany was a country divided. The east was under the control of Stalin's armies and the west was divided into three occupied zones – one British, one French and one American. Nuremberg and its home state of Bavaria belonged to the American zone. Through the Marshall Plan, massive investments were made in the rebuilding of West Germany, and it is now, four or five years after the War that results are starting to show through – that which will be known to posterity as the German "miracle".

But the fruits of new prosperity did not fall to all, and there was a serious lack of food, consumer goods and accommodation during the postwar period. The reborn German democracy was filled with new parties, organisations and societies, and the more Nazi party veterans there were that returned to politics, the more they showed up in the cadre for these organisations. One party that sees the light of day on 2 October 1949: the SRP, *Sozialistische Reichspartei Deutschlands*, which translates as the Socialist Reich Party of Germany. The party exploits effectively the discontent simmering in parts of West Germany.

The Swedish security police (SÄPO) continues to keep an eye on Gustaf Ekström even after the War. Through informants and tipsters, or "sources" as they are referred to in the documents, we discover that Ekström is in frequent and close contact with members the Socialist Reich Party in West Germany. The details are, however, fragmentary. So we decide to find out more. If Ekström was studying, there should be a record of him at the university that can lead us further. This proves harder than we expected. All archivists, officials, private individuals and others whom we have contacted while writing this book have been friendly and helpful in answering our questions. But the university refuses to release even the slightest morsel of information. We decide to contact the Antifascist Press Archive in Berlin to ask if they have anything in their records about what Gustaf Ekström could have been up to in Germany after the War.

A couple of days later we receive a reply. A copy of a letter to the far-right newspaper *Preussische Allgemeine Zeitung* from 25 July 2009. At first, we are doubtful that it will be able to help us piece together the puzzle. Under the heading "In memory of a non-German comrade" the writer, one Helmut Panzer, describes a Swede called "Ekstroem", who fought in northern Finland and then lived in Nuremberg. We put the letter aside for a fortnight or so and thought that even though there might be a connection, the likelihood seemed remote. The first thing we did when we returned to it was to deconstruct the letter. Who wrote it? Is it a pseudonym or a genuine name, and perhaps most pertinently of all, is this Helmut Panzer still alive? Reading the letter again we fancy we see that names and places fit into the pattern surrounding Ekström.

We start looking. If Helmut Panzer is a subscriber, maybe he has written more letters. It turns out that our assumption is correct. Another letter contains a description of the fighting in north Italy towards the end of the War, with Panzer claiming to have fought as a soldier in the Pioneer Battalion of the 4th Parachute Division. We also note that all letters have been sent from the same place in Switzerland. That information leads us to two telephone numbers. We ring them.

It transpires that Helmut Panzer is a former fellow-student of Gustaf Ekström's and a close friend from his time in Germany. Somewhat amazed, we hold a close to 45-minute interview with him. Panzer also promises to write a detailed account and send it to us. A couple of weeks later, two densely written sheets of A4 arrive along with a personal greeting.

Helmut Panzer returned from war imprisonment in the Soviet Union in 1948, and three years later met and became friends with

Gustaf Ekström in Nuremberg. Ekström was studying a couple of classes above Helmut Panzer and they hit it off immediately. Panzer describes Ekström as an odd character, correct, withdrawn, courteous and insightful. He also mentions Gustaf Ekström's, as he puts it, very good relationship with Professor Josef Röll, for whom they both studied. Panzer writes in his report to us:

"[Ekström's] love for Germany was boundless. Especially striking was the concern Gustaf Ekström had for Germany's future." He continues: *"We moved in many different party circles."*

Panzer, with his background as a former prisoner of war and deep aversion to Communism, and Ekström with his Nazi convictions, attended many different meetings of the various parties and organisations that catered for the hundreds of thousands of German refugees that had been driven from their homes in former German areas that had fallen to Poland or the Soviet Union after the War. They also go to meetings arranged by organisations set up specifically for former prisoners of war, such as the Verband der Heimkehrer, Kriegsgefangenen und Vermisstenangehörigen (VdH).

In the early 1950s, they are active members of the far-right Deutsche Gemainschaft's election rallies. Panzer describes Ekström as being highly engaged in these events. According to Panzer, there was the occasional Communist attempt to sabotage the meetings, but with the help of other German veterans they would manage to force the leftist subversives – with violence – to listen, while standing on the tips of their toes, to the assembly singing the first verse of the national anthem "Deutschland über alles".

It is during this time that Gustaf Ekström becomes involved in the Socialist Reich Party, which in only a couple of years has become an established party in Germany. One of the members of the SRP executive was Otto Ernst Remer, a Wehrmacht major and an officer in the Wachbataillon in Berlin, who had played a key part in scuppering the attack on Adolf Hitler on 20 July 1944 and accordingly been promoted by Hitler in person.

The SRP was a neo-Nazi party that garnered considerable attention inside and outside Germany. With a programme that was largely a copy of the former Nazi party's, Remer travelled around delivering speeches at meetings that in many respects were directed along the same lines as the old Hitler rallies of the 1930s. Remer is described in contemporary texts as a fantastically expressive person who honed his oratorical skills in emulation of Hitler, yet was like Goebbels. These meetings often opened with a band playing the marches "Preussens Gloria" and – above all – the Badonweiler March, the one that accompanied Hitler's entrances during Nazi days. The marches were played again and again while the crowds were made to wait for a later appearance by Remer or some other speaker from the party executive. Normally, the main thrust of these speeches was to make Germany great again, or to vaunt the SRP for having donned the mantle of the national socialist revolution.

The SRP made itself out to be the German Nazi party's successor and held Karl Dönitz, who was appointed Reichspräsident (president) by Hitler shortly before his suicide, to be Germany's last legitimate head of state and West German Federal Chancellor Konrad Adenauer's government to be an illegal puppet regime of the USA. The SRP vehemently maintained that the Holocaust had never happened and that the films from the concentration camps were fictions staged by the Allies. The honour of Germany's soldiers was to be reinstated. The party's messages, be they promulgated in speeches, leaflets, newspapers and the like, were dominated by the rallying cry that Germany was due its rightful place in history and in Europe. The SRP regarded the West German government in Bonn as an elite, an establishment erected upon the backs of returning Germans who had betrayed the country by fleeing from Hitler – code, needless to say, for the Jews. The SRP also demanded that the areas in the east should be ceded back to Germany and even spoke of a final solution to the Jewish question.

Ekström and Panzer were invited to the meeting where the local branch of the SRP in northern Bavaria was founded. Ekström was thus active in the SRP's attempts to organise and start operating in Bavaria. He is said to have made such an impression at the meetings that reporters there mistook him for the British fascist leader Oswald Mosley, visiting to assist the SRP. Ekström apparently played along with this and used the name Mosley as an alias during his time there.

The SRP fared so well that in the state election in May 1951 it won a full 11 per cent of the vote in Niedersachsen. In other words, only six years after the War, hundreds of thousands of Germans were openly backing a neo-Nazi party. The German authorities, particularly counter-subversion, treated the SRP as a serious threat and began legal proscription proceedings. The SRP's attempts to become established in Bavaria were less successful. The US professor of political science Kurt Tauber writes in his *Beyond Eagle and Swastika*, the most comprehensive study of German postwar nationalism, that the SRP mobilised a modest 200 or so members in the state and had, at most, some 10,000 members in the whole of West Germany.

Ekström's involvement in the Nazi SRP drew the attention of the German police. According to our sources, he is to have corresponded with members of the SRP executive. In one of the tip-offs to the Swedish security police, a name has unfortunately been blacked out. However, the first letter is clearly an E and the last an R. The length of the name matches that of Ernst Otto Remer, so presumably the SÄPO officer who wrote the memo reversed Otto Ernst Remer's names. Ekström's fervour for the SRP was about to lead to his deportation from West Germany. He is arrested and questioned by the police. In this interview he apparently explained that the common struggle against Bolshevism during the war bound him closely to other veterans. According to Panzer, this is where Professor Röll makes his crucial intervention. He vouches for Ekström and draws upon his personal contacts in the legal world to have his deportation lifted. Ekström and Panzer are then said to have returned to the police station in Nuremberg to taunt the chief of police.

On 23 October 1952, the SRP is brought down. The party is found to be an extension of the German Nazi party and being thus in contravention of the constitution is duly banned. While the executive flees or goes underground, the members drift to other parties. Ekström moves on to Karlsruhe, where he settles down on Nebeniusstrasse and makes a living working at the sewing machine factory Haid & Neu.

As the first Nazi parties try to become established in West Germany, the mammoth task continues of tracing all those who disappeared during the Nazi atrocities of the Second World War. The newspaper Aufbau is packed with thousands of appeals from Jewish survivors seeking loved ones. Millions upon millions of people are missing, as are their belongings.

It is now, in the early 1950s, that testimonies and restitution demands start to be submitted by the relatives of the former residents on Lützowstrasse. While Ekström sings "Deutschland Deutschland über alles" with Otto Ernst Remer's SRP, Getrude Ascher writes down the missing personal effects of Max Ascher, who met his death in Treblinka. Gold, silver, jewellery, a radio and household utensils. On 27 December 1955, his sons send their testimony to Yad Vashem. On 19 September 1955 the niece of Regina Abraham sends a testimony to Yad Vashem along with the photograph reproduced in this book. Slowly but surely information is pieced together on what happened to the people who once lived on Lützowstrasse. Cecilie Sieverts tries to obtain compensation for the property on Hagenstrasse 39-47 and relatives of Betty Karger do the same for her lost jewellery.

Testimony after testimony, memo after memo, demand after demand – everything is collected in archives, newspapers and documents around the world waiting to be put into some sort of order. As late as 15 December 2015 a testimony is submitted on behalf of Nathan Baumgardt by his second cousin's grandchildren. The War has been over for 70 years, but still people want to know what happened to their relatives during the Holocaust. The names, details of where they lived, what they owned and did, who they were, are important for families. For as we have seen, there were organised forces just four or five years after the War who were denying that these people ever existed. Ekström was part of that organisation and that ideology that had committed such horrific crimes and then later becomes actively complicit in the denial that they had ever taken place. And it does not end with his involvement in the SRP.

According to SÄPO sources, Ekström helped to arrange contacts in Germany for Per Engdahl's fascist conference in Malmö in May 1951, the express purpose of which was to bring together fascist and Nazi movements in Europe in what came to be called the Malmö Movement or the European Social Movement (ESB.)

After his stint at the sewing machine factory in Karlsruhe, Ekström gets a job at the atomic research centre in Jülich, where he apparently worked during the 1960s. Gustaf Ekström returns regularly to Sweden to visit relatives. Throughout his time in Germany he has been registered at different addresses in Sweden; for instance, in 1956 he is registered as living in an apartment on Västmannagatan in Stockholm. In the 1960s, his involvement in the Nazi movement seems to have taken a hiatus, presumably on account of his new job. There is no record in SÄPO's public-domain documents of his being active either.

In the 1960s, many Nazi sympathisers end up in more or less quasi-sect organisations; foremost amongst such groups in is the *Nordiska Rikspartiet* (the Nordic Realm Party), but solely as just a peripheral phenomenon. This party serves as a bridge for the far-right and Nazism in Sweden from the postwar period up until the 1980s. However, we have found no evidence that Gustaf Ekström was active in the Nordic Realm Party. What we do know, however, is that he was a member of the NSAP/SSS until the party was disbanded in 1950, from which point he was in the SNF.

Another lobby organisation that establishes itself in postwar Germany is HIAG – or Hilfsgemeinschaft auf Gegenseitigkeit der

Angehörigen der ehemaligen Waffen-SS, which translates as "the Mutual aid association of former Waffen-SS members". In the early 1950s, the organisation grows throughout West Germany when the ban on veteran associations was lifted in 1949. Unlike the veterans of the Wehrmacht – the regular army – SS soldiers were due no pension, a direct consequence of the SS being judged a criminal organisation by the Nuremberg tribunal. Former SS soldiers and convicted war criminals now start to organise to demand what they see as their rights.

At the first HIAG veteran convention in Verden in 1952, the Allies are denounced as the criminals and the SS hailed as heroes, while the Supreme Allied commander Eisenhower is slandered and called "Schweinhund" – pig-dog. The reactions were not slow in coming. Newspapers in West Germany and around the world condemn the meeting. In the 1960s, HIAG works hard to wipe clean the SS's odious history. HIAG's historical revisionism has been described by, amongst others, German historian and author Karsten Wilke in the book *HIAG 1950-1990* and Kurt Tauber in his reference work on German nationalism *Beyond Eagle and Swastika*, whose arguments pivot on two principle claims made by HIAG: that the Waffen-SS was a non-political organisation and that it was innocent of war crimes, outrages and murder. It is not only Tauber and Wilke who dismiss these claims outright; historians around the world do the same. As we have seen, the Nuremburg tribunal ruled that the SS and its associate organisations, the Waffen-SS included, stand out for the very reason that they were political. It has also been established from the overwhelming evidence presented that the Waffen-SS was a critical participant in the war crimes and the persecutions of the Jews and others.

The attempts to have the Waffen-SS juridically rehabilitated in West Germany fail, and HIAG becomes even more radicalised. The veteran conventions in West Germany, where the major Auschwitz and Treblinka trials are in full swing, are PR nightmares. At their meetings, the SS veterans sing forbidden Nazi songs. SS veterans affiliated with HIAG dismiss the Holocaust and express anti-Semitic sentiments in the newspapers. In the end, the West German counter-subversion unit begins to monitor the organisation. HIAG is classed as a far-right organisation but manages to be spared proscription.

During the time that HIAG was active, they produced a whole genre of literature, newspapers and magazines that portray the Waffen-SS in a revisionist light. The organisation's own publishing house, Munin-Verlag, published 57 titles on the Waffen-SS until 1992, and had around 50 years of newspaper publication. The organisation also published its own newspaper, *Der Freiwillige* (The Volunteer), which is full of flattering articles about the Waffen-SS. An important aspect of this genre is to differentiate between the Waffen-SS from its sister SS organisation Allgemeine-SS, on which it pins all crimes. This false and revisionist version of history has become astonishingly widespread, and we were a little surprised to find HIAG's historical revisionism reiterated in military historian Jan von Konow's foreword to Lennart Westberg's essay on Swedish volunteers in the German Waffen-SS, published in the Swedish Army Museum's bulletin 45–46 from 1986:

"But it can be noted in this context that there was a significant difference between different SS categories: there was a distinct boundary of respectability between on the one hand...the Allgemeine-SS and on the other...the Waffen-SS, who fought on the fronts alongside the regular German army, and thus strove to uphold the basic ethical code of military honour."

Jan von Konow's foreword is a clear illustration of the kind of uncritical apology for the Waffen-SS that echoes HIAG's political views. Von Konow completely disregards the verdict of the Nuremberg tribunal, namely that no distinction can be drawn between the different parts of the SS. The Waffen-SS exploited the persecution of Jews to enable their own bureaucratic expansion in Berlin as we have described in this book. It participated in massacres behind the front and supplied the Einsatzgruppen with personnel for murdering Jews in occupied areas. It schooled its troops in the racial ideology that fed the Holocaust. Any talk of there being some form of "ethical code" for the Waffen-SS is quite simply false.

HIAG was, however, intrinsically doomed. Veterans age and with time the pool of possible recruits dried up for the simple reason that one by one the veterans eventually died.

In the early 1990s, the organisation's own organ *Der Freiwillige* becomes increasingly a vehicle for obituaries and tributes to deceased veterans. In 1992, HIAG is disbanded at a federal level in Germany, even though Der Freiwillige survives for a few more years. In the May 1996 issue, we find Gustaf Ekström's obituary.

HIAG never properly managed to secure legal recognition or pensions for its members. However, the legacy of HIAG's publication business persists. A large amount of literature based on HIAG's views is published every year by far-right publishing houses the world over. Some spew unapologetically explicit extremist opinions, others are inclined more towards whitewashing and idolisation.

Ekström moves to Lund at the end of the 1970s, where he spends much of his life as a pensioner, sitting in libraries reading history books. In 1976 he corresponds with the Nationaldemokratische Hochschulbund (the National Democratic University Federations), a far-right organisation that tries to recruit students at German universities. Ekström is also in touch with another far-right organisation, the German-Rhodesia Association.

At the end of the 1960s, a new party, the Nationaldemokratische Partei Deutschland (NPD, National Democratic Party of Germany) begins to make headway in West Germany. Some of the old Nazis sign up to this party, Gustaf Ekström amongst them. In August 1977 he pays a visit to the NPD executive and the circle surrounding party leader Martin Mussgnug. In 1977 Ekström takes out a subscription for the party's organ Deutsche Stimme. Its articles bristle with historical revisionism, racism and anti-Semitism, and many claim that the Holocaust is a lie. On 4–13 November 1977 Ekström pays a return visit to the NPD, this time to its Lübeck branch.

The NPD is regarded as a pure Nazi party. Like the SRP of the 1950s, NPD sings the praises of the original Nazi party from the War years. The NPD holds that the West German government is illegal and that national solidarity is the alternative to democracy. The NPD has long had the eyes of the German authorities on it as a possible subversive element, just like the SRP. Following a lengthy investigation lasting several years, the German constitutional court announces on 17 January 2017 that the NPD is unconstitutional, but given that it lacks influence and clout to carry out its policies no ban is enforced.

In the 1980s, Ekström takes regular part in the 30 November parades in Lund in celebration of the death of Karl XII. Such demonstrations have a long tradition amongst Swedes of a far-right and nationalist persuasion dating back to the turn of the century. Here he meets Gösta Bergquist, his old party colleague from the NSAP/SSS. Bergquist is younger than Ekström, and was active in the Nordic Youth in the 1930s, the organisation of which Ekström was once the secretary. They are both equally zealous about the "national forces" in Sweden getting the wind back in their sails. They miss the movement of the 1930s.

The 30 November demonstrations in the early 1980s become a platform for the first generational interaction between younger nationalists, right-wing extremists and neo-Nazis, and the older generation of Nazis from the interbellum – the generation to which Ekström and his somewhat younger companion Gösta Bergquist belong. Marching along in the torchlit parades are men dressed in the uniforms of Karl XII's soldiers and hooded leafletters from the racist organisation Bevara Sverige Svenskt (Keep Sweden Swedish) along with smartly dressed elderly gentlemen delivering unabashed Hitler salutes to the newspaper and TV photographers sent to cover the proceedings. On 30 November these generations meet. But still in the early 1980s there is no real party in Sweden to bring all these ideas together. In due course, however, Gustaf

Ekström and Gösta Bergquist will find a new party with which to become involved.

Chapter 19
From SS to SD

The date is 21 February 1988. The two Nazi veterans Gustaf Ekström and Gösta Bergquist attend the first annual meeting of the Sweden Democrats (SD) in Malmö. According to the minutes, they are two of the 23 people at the meeting, which took place at the Saint Gertrud conference centre at Östergatan 7b. The SD national organisation had been founded barely a fortnight previously – on 6 February 1988 – in a flat in Stockholm.

Founding a party is a collective act that takes place over time and requires many convinced people to be on board from the get-go. Minutes need taking, premises booking and documents copying, and someone has to insert meeting invitations into envelopes and distribute them. Accounts have to be opened, grants and permits applied for, and local branches, such as that in Malmö, started and made politically active. All this, the old Nazis help with. Gösta Bergquist is the meeting secretary. The minutes are important, because with their help SD can apply for a broadcast license for local radio. Gustaf Ekström is elected accountant at the meeting of 21 February 1988. The position is essential to the functioning of an organisation or party.

Ekström works his way up the SD party organisation. He is

elected accountant to the party executive and the party as a whole at the first national conference on 10 June 1989.

As the Sweden Democrats become more established as a party and participate officially in the 30 November demonstrations, the gatherings become increasingly violent. In their newsletters, the party refers to these events as kampdagar – a word meaning "days of action" but with militant, combative connotations. Ekström lets young SD members sleep over in his apartment on Kämnärsvägen when visiting Lund to take part in demonstrations and the like. It is now no longer just a matter of the raising of hands by a cluster of disgruntled men; now there are rhythmic chants of "Sieg Heil" and "ut med packet" (roughly "kick out the scum"). The openly Nazi organisation Vitt Ariskt Motstånd (White Aryan Resistance) is welcomed in by the Sweden Democrats.

Alongside his duties as party accountant, Ekström helps to grow the party's Malmö branch into what the Sweden Democrats' own party organ describes as the most active in the country. He is active as a leafletter and in the party's outreach work. He takes parts at rallies in his hometown of Lund and around Skåne and even travels to some of the SD events arranged in Stockholm. His participation in different party activities is documented on film available in the unofficial SD archive.

When Gustaf Ekström, Gösta Bergquist and a handful of other party members arrange an open meeting on Rådhustorget in Landskrona on 11 April 1992 they bring with them a cameraman to film the whole affair. In the almost 10-minute long video recording, Gustaf Ekström is seen in lengthy sequences enthusiastically handing out leaflets and talking to passers-by in front of a large banner bearing the legend "National Solidarity". Some people stop, exchange a few words with him before taking a leaflet. Others hurry past. There is a little table there where on which they have placed stacks of leaflets and stickers. During the days following the 11 April 1992, the campaign team that Ekström was a part of handed out several thousands of leaflets in the Landskrona area.

The man speaking through a megaphone at the meeting

proclaims the myth that if immigration is not stopped, Swedish people will be in the minority by the early 21st century. The wording echoes the propaganda that Gustaf Ekström helped to produce during his time at the SS-Hauptamt. Two slogans promulgated by SD on the stickers and elsewhere are taken straight from Nazi Germany too: "Do not defile your race!" and "Sweden Awake!", the former being a translation of the Nazi term *Rassenschande* (race defilement). Women and men who had relations with each other, where the Nazis defined the one as "Aryan" and the other as "non-Aryan", were arraigned as racial defilers and publicly named and shamed, mocked, beaten and persecuted – all in full compliance with the Nuremberg Laws. While normal Jews were made to wear a yellow Star of David, a Jewish man who had had relations with an "Aryan" woman had to wear a star comprising a yellow triangle with a black hollow triangle superimposed on it; the "Aryan" woman, for her part, was made to wear a yellow triangle on top of a black.

"Sverige vakna" (Sweden awake) is a direct translation of *Deutschland erwache* (Germany awake). This was a slogan emblazoned on Nazi party standards, a clarion call to the people to arise out of their slumber to eradicate and conquer "Jewishness", and was used repeatedly in propaganda, both in music and on posters, and in the rhetoric of Adolf Hitler. In Germany, counter-subversion measures have made the wording illegal; in the late 1980s and early 1990s, these two phrases are revived by the Sweden Democrats.

The Sweden Democrats sometimes closed their public rallies with Richard Wagner's *The Ride of the Valkyries*; at the meeting in Landskrona in 1992, however, they make do with a rendition of the Swedish national anthem via the megaphone.

In 1993 Swedish Television conducts the most extensive interview with Gustaf Ekström ever published. In it, Ekström is given an opportunity to reflect upon his past, to share his views on anti-Semitism, to talk about his time in the SS and to give his opinions on the Holocaust. But Ekström shows no remorse:

"I regret nothing because I believe people are weak and must be treated as weak people."

Ekström is asked about the Holocaust and the concentration camps. About this he says the following:

"No sensible person believed a word about these concentration camps. We all understood it to be war propaganda. It had started already during and before the war and persisted after the war. So every sensible person was highly sceptical towards these horror stories."

"You still don't believe them?" asks the interviewer. Ekström laughs and says:

"What a question! What can I say? Every country has its horror stories. No one's perfect, so we're all just as bad as each other, I'd say."

Ekström had several chances to denounce Nazism. But a Nazi he remained until his dying day.

In 1994 Gustaf Ekström attends his last 30 November demonstration in Lund. This year, there are fewer Sweden Democrats than before since the party is not officially a participant.

Because of the brawls that occurred in previous years, the police hold a tight rein on the demonstration. The 30 November Association is denied permission to congregate at the statue of Swedish writer Esaias Tegnér in Lundagård and a torchlight parade is out of the question. Instead, the association is directed to the Klostergården sports ground on the outskirts of the city. After a decision by the County Administrative Court, however, the association is allowed to hold a stationary demonstration between noon and 1:30.

465 riot police watch over the area and the streets of Lund are closed off with sandbags and chains. This year, however, only 32 people show up, largely elderly men who have gathered in honour of the hero king but also several active members of the Sweden

Democrats. There are twice as many reporters and photographers as there are members of the 30 November Association.

Gustaf Ekström is caught on camera by Jonn Leffman standing by the plinth of the Tegnér stature. He is leaning on his cane and doffs his Tyrolean-like hat when the association chairman, Lars Hulthén, lays a wreath in honour of Karl XII.

A few weeks into December 1994 Jimmie Åkesson decides to contact the Sweden Democrats and form the local youth organisation SDU-Sölvesborg. The party leader-to-be joins at a time when the Nazi Gustaf Ekström is still active.

A few months later, on 16 July 1995, the 87-year-old Gustaf Ekström dies and is buried in the family grave in Färila church cemetery. But the political ideas that Ekström spent a lifetime fighting for live on.

Chapter 20
Triumph

In 1988, the same year that Gustaf Ekström helps to found the Sweden Democrats, Renate Golinski is baking bread, like she probably did when she worked in the kitchen at the nursing home on Lützowstrasse 47 years earlier. Her eldest son has finished building his own house and she wants to take him a loaf and some salt, the traditional assurance that a house will never want for food. She also has a mezuzah, a roll of parchment to attach to the doorpost. She will die a few weeks later, but for the moment is happy that she has managed to rebuild her family.

43 years previously, in early May 1945, Renate Golinski was liberated from Mauthausen concentration camp by US troops. She then made her way on Tel Hai, one of the Jewish refugee ships, to the coastal city of Haifa in Mandatory Palestine. She arrives together with over 700 refugees on 3 April 1946. As one of many illegal immigrants she was interned in the Atlit detainee camp to the south of the city. Soon after the state of Israel was proclaimed and Renate Golinski moved to the Kibbutz Ma'ayan Zvi in the town of Zikhron Ya'akov.

Farm work on the Kibbutz was hard, starting at 6.30 every morning, and before the marshes along the shore were drained, was plagued by mosquitoes. At first Renate lived in a tent before the first wooden houses were built. She liked the long working days in the sun. Her neighbours noted her industriousness.

Renate Golinski looked forward, not back, and always tried to remain upbeat, even if the people closest to her could detect an underlying sadness. She built a new life, which was soon enriched by a husband and the arrival of their three children. After a while, Renate changed her first name to Devorah and her surname to Golan, a Hebrew version of Golinski. Her husband also took the name. Otherwise, she would have been the last of her line, her father, mother and brother having been murdered. Her children eventually went on to have children and grandchildren of their own in their new homeland. Devorah Golan's personal triumph over Nazism had come at last.

Epilogue

Gustaf Ekström was never convicted of any crime in Sweden at the end of the War, and no full police investigation was ever conducted of his time with the Waffen-SS. All there is is the interview held with him while in quarantine in Älmhult, in which Ekström himself is generally the source and the questions hardly probing. It seems that the police are only interested in confirming that Ekström was not actually Thorwald Calais, and rather indifferent towards exploring Ekström's own role as a partner of the wanted spy Calais. Since the Swedish Foreign Ministry had helped him escape home to Sweden on the Red Cross's White Buses, he also avoided being arrested, interned and interrogated by the American occupation forces. As a volunteer in the Waffen-SS, Ekström would have faced immediate arrest had he remained in Germany. So Ekström was not an object of interest for the Swedish courts or any of the victors. However, there are postwar researches and hearings that can give us some sort of objective answer about his role and his culpability as a Waffen-SS volunteer, both legally and morally.

Firstly, whoever writes an account of a Swedish Nazi and Waffen-SS volunteer will inevitably need to describe the persecution and murder of Jews. The more we found out about the properties and places he had been in, the clearer the picture became of the inescapable fact lurking at the heart of Nazism: the Holocaust. In this regard, Gustaf Ekström is naturally complicit in the Holocaust, although that says little about his actual personal accountability.

Secondly, the Holocaust was such a fierce and comprehensive social project that it was impossible to construct a single system to implement it. It required the participation of all existing institutions: the German railway, postal and communication services, logistics, travel agencies, shipping agencies, public transport, exchange bureaus, official decision-makers, the police, merchants to auction off stolen property, bureaucrats and secretaries to write documents and lists of names – to name but a few. All of society was implicated; but this does not mean that all individuals are equally blameworthy. However, the organisation to which Ekström belonged – the SS – was the very engine that drove the Holocaust.

The Holocaust did not begin at the barbed-wire-fenced concentration camp in a remote part of Poland; nor did it begin in Deutsche Reichsbahn's punctual trains with their cattle trucks packed with victims or at the station loading ramps; nor did it begin at the various transit camps in the middle of Berlin. Maybe it could be said that the Holocaust began when the Jews had their deportation orders shoved into their hands. But that would be forgetting that all this is predicated on a system and a society that enables people to be expelled and deported simply on the grounds of their ethnic origin. Of course, it is obvious that Gustaf Ekström never actually worked at a concentration camp and that he was to all intents and purposes a pen-pusher. But he did work just as obviously for the ideology that had the Holocaust as its explicit objective. Without the propaganda that Ekström helped to create, that defined Jews as subhuman, it would have been much harder for the Nazis to get society on board with its nefarious plans.

To ascertain Ekström's actual role, we need to codify the different parts of the Holocaust. Professor Michael Berenbaum at the

American Jewish University in California has done just this. His six-fold categorisation makes it easier to grasp the Holocaust as a phenomenon. His six terms are: *definition, expropriation, concentration, Einsatzgruppen, deportation* and *death camps*.

Nazism's definition of Jews as non-Germans conspiring against the people began as the ideology started to emerge. To start with, Jews are *defined* through tracts, agitation, leaflets and violence from the Nazis on Germany's streets. Once the Nazis assume power, they take the next step – definition by legislation. By defining Jews as non-Germans while depriving Jews of full citizenship by force of law, the state is able to *expropriate* their belongings and property. The first of Michael Berenbaum's six terms facilitates the second.

The third Berenbaum step is the *concentration* of Jews, which is a consequence of state theft of Jewish property: the Jews have to go somewhere. Initially they are concentrated into special buildings. The Jews evicted from the nursing home, for instance, are crammed together into other properties in the way we have described. They are later transferred to transit camps and on to ghettos and, ultimately, concentration camps. They are constantly subjected to increasing brutality, and all in accordance with ad-hoc Nazi laws. As the War spreads, opportunities arise to start what Nazism will later refer to as "the final solution". The German conquests in the east created more territorial space, more people to kill and more potential volunteers to their programme of mass-slaughter. This introduces Berenbaum's fourth term: *Einsatzgruppen*, the special SS units whose only raison d'être was the wholesale execution of Jews and other non-persons in the occupied areas as well as the *deportation* and mass slaughter in the *death camps*, the fifth and sixth Berenbaum terms.

By tracing the fates of the former residents of the nursing home on Lützowstrasse that the SS sequestered and where Gustaf Ekström worked, the process unfolds in stark clarity. It took just ten years for 256 people at one of Berlin's Jewish nursing homes to be denied their rights, evicted, robbed of their property, deported, concentrated in camps and finally exterminated. Their fate can then be placed in the larger context of the ultimate genocide of six million of their fellow Jews.

It is tempting to dismiss all Nazis as monsters or suspect them of being mentally instable or even psychopathic, but such excuses are merely a convenience for those who refuse to accept that the exploits of Nazism would have been impossible without the widespread support of normal German people. Holocaust scholars often divide people into *victim*, *perpetrator*, *spectator* and *profiteer*. As far as we know, Gustaf Ekström never set foot in a concentration camp, and was geographically far away from the SS Einsatzgruppen's mass-killings. His relatives describe him as mild-mannered, kind, solitary and intellectual. He liked going to churches to listen to choirs. He would often drive up from Germany in his dark-green Karmann Ghia to spend time with his family over some home cooking and a glass of Aalborg. His personal friend, Helmut Panzer, calls him polite and courteous and says that after the War he helped to set up the Save the Children orphanage for poor German children in Nuremberg. Ekström was highly educated and spoke numerous languages. He was brought up with his two brothers and one sister in the secure environment of the village of Lindesberg, from where he would go on summer excursions to Färila, the village of his birth in the charming Hälsingland countryside. He had every opportunity during his life to choose other paths.

He could have drawn a line under his Nazi involvement when he returned from the USA in 1932. He could also have refused Nazism when he saw that it hampered his career in Sweden after his standby service in connection with Germany's occupation of Norway. He had all the opportunities in the world to reconsider his decision to travel to Norway and sign up for the Waffen-SS. But Ekström, like other Nazis, was a staunch believer in the racial theories and anti-Semitism that formed the bedrock of the movement he represented. Ekström took active part in German anti-Jewish propaganda; in other words, he was *active in the definition* of Jews according to Nazi ideology, and by virtue of that is a kind of perpetrator, albeit a lower ranking one with limited liability. To some degree, Ekström is also a *profiteer* as his private career was indirectly abetted, in part, at the expense of the residents of the nursing home on Lützowstrasse.

Gustaf Ekström was also a *spectator* of the results of the *expropriation* and *concentration* of Jews that was going on in Berlin. In spite of this, he still *denies* the Holocaust as late as the SVT interview in 1993. He *denies* that six million Jews were murdered. This means that he also *denies* that the 256 people whom we have traced, the mostly elderly Jews who had once lived on Lützowstrasse, were evicted, robbed of their property and then murdered. Such denials can still attract a maximum of five years' imprisonment in Germany.

Another way of analysing Ekström's role during the Second World War and the Waffen-SS is to approach it from the angle of Allied Control Council Directive No 38. The Control Council was the highest public authority in postwar Germany and comprised representatives of the Soviet Union, the USA, the UK and France. Directive No 38 was passed on 12 October 1946 and contains directions on the arrest and punishment of war criminals, Nazis and militarists and the internment, control, and surveillance of potentially dangerous Germans. The directive sought to create a unified conceptual structure during the extensive denazification process of Germany after the War.

Directive 38 divides war criminals, Nazis and militarists into the following categories:

(1) Major offenders
(2) Offenders – with the following sub-categories:

a) activists
b) militarists
c) profiteers

(3) Lesser offenders
(4) Followers
(5) Persons exonerated

Major Offenders
For the Waffen-SS this means all those who were officers at the rank of SS-Sturmbannführer (major) and above, all members of the Totenkopfverbände and the SS-Helferinnen and SS-Kriegshelferinnen who served at concentration camps.

Offenders
For the Waffen-SS this means all personnel, with the exception of those enlisted against their will (unless promoted to the rank of non-commissioned officer) and all concentration camp personnel.

Lesser offenders
A lesser offender is anyone who otherwise belongs to the category of Offender but because of special circumstances seems worthy of a milder judgment and can be expected according to his character to fulfil his duties as a citizen of a peaceful democratic state after he has proved himself in a period of probation; this also applies to former members of the armed forces.

Followers
A follower is anyone who was not more than a nominal participant in, or a supporter of, the national socialistic tyranny.

Persons exonerated
A person exonerated is anyone who, in spite of his formal membership of the Nazi party not only showed a passive attitude but also actively resisted the national socialistic tyranny to the extent of his powers and thereby suffered disadvantages.

According to Directive 38, Gustaf Ekström, on account of his membership of the Waffen-SS, would end up in the Offenders category, one that the Council decreed warranted thorough investigation. Since Ekström actively participated in words and deeds by producing and spreading the Nazi ideology both in speech and writing, he might well fall under the sub-category of activist or even perhaps, given that he disseminated militaristic doctrines and programmes by word and deed and volunteered for an organisation serving the advancement of militaristic ideas, the sub-category of militarist.

Article 9 of the Directive details the sanctions to be imposed. Depending on the degree of culpability, whoever was eventually judged an Offender could be subjected to one or more of the following sanctions:

a) Imprisonment or internment for a period up to ten years in order to perform reparation and reconstruction work.
b) Prohibition from holding any public office, including that of notary or attorney.
c) Loss of any legal claims to a pension or allowance payable from public funds.
d) Loss of the right to vote, the capacity to be elected, and the right to be politically active in any way or to be members of a political party.
e) Prohibition from joining a trade union or business or vocational association.
f) Prohibition, for a period of not less than five years after their release, from being active in a profession other than ordinary labour.
g) Prohibition, for a period of not less than five years after their release, from being active as a teacher, preacher, editor, author, or radio commentator.
h) Restriction as regards living space and place of residence.
i) Loss of all licenses, concessions and privileges and the right to keep a motor vehicle.
j) Prohibition, at the discretion of Zone Commanders (Germany

was divided into occupied zones – authors' note), from leaving a Zone without permission.

It is important to point out that we cannot say for sure that Ekström would have been judged an Offender and punished under the denazification process initiated by the Allies. The process was not followed through completely and was riddled with flaws. For one thing, there were so many people to be examined – we are talking millions of Germans – that the Allies soon passed the task on to the German authorities. It was also easy for people to have themselves placed in a lower category through the testimonies of friends and neighbours, or to drag out the process until new amnesty laws came into effect.

This said, thousands of Nazis received Directive 38 sanctions and were sentenced to prison or labour camps, or deprived of other rights. Sven Helander, the Nazi who helped Ekström escape on the White Buses, spent many years in custody of the US forces in West Germany. But Gustaf Ekström was never imprisoned. By the time he returned to Nuremberg, the denazification process had effectively drawn to a close.

In Sweden there was no corresponding process for the Nazis returning after the War, so Gustaf Ekström was able to continue his political activities serving the advancement of Nazi ideas both in Sweden and in Germany – despite the fact that all the Holocaust cards were on the table.

As mentioned, Ekström was not alone in representing the old Nazis in the Sweden Democrats; Gösta Bergquist was there too, as well as other Nazis of Ekström's generation. In the Sweden Democrat organ SD-Kuriren No 7–8 1989, Erik Walles writes about the lessons that SD can draw from the NSAP/SSS – the Nazi party of which he, Ekström and Bergquist had been members. One section of his article is particularly salient. In it, Walles concludes that the Sweden Democrats need not feel any shame to be likened to the Swedish Nazis:

"What SD has in common with the old national movement is a serious endeavour to rescue the Swedish nation and its distinctiveness from impending danger. Thus far Heléne Lööw is right (the article is partly a response to Lööw's book Hakkorset och Vasakärven – authors' note) when she says that SD and others of a similar mind are spiritually akin to the old Nazis, and it is absolutely nothing to be ashamed of."

Erik Walles, former deputy leader of the Nazi NSAP/SSS, considered, like Ekström and Bergquist, the Sweden Democrats to be his party. As we saw in chapter 4, Erik Walles was also the owner of the list of Jews that was found in Lisell Hall in Malung in 1997. Why he kept this list his whole life we will probably never know.

Many of the ideas for which Ekström fought live on in the Sweden Democrats. Arguably the most alarming recent demonstration of this was when one of the party's leading figures, Björn Söder, defined Jews as non-Swedes in an interview with the mainstream newspaper Dagens Nyheter on 14 December 2014. He repeated the sentiment in June 2018.

***

Shortly after the War, Ekström met Nazi leader Sven Olov Lindholm at a conference. Ekström recalls their conversation in the 1993 SVT interview:

"I met party leader Lindholm afterwards, a month or so after the War. Some time in July 1945 it was. And he was very calm and collected and determined and said that we now had to acknowledge the new circumstances and that we had to hold out as best we could. Better times might soon be just around the corner."

Gustaf Ekström held out for over 50 years. In the Sweden Democrats he saw his chance to pass the baton on to the next generation.

Appendix

The residents of Lützowstrasse 48/49

This section contains the personal details of the 256 Jews who lived at the Jüdische Altersheim e.V., W35 at Lützowstrasse 48/49 in Berlin according to the census taken on 17 May 1939. It is important to point out that the census information as catalogued by Tracing the past e.V. might contain inaccuracies resulting from errors in data processing. The volume of material that has been made searchable in their database is immense, and the list of the residents might therefore change as new details emerge, most likely concerning a new person or the death dates of people who were not deported. Information about the fates of the different individuals has been taken from four main sources: *Yad Vashem's central database of Shoah victims*, the *Bundesarchiv's memorial book of victims of the Jewish Holocaust during the Nazi tyranny of 1933–1945*, *Gedenkbuch Berlins*, and the *Memorial book of the prisoners and victims of Theresienstadt*. Some individual's addresses are given after their eviction from the nursing home as stated in the transport lists drawn up by the Gestapo. We have decided to write the addresses exactly as they appear on these lists, which means that the same address is sometimes given a different spelling. The lists can be found in the Yad Vashem archive and in the National Archives, Maryland, catalogue number AR3355.

Of the 256 residents of the nursing home, 184 were women, 72 men. We have been able to establish the fate of 237 of these 256 individuals, while that of the remaining 19 remains unknown to us. Most of these 19 people were relatively old in 1939 when the census was taken. It is therefore reasonable to assume that many of them died during the War. A few of the 19 were younger than 40, and it is perfectly possible that one or more of them survived by fleeing the country or going into hiding. As more information comes to light, it should be possible to ascertain the fates of all the people. 166 were murdered during the Holocaust. They were not only gassed or shot to death; they were also burned, driven to exhaustion and death through starvation and slave labour. They were denied healthcare and medicine and were kept in deplorable sanitary conditions. Five people were driven to suicide by the pogrom.

Of the 166 who were murdered, 30 were deported to one of the ghettos or killing fields of the east in Riga, Warsaw, Litzmannstadt (Lodz), Piaski Luterskie or Maly Trostenets outside Minsk. One person was deported direct from Berlin to the Sobibór extermination camp and another three direct to Auschwitz. 130 people were deported to Theresienstadt concentration camp, where 76 were murdered. 38 people were then deported from Theresienstadt to Treblinka and 14 to Auschwitz, where they were murdered. The oldest resident to be deported was 89 and the youngest, born in 1924, 17. A total of eleven of the 256 Jews who once lived on Lützowstrasse survived the War; three of them survived the horrors of the camps, eight managed to escape by fleeing Germany.

The director of the nursing home on Lützowstrasse, Dr Martin Salomonski, was also deported to Theresienstadt on Transport I/9 on 19 June 1942. On 16 October 1944, Salomonski was transferred on Transport Er to Auschwitz, where he was murdered. The owner of the photograph album containing the pictures of the nursing home, Heinrich Stahl, was deported on 12 June 1942 on Transport I/6 to Theresienstadt, where he died, partly through lack of medical attention, of pneumonia on 4 November 1942.

The Jewish architect Gustav Bauer, who designed the nursing home on Lützowstrasse, was involved in the resistance movement against the Nazi regime. He was arrested on 17 August 1938 and taken to Buchenwald concentration camp. In 1940 he was stripped of his German citizenship, but after that his fate is unknown. He was probably murdered. Ester Golan's mother, who worked at the home, and father were both murdered during the Holocaust.

Transports coded I/(number) are those from Berlin to Theresienstadt, where I stands for Berlin and the number the sequential order of the transport. A transport with a number only (e.g. Transport 36) is an "East transport" that went direct from Berlin to a ghetto, killing field or extermination camp such as Auschwitz, Sobibór or Treblinka. Transports with a letter only went from Theresienstadt to an extermination camp. B stands for Treblinka and E for Auschwitz; the letter that follows gives the order in which the transports were carried out (e.g. Er to Auschwitz and Bo to Treblinka).

Transport I/46, also known as 1 Grosse Altertransport (the first large elderly transport), deported the largest number of residents of Lützowstrasse on a single occasion: 40 of them were sent on this train from Berlin to Theresienstadt on 17 August 1942. There were a total of 997 individuals on board. All but 15 were murdered.

***

Abraham, Regina *19.08.1887, Podwolozyska/Skalat. Deported from Berlin, Schönhauser Allee 23/25 to Theresienstadt on Transport I/60 on 07.09.1942. Deported from Theresienstadt to Auschwitz on 18.04.1944 on Transport Eb. Murdered.

Arndt, Louis *23.05.1868, Eichfier. Died in Berlin on 29.03.1941.

Aronsohn, Cerine *24.02.1862 (also given as 23.02.1861 and 24.02.1860), Jastrow. Deported from Berlin, N58 Schönhauser Allee 22, to Theresienstadt on Transport I/46 on 17.08.1942. Died at Theresienstadt on 23.08.1942. Murdered.

Ascher, Max *28.03.1869, Naugard. Deported from Berlin, Gerlachstrasse 18/21, to Theresienstadt on Transport I/46 on 17.08.1942. Deported from Theresienstadt to Treblinka on 19.09.1942 on Transport Bo. Murdered.

Auerbach, Catharina *29.10.1867, Landsberg Warthe. Died in Berlin on 23.05.1940.

Auerbach, Salomon *20.08.1859, Labiszyn. Died in Berlin on 23.05.1940.

Auerbach, Selma *12.10.1869, Briesen. Deported from Berlin, N58 Schönhauser Allee 22, to Theresienstadt on Transport I/46 on 17.08.1942. Died at Theresienstadt on 08.01.1943. Murdered.

Baumgardt, Nathan *15.07.1857, Hohensalza. Deported from Berlin, Artilleriestrasse 31, to Theresienstadt on Transport I/46 on 17.08.1942. Died at Theresienstadt on 10.09.1942. Murdered.

Behrendt, Auguste *23.07.1867, Baerting. Deported from Berlin, N4 Artilleriestrasse 31, to Theresienstadt on Transport I/46 on 17.08.1942. Deported from Theresienstadt to Treblinka on 19.09.1942 on Transport Bo. Murdered.

Benheim, Margarete *24.12.1870, Berent. Deported from Berlin, N65 Iranischestrasse 2, to Theresienstadt on Transport I/22 on 14.07.1942. Died at Theresienstadt on 22.05.1944. Murdered.

Bernhard, Arthur *03.09.1866, Ziegenhals. Deported from Berlin, W35 Derfflingerstrasse 17, to Theresienstadt on Transport I/23 on 15.07.1942. Died at Theresienstadt on 02.09.1943. Murdered.

Bernhard, Lina *19.07.1879, Riga. Deported from Berlin, W35 Derfflingerstrasse 17, to Theresienstadt on Transport I/23 on 15.07.1942. Deported from Theresienstadt to Auschwitz on 23.10.1944 on Transport Et. Murdered.

Berwin, Else *16.07.1899, Reetz. Fate unknown.

Bittermann, Hildegard *11.03.1907, Berlin. Deported from Berlin, Grosse Hamburgerstrasse 26, to Theresienstadt on Transport I/44 on 13.08.1942. Died at Theresienstadt on 02.12.1943. Murdered.

Bittermann, Meta *08.04.1879, Berlin. Deported from Berlin, Grosse Hamburgerstrasse 26, to Theresienstadt on Transport I/44 on 13.08.1942. Deported from Theresienstadt to Auschwitz on 23.10.1944 on Transport Et. Murdered.

Bloch, Ida *31.01.1857, Märkisch Friedland. Died in Berlin on 22.01.1941.

Borchardt, Elisabeth *25.06.1879, Grunberg. Deported from Berlin, W62 Derflingenstrasse 72, to Riga on Transport 9 on 19.01.1942. Murdered.

Borchardt, Hans *06.07.1865, Berlin. Died in Berlin on 23.05.1939.

Boss, Richard *16.07.1882, Berlin. Deported from Berlin, Elsässerstrasse 85, to Theresienstadt on Transport I/33 on 29.07.1942. Died in Theresienstadt. Murdered.

Brandenburg, Auguste *08.09.1859, Posen. Deported from Berlin, W35 Lützowstrasse 77, to Theresienstadt on Transport I/23 on 15.07.1942. Died at Theresienstadt on 19.10.1942. Murdered.

Brandenburg, Heinrich *17.02.1857, Berlinchen. Died in Berlin on 24.12.1941.

Bredt, Clara *26.02.1861, Jutrosin. Died in Berlin on 11.09.1942.

Bromberger, Louise *18.06.1885, Miejska Gorka. Deported from Berlin to Theresienstadt on Transport I/95 on 28.05.1943. Died in Theresienstadt on 23.05.1944. Murdered.

Bütow, Selma *01.08.1864, Egeln. Emigrated to the USA on 11.07.1939.

Buttermilch, Hedwig *26.06.1863, Strelno. Deported from Berlin, N4 Artilleriestrasse 31, to Theresienstadt on Transport I/46 on 17.08.1942. Died at Theresienstadt on 22.12.1942. Murdered.

Calvary, Johanna *03.01.1896, Munich. Deported from Berlin, Schönhauser Alle 22, to Maly Trostenets, Minsk on Transport 16 on 23/26.06.1942. Murdered.

Casparius, Siegfried *02.07.1854, Neuwedell. Deported from Berlin, W35 Lützowstrasse 77, to Theresienstadt on Transport I/28 on 22.07.1942. Deported from Theresienstadt to Treblinka on 21.09.1942 on Transport Bp. Murdered.

Caspary, Felix *30.07.1873, Bussin. Died in Berlin on 16.11.1939.

Cohn, Alma *30.01.1880, Pyritz. Deported from Berlin, N4 Brunnenstrasse 41, to Theresienstadt on Transport I/46 on 17.08.1942. Commited suicide in Theresienstadt on 13.10.1942.

Cohn, Elsa *20.01.1868, Offenbach. Died in Berlin on 25.05.1942.

Cohn, Hermann *02.12.1868, Sierakow. Deported from Berlin, Brunnenstrasse 41, to Theresienstadt on Transport I/46 on 17.08.1942. Died at Theresienstadt on 29.10.1942. Murdered.

Cohn, Margarete *17.04.1873, Eillichau. Deported from Berlin, Grosse Hamburgerstrasse 26, to Riga on Transport 10 on 25.01.1942. Murdered.

Cohn, Siegfried *02.09.1874, Inowroclaw. Deported from Berlin, N65 Iranischestrasse 3, to Theresienstadt on Transport I/15 on 03.07.1942. Deported from Theresienstadt to Treblinka on 19.09.1942 on Transport Bo. Murdered.

Conrad, Else *15.04.1896, Zerkow. Deported from Berlin, C2 Gerlachstrasse 20, to Theresienstadt on Transport I/52 on 26.08.1942. Deported from Theresienstadt to Auschwitz on 09.10.1944 on Transport Ep. Murdered.

Czempin, Melanie *09.05.1866, Zaniemysl. Died in Berlin on 04.08.1940.

Cronheim, Johanna *16.10.1864, Gleiwitz. Deported from Berlin, W35 Derfflingerstrasse 17, to Theresienstadt on Transport I/23 on 15.07.1942. Died at Theresienstadt on 10.12.1942. Murdered.

Cronheim, Leopold *16.07.1862, Berlin. Deported from Berlin, W35 Derfflingerstrasse 17, to Theresienstadt on Transport I/23 on 15.07.1942. Died at Theresienstadt on 03.03.1943. Murdered.

David, Martin *08.04.1884, Landsberg. Deported from Berlin to Theresienstadt on Transport I/95 on 29.05.1943. Died at Theresienstadt on 26.01.1944. Murdered.

Davidowsky, Jenny *15.02.1865, Guestrow. Deported from Berlin, N65 Iranischestrasse 3, to Theresienstadt on Transport I/7 on 17.06.1942. Deported from Theresienstadt to Treblinka on 19.09.1942 on Transport Bo. Murdered.

Davidsohn, Rosa *17.04.1860, Podewitz. Died in Berlin on 18.12.1939.

Dienstfertig, Mathilde *23.05.1866, Breslau. Deported from Berlin, C2 Gerlachstrasse 18/21, to Theresienstadt on Transport I/46 on 17.08.1942. Deported from Theresienstadt to Treblinka on 19.09.1942 on Transport Bo. Murdered.

Doerpholz, Anna *15.03.1898, Berlin. Fate unknown.

Elkan, Sophie *29.01.1874, Hamburg. Deported from Berlin, N4 Artilleriestrasse 31, to Theresienstadt on Transport I/46 on 17.08.1942. Deported from Theresienstadt to Treblinka on 19.09.1942 on Transport Bo. Murdered.

Engel, Gustav *29.12.1861, Widminnen. Died in Berlin on 24.01.1942.

Fabian, Laura *22.04.1861, Tuchel. Deported from Berlin, N4 Grosse Hamburgerstrasse 26, to Theresienstadt on Transport I/1 on 02.06.1942. Died at Theresienstadt on 15.09.1942. Murdered.

Fabian, Rosa *15.04.1864, Tuchel. Died in Berlin on 24.02.1942.

Fabian, Sabine *10.11.1859, Warszawa. Died in Berlin on 11.07.1942

Fabian, Sally *02.06.1852, Lubiewo. Died in Berlin on 27.06.1942

Fabian, Sally *24.08.1853, Tuchel. Died in Berlin on 05.11.1942.

Falk, Clara *18.08.1877, Schlochau. Deported from Berlin, Grosse Hamburgerstrasse 26, to Riga on Transport 10 on 25.01.1942. Murdered.

Falk, Philipp *04.10.1863, Deutsch Krone. Died in Berlin on 04.01.1941.

Feige, Marie *15.11.1867, Bromberg. Deported from Berlin, N65 Iranischestrasse 3, to Theresienstadt on Transport I/9 on 19.06.1942. Deported from Theresienstadt to Treblinka on 19.09.1942 on Transport Bo. Murdered.

Feilchenfeld, Wilhelm *17.03.1860, Glogau. Deported from Berlin, N56 Schönhauser Allee 22, to Theresienstadt on Transport I/46 on 17.08.1942. Died in Theresienstadt. Murdered.

Fischel, Rosa *28.03.1869/ 24.03.1869, Miloslaw/Posen. Deported from Berlin, Gerlachstrasse 19/20, to Theresienstad on Transport I/80 on 05.12.1942. Died at Theresienstadt on 19.08.1943. Murdered.

Franck, Martin *13.06.1861, Magdeburg. Died in Berlin on 28.05.1939.

Frauck, Jenny *02.01.1861, Lüthorst. Died in Berlin on 12.03.1940.

Friedländer, Isidor *24.11.1867, Czarnkow. Deported from Berlin to Theresienstadt on Transport I/46 on 17.08.1942. Deported from Theresienstadt to Treblinka on 21.09.1942 on Transport Bp. Murdered.

Fürst, Natalie *15.02.1868, Berlin. Deported from Berlin, N4 Grosse Hamburgerstrasse 26, to Theresienstadt on Transport I/46 on 17.08.1942. Died on 28.08.1942 in Theresienstadt. Murdered.

Gans, Therese *06.12.1871, Hamburg. Deported from Berlin to Theresienstadt on Transport I/20 on 10.07.1942. Died in Theresienstadt. Murdered.

Geismar, Bertha *25.06.1866, Bad Kreuznach. Died in Berlin on 12.05.1942.

Gerson, Emma *17.09.1875, Schönlanke. Deported from Berlin to Riga on Transport 17 on 15.08.1942. Died in Riga 17.08.1942. Murdered.

Gerstel, Laura *18.12.1855, Beuthen. Deported from Berlin to Theresienstadt on Transport I/46 on 17.08.1942. Died at Theresienstadt on 05.10.1942. Murdered.

Gerstel, Anna *17.07.1869. Deported from Berlin to Theresienstadt on Transport I/22 on 14.07.1943. Died in Theresienstadt on –.03.1944. Murdered.

Goldschmidt, Ottilie *05.09.1861, Breslau. Deported from Berlin, Gerlachstrasse 21, to Theresienstadt on Transport I/46 on 17.08.1942. Died on 14.11.1942 in Theresienstadt. Murdered.

Golinski, Erich *17.04.1922, Kotzenau/Lüben. Deported from Berlin, Elsässerstrasse 54, to Theresienstadt on Transport I/90 on 17.03.1943. Deported from Theresienstadt to Auschwitz on 29.09.1944 on Transport El. Died in Gross-Rosen. Murdered.

Golinski, Paula *25.08.1892, Briesen/Wabrzezno. Deported from Berlin, Elsassaerstrasse 54, to Theresienstadt on Transport I/90 on 17.03.1943. Deported from Theresienstadt to Auschwitz on 04.10.1944 on Transport En. Murdered.

Golinski, Renate *11.05.1924, Kotzenau/Lüben. Deported from Berlin, Landwerk Neuendorf, to Theresienstadt on Transport I/90 on 17.03.1943. Deported from Theresienstadt to Auschwitz on 04.10.1944 on Transport En. Deported on 12.10.1944 from Auschwitz to Freiberg, Flossenbürg then to Mauthausen. Liberated in Mauthausen in May 1945. Survived.

Golinski, Nathan *16.11.1893, Lissa. Deported from Berlin, Elsässerstrasse 54, to Theresienstadt on Transport I/90 on 17.03.1943.

Deported from Theresienstadt to Auschwitz on 29.09.1944 on Transport El. Murdered.

Gossels, Gottfried *09.05.1874, Emden. Deported from Berlin to Riga on Transport 7 on 27.11.1941. Died in Riga. Murdered.

Götze, Samuel *08.11.1863, Bydgoszcz. Died 17.03.1941.

Grassheim, Hedwig *14.04.1855 Berlin. Died 23.09.1939.

Gruetzmacher, Marianne *07.09.1876. Commited suicide on 22.11.1941.

Grünewald, Helene *24.12.1886, Peterswalde. Deported from Berlin to Riga on Transport 10 on 25.01.1942. Murdered.

Gurau, Emma *27.01.1862, Berlin. Deported from Berlin to Theresienstadt on Transport I/46 on 17.08.1942. Died at Theresienstadt on 27.08.1942. Murdered.

Guttmann, Flora *09.01.1863, Wronke. Deported from Berlin, W35 Lützowstrasse 77, to Theresienstadt on Transport I 28. Died at Theresienstadt on 11.09.1942. Murdered.

Hagelberg, Jenny *04.03.1874, Dramburg. Deported from Berlin, W35 Derfflingerstrasse 17, to Theresienstadt on Transport I/23 on 15.07.1942. Deported from Theresienstadt to Treblinka on 19.09.1942 on Transport Bo. Murdered.

Hanow, Hedwig *18.04.1859, Danzig. Deported from Berlin, Gormannstrasse 3, to Theresienstadt on Transport I/46 on 17.08.1942. Died on 29.08.1942 in Theresienstadt. Murdered.

Havelburg, Ida *29.09.1878, Pasewalk. Deported from Berlin to Theresienstadt on Transport I/22 on 14.07.1942. Deported from

Theresienstadt to Auschwitz on 16.05.1944 on Transport Ea. Murdered.

Heilbronn, Bertha *13.12.1850, Horstmar/Steinfurt. Died in Berlin on 23.10.1940.

Heim, Irene *24.09.1911, Borck/Posen. Deported from Berlin to Litzmannstadt (Lodz) on Transport 3 on 27.10.1941 or 29.10.1941. Deported from Litzmannstadt to Chelmno on 05.05.1942. Murdered.

Herzog, Lina *11.04.1884, Neukrug. Deported from Berlin, W35 Lützowstrasse 77, to Theresienstadt on Transport I/28 on 22.07.1942. Deported from Theresienstadt to Treblinka on 21.09.1942 on Transport Bp. Murdered.

Herzog, Sally *25.08.1873, Hochstüblau. Deported from Berlin, W35 Lützowstrasse 77, to Theresienstadt on Transport I/28 on 22.07.1942. Deported from Theresienstadt to Treblinka on 21.09.1942 on Transport Bp. Murdered.

Heskel, Chaje *26.04.1867, Deutsch Krone. Died in Berlin on 22.03.1940.

Hirschberg, Jette *30.10.1872, Fischbach. Deported from Berlin, W35 Lützowstrasse 77, to Riga on Transport 10 on 19.01.1942. Murdered.

Hirschberg, Joseph *20.04.1877, Sichitskau. Deported from Berlin, W35 Lützowstrasse 77, to Riga on Transport 10 on 19.01.1942. Murdered.

Hirsch, Elise *11.04.1873. Died in Berlin on 18.10.1941.

Hirsch, Heinz *28.09.1860. Died in Berlin on 12.03.1942.

Hirschmann, Salomon *15.10.1852, Neustadt. Deported from Berlin to Theresienstadt on Transport I/46 on 17.08.1942. Died at Theresienstadt on 30.08.1942. Murdered.

Hirschfeld, Selma *08.06.1862, Berlin. Died 18.02.1941.

Hoffmann, Minna *16.06.1909, Berlin. Deported from Berlin to Riga on Transport 22 on 26.10.1942. Died in Riga. Murdered.

Holzheim, Klara *04.02.1879, Deutsche Krone. Deported from Berlin, W35 Derfflingerstrasse 17, to Theresienstadt on Transport I/23 on 15.07.1942. Died in Theresienstadt. Murdered.

Holzheim, Max *22.10.1869, Deutsche Krone. Deported from Berlin, W35 Derfflingerstrasse 17, on Transport I/23 on 15.07.1942 to Theresienstadt. Died in Theresienstadt. Murdered.

Holzheim, Doris *19.01.1873, Frankfurt an der Oder. Emigrated to Brazil on 19.08.1940.

Holzheim, Moritz *10.07.1865, Deutsche Krone. Emigrated to Brazil on 19.08.1940.

Holzheim, Pauline *24.09.1874, Lobsens. Deported from Berlin, N4 Grosse Hamburger Strasse 27, to Riga on Transport 10 on 25.01.1942. Murdered.

Jablonowski, Leopold *29.09.1872, Seehesten/Sensburg. Emigrated to Brazil on 07.06.1939.

Jablonowski, Regina *15.06.1873, Lidzbark. Emigrated to Brazil on 07.06.1939.

Jacobsohn, Sophie *03.04.1864, Swinemünde. Deported from Berlin, W35 Lützowstrasse 77, to Theresienstadt on Transport I/28 on 22.07.1942. Died at Theresienstadt on 29.12.1942. Murdered.

Jacoby, Helene *30.06.1878, Neustettin. Deported from Berlin, C2 Gerlachstrasse 18, to Riga on Transport 10 on 20.01.1942. Murdered.

Jacoby, Martha *14.09.1862, Berlin. Deported from Berlin to Theresienstadt on Transport I/46 on 17.08.1942. Deported from Theresienstadt to Treblinka on 26.09.1942 on Transport Br. Murdered.

Jacubowski, Ernstine *05.09.1862, Swiecie. Fate unknown.

Jacubowski, Michael *28.12.1868, Znin. Deported from Berlin to Theresienstadt on Transport I/76 on 15.12.1942. Ransomed and transported to Switzerland on 05.02.1945.

Kahn, Sophie *14.01.1858, Markt Erlbach/Neustadt a. d. Aisch. Fate unknown.

Kalenscher, Rose *18.08.1883, Chelmno. Emigrated to Brazil on 25.12.1939.

Karo, Pauline *22.05.1855, Lüben. Deported from Berlin, N65 Iranischestrasse 3, to Theresienstadt on Transport I/17 on 07.07.1942. Died at Theresienstadt on 02.01.1943. Murdered.

Katz, Martha *25.05.1879, Leszno. Died in Berlin on 13.10.1941.

Katzenstein, Emilie *07.03.1860, Bydgoszcz. Deported from Berlin to Theresienstadt on Transport I/36 on 03.08.1942. Died in Theresienstadt. Murdered.

Keiler, Agnes *28.08.1865, Berlin. Emigrated to the USA on 20.03.1940.

Kirstein, Jenny *16.10.1858 or 16.10.1867, Tempelburg/Neustettin. Deported from Berlin to Theresienstadt on Transport I/10 on 23. 06.1942. Deported from Theresienstadt to Treblinka on 23.09.1942 on Transport Bq. Murdered.

Kirstein, Luise *16.10.1867, Tempelburg. Deported from Berlin, Iranischestrasse 3, to Theresienstadt on Transport I/10 on 23.06.1942. Deported from Theresienstadt to Treblinka on 21.09.1942 on Transport Bp. Murdered.

Koppel, Rosa *15.05.1881, Breslau. Deported from Berlin to Auschwitz on Transport 23 on 29.11.1942. Murdered.

Koslowski, Adolf *18.08.1859, Königsberg. Died in Berlin on 17.08.1940.

Koslowski, Recha *23.05.1870, Leszno. Died in Berlin on 09.01.1941.

Kroner, Auguste *29.10.1863, Rawicz. Died in Berlin on 02.12.1939.

Kuttner, Fanny *14.08.1867, Lübeck. Died in Berlin on 23.01.1940.

Lachmann, Laura *26.01.1862, Leszno. Died in Berlin on 10.02.1942.

Lack, Dorothea *15.01.1860, Bath, UK. Deported from Berlin, N33 Schönhauser Allee 22, to Theresienstadt on Transport I/6 on 12.06.1942. Died at Theresienstadt on 30.08.1942. Murdered.

Leander, Käthe *18.04.1874, Berlin. Died in Berlin on 30.10.1940.

Lebenstein, Clara *29.04.1854, Grudziadz. Died in Berlin on 12.12.1940.

Ledermann, Recha *26.03.1863, Smigiel. Deported from Berlin to Theresienstadt on Transport I/27 on 21.07.1942. Died at Theresienstadt on 25.08.1942. Murdered.

Levy, Mathilde *01.06.1864 (10.06), Schivelbein. Deported from Berlin, W35 Derfflingerstrasse 17, to Theresienstadt on Transport I/23 on 15.07.1942. Deported from Theresienstadt to Treblinka on 19.09.1942 on Transport Bo. Murdered.

Lewin, Louis *19.07.1866, Neu-Mecklenburg. Deported from Berlin, W35 Lützowstrasse 77, to Theresienstadt on Transport I/28 on 22.07.1942. Deported from Theresienstadt to Treblinka on 21.09.1942 on Transport Bp. Murdered.

Lewin, Marie *01.02.1871, Dabrowa Biskupia. Deported from Berlin to Theresienstad on Transport I/18 on 08.07.1942. Died in Theresienstadt -.10.1943. Murdered.

Lewin, Rosa *26.05.1855, Regenwalde. Fate unknown.

Lewin, Sanme *07.07.1848, Nekla. Died in Berlin on 30.08.1939.

Lewin, Tine *22.07.1859, Kornik. Died in Berlin on 14.03.1941.

Lewinson, Anna *19.01.1877, Brodnica. Deported from Berlin, W35 Lützowstrasse 77, to Theresienstadt on Transport I/28 on 22.07.1942. Deported from Theresienstadt to Treblinka on 21.09.1942 on Transport Bp. Murdered.

Lewinson, Gustav/Georg *01.01.1868, Landsberg a. d. Warthe. Deported from Berlin, W35 Lützowstrasse 77, to Theresienstadt on Transport I/28 on 22.07.1942. Deported from Theresienstadt to Treblinka on 21.09.1942 on Transport Bp. Murdered.

Lewinson, Paul *06.01.1871, Landsberg a. d. Warthe. Deported from Berlin, W35 Lützowstrasse 77, to Theresienstadt on Transport I/28 on 22.07.1942. Died at Theresienstadt on 08.09.1942. Murdered.

Lewy, Johanna *19.12.1877, Krotoschin. Deported from Berlin, W35 Lützowstrasse 67, to Warszawa on Transport 12 on 02.04.1942. Murdered.

Lewy, Johanna *20.06.1875, Schrimm. Deported from Berlin, N65 Iranischestrasse 3, to Riga on Transport 10 on 25.01.1942. Murdered.

Lewy, Richard *25.08.1875, Dennewitz. Deported from Berlin, W35 Lützowstrasse 67, to Warszawa on Transport 12 on 02.04.1942. Murdered.

Levy, Klara *05.09.1873, Rodenberg. Deported from Berlin to Theresienstadt on Transport I/26 on 20.07.1942. Deported from Theresienstadt to Auschwitz on 16.05.1944 on Transport Ea. Murdered.

Lichtenbaum, Klara *01.05.1902, Stryj. Deported from Berlin to Auschwitz on Transport 24 on 09.12.1942. Murdered.

Liebermann, Johanna *30.01.1876, Gniew. Died in Berlin on 18.05.1939.

Lindenstädt, Cäcilie *23.03.1852/ 23.08.1867, Massow. Deported from Berlin to Theresienstadt on Transport I/77 on 03.10.1942. Died at Theresienstadt on 01.12.1943. Murdered.

Lipstein, Leo *31.03.1863, Slonim. Died in Berlin on 24.04.1942.

Lippmann, Hugo *09.02.1867, Berlin. Deported from Berlin,

W35 Lützowstrasse 77, to Theresienstadt on Transport I/28 on 22.07.1942. Died at Theresienstadt on 15.11.1942. Murdered.

Lippmann, Regine *07.02.1874, Berlin. Deported from Berlin, W35 Lützowstrasse 77, to Theresienstadt on Transport I/28 on 22.07.1942. Deported from Theresienstadt to Auschwitz on 16.05.1944 on Transport Ea. Murdered.

Loeffler, Franziska *05.06.1869, Berlin. Died in Berlin on 20.01.1941.

Loeffler, Gustav *07.12.1869, Marienburg. Died in Berlin on 04.07.1939.

Loewenberg, Richard *31.10.1871, Berlin. Deported from Berlin, N54 Hermannstrasse 3, to Theresienstad on Transport I/46 on 17.08.1942. Died at Theresienstadt on 08.09.1942. Murdered.

Loewenstein, Hertha *07.12.1866, Wielen nad Notecia. Fate unknown.

Looser, Bertha *28.03.1870, Szamotuly. Deported from Berlin to Theresienstadt on Transport I/46 on 17.08.1942. Deported from Theresienstadt to Treblinka on 19.09.1942 on Transport Bo. Murdered.

Lowin, Tilly *22.04.1869, Trier. Died in Berlin on 25.11.1941.

Luft, Else *16.03.1861 Harzgerode. Deported from Berlin to Theresienstadt on Transport I/46 on 17.08.1942. Died at Theresienstadt on 28.08.1942. Murdered.

Manasse, Regina *18.05.1876, Pasewalk. Deported from Berlin, Altonaerstrasse 4, to Riga on Transport 10 on 25.01.1942. Murdered.

Mann, Hedwig *18.02.1873, Ziebingen. Deported from Berlin, N58 Schönhauser Allee 22, on Transport I/46 on 17.08.1942 to Theresienstadt. Died at Theresienstadt on 28.08.1942. Murdered.

Mann, Max *28.07.1869 Tirschtiegel. Deported from Berlin, N58 Schönhauser Allee 22, to Theresienstadt on Transport I/46 on 17.08.1942. Died at Theresienstadt on 28.12.1942. Murdered.

Mannheim, Emma *05.03.1893, Landsberg. Deported from Berlin to Theresienstadt on Transport I/33 on 29.07.1942. Deported from Theresienstadt to Treblinka on 26.09.1942 on Transport Br. Murdered.

Mannheim, Hugo *09.10.1871, Landsberger Holländer/Landsberg. Deported from Berlin to Theresienstadt on Transport I/33 on 29.07.1942. Died in Theresienstadt. Murdered.

Methis, Regina *01.03.1876. Deported from Berlin, C2 Gerlachstrasse 18/21, to Theresienstadt on Transport I/46 on 17.08.1942. Died at Theresienstadt on 03.09.1942. Murdered.

Mayer, Rosa *25.09.1868, Wittlich. Deported from Berlin to Theresienstadt on Transport I/46. Died at Theresienstadt on 29.09.1942. Murdered.

Melhaus, Hertha *11.11.1923, Sommerfeld. Fate unknown.

Melhaus, Hulda *25.05.1894, Mrocza. Fate unknown.

Meyer, Käte, Katherine *03.05.1872, Berlin. Deported from Berlin to Theresienstadt on Transport I/36 on 03.08.1942. Died at Theresienstadt on 09.02.1942. Murdered.

Meyer, Hulda *19.07.1870, Zempelburg. Deported from Berlin, N4 Artelleriestrasse 31, to Theresienstadt on Transport I/46 on 17.08.1942. Deported from Theresienstadt to Treblinka on 19.09.1942 on Transport Bo. Murdered.

Meyersohn, Flora *26.04.1854, Chodzicz. Died in Berlin on 21.02.1941.

Michaelis, Paula *14.12.1868, Guttentag. Deported from Berlin to Theresienstadt on Transport I/47 on 19.08.1942. Deported from Theresienstadt to Treblinka on 26.09.1942 on Transport Br. Murdered.

Michaelis, Sophie *22.11.1866, Guttentag. Deported from Berlin to Theresienstadt on Transport I/47 on 19.08.1942. Deported from Theresienstadt to Treblinka on 26.09.1942 on Transport Br. Murdered.

Müller, Flora *07.02.1862, Schwerin. Deported from Berlin to Theresienstadt on Transport I/22 on 14.07.1942. Died at Theresienstadt on 13.08.1942. Murdered.

Müller, Recha *27.01.1865, Birnbaum. Died in Berlin on 05.02.1942.

Müllerheim, Hedwig *18.05.1877, Schwerin. Deported from Berlin to Theresienstadt on Transport I/21 on 13.07.1942. Deported from Theresienstadt to Treblinka on 19.09.1942 on Transport Bo. Murdered.

Münzer, Bertha *05.09.1869/05.09.1859, Koschmin. Deported from Berlin to Theresienstadt on Transport I/46 on 17.08.1942. Deported from Theresienstadt to Treblinka on 26.09.1942 on Transport Br. Murdered.

Nathan, Bernhard *08.12.1864, Lyck. Deported from Berlin to Auschwitz. Date unknown. Murdered.

Nathan, Josefa/Sophie-Josephe *21.04.1866/24.04.1866, Berlin. Deported from Berlin to Theresienstadt on Transport I/13 on 30.06.1942. Died at Theresienstadt on 12.08.1942. Murdered.

Naumann, Elsbeth *30.03.1871, Schwedt. Deported from Berlin to Theresienstadt on Transport I/46 on 17.08.1942. Deported from Theresienstadt to Treblinka on Transport Br on 26.09.1942. Murdered.

Neuländer, Fanny *14.04.1862, Beuthen. Deported from Berlin, Gerlachstrasse 18/21, on Transport I/46 on 17.08.1942. Died at Theresienstadt on 26.08.1942. Murdered.

Neuthal, Moritz *09.05.1869, Riesenburg. Deported from Berlin, W35 Lützowstrasse 77, to Theresienstadt on Transport I/28 on 22.07.1942. Died at Theresienstadt on 05.09.1942. Murdered.

Neuthal, Natalie *03.051872, Neuenburg. Deported from Berlin, W35 Lützowstrasse 77, to Theresienstadt on Transport I/28 on 22.07.1942. Deported from Theresienstadt to Treblinka on 21.09.1942 on Transport Bp. Murdered.

Norden, Elise *12.06.1875, Breslau. Deported from Berlin, W35 Derfflingerstrasse 17, to Theresienstadt on Transport I/23 on 15.07.1942. Murdered.

Norden, Oskar *29.08.1871, Berlin. Died in Berlin on 21.04.1940.

Oppenheim, Helene *21.12.1882, Insterberg, Ost-Preussen. Deported from Berlin, N65 Iranischestrasse 3, to Riga on Transport 10 on 25.01.1942. Murdered.

Oppenheim, Martin *25.12.1878, Stettin. Deported from Berlin, N65 Iranischestrasse 3, to Riga on Transport 10 on 25.01.1942. Murdered.

Oppenheimer, Siegmund *28.01.1865, Hemer. Deported from Berlin, Brunnenstrasse 41, to Theresienstadt on Transport I/46 on 17.08.1942. Deported from Theresienstadt to Treblinka on 19.09.1942 on Transport Bo. Murdered.

Orbach, Frieda *10.02.1897, Mohrungen. Deported from Berlin, N4 Auguststrasse 14-16, to Auschwitz on Transport 36 on 12.03.1943. Murdered.

Ordower, Salomon *30.07.1867, Brody. Deported from Berlin, W35 Lützowstrasse 77, to Theresienstadt on Transport I/28 on 22.07.1942. Deported from Theresienstadt to Treblinka on 21.09.1942 on Transport Bp. Murdered.

Ordower, Scheindel 28.12.1870, Drohobycz. Deported from Berlin, W35 Lützowstrasse 77, to Theresienstadt on Transport I/28 on 22.07.1942. Deported from Theresienstadt to Treblinka on 21.09.1942 on Transport Bp. Murdered.

Palnitzki, Olga *11.10.1863, Hohenstein. Deported from Berlin to Theresienstadt on Transport I/22 on 4.07.1942. Died at Theresienstadt on 07.11.1942. Murdered.

Pinner, Thekla *08.11.1863, Landsberg Warthe. Died in Berlin on 15.01.1941.

Posner, Betty *18.03.1871, Dramburg. Deported from Berlin to Theresienstadt on Transport I/46 on 17.08.1942. Deported from Theresienstadt to Treblinka on 19.09.1942 on Transport Bo. Murdered.

Preiss, Ida *25.07.1867, Beuthen. Died in Berlin on 21.05.1943.

Presser, Eveline *01.06.1869, Mikolow. Died in Berlin on 01.10.1941.

Presser, Max *14.12.1860, Miloslaw. Died in Berlin on 13.08.1942.

Preuss, Marie *24.03.1868, Szamotuly. Deported from Berlin to Theresienstadt on Transport I/52 on 26.08.1942. Died in Theresienstadt -.05.1943. Murdered.

Reinhardt, Jenny *16.09.1861, Märkisch Friedland. Deported from Berlin to Theresienstadt on Transport I/46 on 17.08.1942. Died at Theresienstadt on 14.09.1942. Murdered.

Ring, Laura *09.05.1866, Kulm. Deported from Berlin, Grosse Hamburgerstrasse 26, to Theresienstadt on Transport I/3 on 05.06.1942. Died in Theresienstadt. Murdered.

Ritter, Martha *05.12.1865, Berlin. Died in Berlin on 26.10.1939.

Ritter, Paula *08.06.1862, Berlin. Died in Berlin on 25.10.1941.

Rosenbaum, Paula *05.05.1871, Grudziaz. Emigrated to Cuba on 25.10.1941.

Rosenbaum, Sophie *14.09.1864, Birnbaum. Deported from Berlin, W35 Lützowstrasse 67, to Theresienstadt on Transport I/23 on 15.07.1942. Deported from Theresienstadt to Treblinka on 21.09.1942 on Transport Bp. Murdered.

Rosenberg, Martha *25.03.1870, Lasin. Died in Berlin on 21.12.1940.

Rosenthal, Felix *09.01.1872, Magdeburg. Deported from Berlin, N65 Iranischestrasse 3, to Riga on Transport 10 on 25.01.1942. Murdered.

Rosenthal, Ida *17.03.1879, Düren. Deported from Berlin, N65

Iranischestrasse 3, to Riga on Transport 10 on 25.01.1942. Murdered.

Rosenthal, Rosa *07.06.1870, Bentschen. Deported from Berlin, W35 Lützowstrasse 77, on Transport I/28 on 22.07.1942 to Theresienstadt. Deported from Theresienstadt to Treblinka on Transport Bp on 21.09.1942. Murdered.

Rosenthal, Amalia *23.08.1868, Berlin. Deported from Berlin to Theresienstadt on Transport I/46 on 17.08.1942. Ransomed and transported to Switzerland on 07.02.1945.

Roth, Emma *25.03.1858, Rheinsberg. Deported from Berlin to Theresienstadt on Transport I/46 on 17.08.1942. Died at Theresienstadt on 03.09.1942. Murdered.

Rothmann, Jenny *08.02.1868, Gniezno. Deported from Berlin to Theresienstadt on Transport I/15 on 03.07.1942. Deported from Theresienstadt on 19.09.1942 on Transport Bo. Murdered.

Rothmann, Regina *09.11.1870, Gniezno. Fate unknown.

Röhricht, Hermann *22.07.1868, Danzig. Fate unknown.

Röhricht, Selma *21.08.1870, Berlin. Fate unknown.

Salinger, Martha *29.05.1867, Marienburg. Deported from Berlin, W35 Lützowstrasse 77, to Theresienstadt on Transport I/28 on 22.07.1942. Deported from Theresienstadt to Treblinka on 26.09.1942 on Transport Br. Murdered.

Salinger, Minna *18.07.1874, Deutsch-Krone. Deported from Berlin, W35 Lützowstrasse 77, on Transport I/28 on 22.07.1942 to Theresienstadt. Deported from Theresienstadt to Treblinka on Transport Br on 26.09.1942. Murdered.

Salinger, Bertha *08.07.1863, Jakobsdorf. Died in Berlin 06.04.1941.

Salomon, Bernhard *29.01.1856, Kornik. Died in Berlin 06.07.1939.

Salomon, Heinrich *11.05.1874, Regenwalde. Died in Berlin 26.04.1941.

Salomon, Rosa *03.05.1880, Randow/Stettin. Deported from Berlin to Piaski Luterskie on Transport 11 on 28.03.1942. Murdered.

Scheidemann, Edith *02.03.1921, Rosenberg. Deported from Berlin to Riga on Transport 7 on 27.11.1941. Died in Riga on 30.11.1941 during the massacre in Rumbulaskogen. Murdered.

Scheidemann, Ernestine *14.02.1874, Wrzesnia. Deported from Berlin to Theresienstadt on Transport I/22 on 14.07.1942. Died in Theresienstadt. Murdered.

Scheidemann, Sally *02.12.1872, Lauenburg. Deported from Berlin, Altonaerstrasse 4, to Theresienstadt on Transport I 22 on 14.07.1942. Died at Theresienstadt on 21.09.1942. Murdered.

Scherek, Rebekka *21.01.1871, Krotoszyn. Fate unknown.

Schindler, Margarete *23.11.1874, Berlin. Deported from Berlin to Riga on Transport 10 on 25.01.1942. Died in Riga. Murdered.

Schindler, Martha *29.07.1865, Berlin. Deported from Berlin, Bayerische Strasse 29, to Theresienstadt on Transport I/46 on 17.08.1942. Died at Theresienstadt on 05.10.1942. Murdered.

Schidorowski, Auguste *24.03.1872, Brodnica. Fate unknown.

Schlesinger, Anna *12.02.1868, Berlin. Deported from Berlin to Theresienstadt. on Transport I/46 on 17.08.1942. Deported from Theresienstadt to Treblinka on 19.09.1942 on Transport Bo. Murdered.

Schoeps, Emstine *28.10.1859, Neuenburg. Fate unknown.

Schwarzwald, Hulda *03.12.1865, Berlin. Deported from Berlin, Auguststrasse 14, to Theresienstadt on Transport I/24 on 16.07.1942. Died at Theresienstadt on 03.08.1942. Murdered.

Schweitzer, Charlotte *10.10.1866, Broslawitz. Fate unknown.

Schweitzer, Emelie *14.03.1866, Broslawitz. Deported from Berlin, SW 29 Heimstrasse 20, to Theresienstadt on 15.09.1942. Died on 18.11.1942 in Theresienstadt. Murdered.

Schweitzer, Mathilde *14.08.1868, Broslawitz. Fate unknown.

Seelig, Rosa *09.08.1862, Szamotouly. Fate unknown.

Seligsohn, Felix *19.09.1868, Berlin. Commited suicide on 29.07.1942.

Siegheim, Frieda *23.11.78, Berlin. Commited suicide on 13.01.1942.

Siegmann, Georg *21.05.1869, Berlin. Deported from Berlin, W35 Lützowstrasse 77, to Theresienstadt on Transport I/24 on 16.07.1942. Deported from Theresienstadt to Auschwitz on 28.10.1944 on Transport Ev. Murdered.

Siegmann, Helene *07.04.1884, Frankfurt a Main. Deported from Berlin, W35 Lützowstrasse 77, to Theresienstadt on Transport

I/24 on 16.07.1942. Deported from Theresienstadt to Auschwitz on 28.10.1944 on Transport Ev. Murdered.

Silbermann, Anna *28.12.1860, Greifenberg. Deported from Berlin, W35 Lützowstrasse 77, on Transport I/28 on 22.07.1942 to Theresienstadt. Died in Theresienstadt. Murdered.

Silbermann, Röschen *07.02.1860, Gleiwitz. Deported from Berlin, N4 Grosse Hamburgerstrasse 26 to Theresienstadt on Transport I/2 on 04.06.1942. Died on 23.07.1942 in Theresienstadt. Murdered.

Silberstein, Ella *16.12.1869, Berlin. Died in Berlin 05.04.1941.

Silberstein, Franziska *27.06.1862, Preussisch-Friedland. Deported from Berlin, W35 Lützowstrasse 77, to Theresienstadt on Transport I/28 on 22.07.1942. Died at Theresienstadt on 20.08.1942. Murdered.

Stadthagen, Goldinchen *03.04.1866, Hamburg. Deported from Berlin, N4 Grosse Hambugerstrasse 26, to Theresienstadt on Transport I/46 on 17.08.1942. Died at Theresienstadt on 30.08.1942. Murdered.

Stahl, Hermann *12.02.1872, Kozmin. Deported from Berlin to Theresienstadt on Transport I/46 on 17.08.1942. Murdered.

Stahl, Rosalie *06.12.1869, Kozmin. Deported from Berlin, Schönhauser Allee 22, to Theresienstadt on Transport I/46 on 17.08.1942. Died at Theresienstadt on 14.01.1943. Murdered.

Stargardt, Meta *03.07.1882, Landsberg Warthe. Deported from Berlin to Riga on Transport 10 on 25.01.1942. Murdered.

Steigerwald, Karoline *12.12.1854, Landenbach. Deported from

Berlin to Theresienstadt on Transport I/22 on 14.07.1942. Died in Theresienstadt 12.08.1942. Murdered.

Stein, Adele *28.06.1866, Berlin. Died in Berlin 22.01.1943.

Steinhardt, Julius *15.07.1871, Tauberbischofsheim. Deported from Berlin, N65 Iranischestrasse 2, to Theresienstadt on Transport I/65 on 15.09.1942. Died at Theresienstadt on 20.01.1943. Murdered.

Stern, Therese *15.12.1875, Berlin. Deported from Berlin to Riga on Transport 10 on 25.01.1942. Murdered.

Stern, Willy *22.03.1873, Berlin. Deported from Berlin, C2 Gerlachstrasse 21, to Riga on Transport 10 on 25.01.1942. Murdered.

Sternberg, Emilie *11.03.1865, Löbau. Deported from Berlin, N58 Schönhauser Allee 22, to Theresienstadt on Transport I/6 on 12.06.1942. Died at Theresienstadt on 17.08.1942. Murdered.

Sternberg, Sara *05.03.1854, Deutsch-Eylau. Deported from Berlin, Grosse Hamburgerstrasse 26, on Transport I/2 on 06.06.1942 to Theresienstadt. Died at Theresienstadt on 07.08.1942. Murdered.

Storch, Franziska *10.06.1871, Widminnen. Deported from Berlin, W35 Lützowstrasse 67, to Theresienstadt on Transport I/23 on 15.07.1942. Died at Theresienstadt on 03.01.1943. Murdered.

Tischler, Eugen *18.06.1865, Gostyn. Died in Berlin 16.03.1940.

Tischler, Hedwig *05.09.1872, Srem. Fate unknown.

Waldt, Tressi *26.04.1872, Williamsburg. Deported from Berlin to Theresienstadt on Transport I/22 on 13.07.1942. Died on 28.10.1943 in Theresienstadt. Murdered.

Wagner, Amelie *14.04.1873, Berlin. Deported from Berlin, Grosse Hamburgerstrasse 26, to Riga on Transport 10 on 25.01.1942. Murdered.

Warschauer, Valeska *14.08.1868, Kanth. Deported from Berlin, W35 Lützowstrasse 77, to Theresienstadt on Transport I/28 on 22.07.1942. Murdered.

Wassermann, Johanna *15.01.1867, Filehne. Died in Berlin 14.02.1943.

Weil, Mathilde *22.04.1854, Landberg Warthe. Fate unknown.

Westenberg, Isidor *04.02.1875, Gleidingen. Fate unknown.

Westenberg, Selma *05.03.1873, Pasewalk. Deported from Berlin, Altonaerstrasse 4, to Riga on Transport 10 on 25.01.1942. Murdered.

Wilde, Mathilde *15.01.1862, Berlin. Died in Berlin 08.01.1942.

Wollstein, Emma *05.10.1858, Dirschau. Deported from Berlin to Theresienstadt on Transport I/18 on 08.07.1942. Died 16.02.1943 in Theresienstadt. Murdered.

Wulff, Selma *06.09.1876, Köpeniek. Deported from Berlin, W35 Derfflingerstrasse 17, to Warszawa on Transport 12 on 02.04.1942. Murdered.

Wurzel, Mathilde *07.10.1869, Znin. Deported from Berlin to Theresienstadt on Transport I/27 on 21.07.1942. Deported from

Theresienstadt to Treblinka on 21.09.1942 on Transport Bp. Murdered.

Zander, Hedwig *14.12.1880, Beuthen. Commited suicide on 25.01.1942.

Zeidler, Hulda *27.08.1886, Schwerin. Deported from Berlin to Sobibór on Transport 15 on 13.06.1942. Murdered.

Restitution demands linked to the property at Hagenstrasse 39–47

The table shows the restitution demands linked to the property (Grundstück) and its furnishings at Hagenstrasse 39–47 from the Society of the Sacred Heart against the German Reich and from Cecilie Sieverts against Paula Werhahn, the person who acquired the property on the society's behalf (Adelheid Verein e.V., Ordensfrauen vom Heiligen Herzen Jesu) 1938.

Claimant	Claim against	Item	Doc. No
Adelheid Verein e.V., Ordensfrauen vom Heiligen Herzen Jesu, Pützchen bei Bonn	The German Reich	Fixtures and fittings from the property in Berlin-Grunewald, Hagenstrasse 39-47	23 WGA 980/62
Cecilie Sieverts, née Behrendt, Thiensville, Wisc., USA	Paula Werhahn, Berlin-Charlottenburg, Insterburg Allee 8	The property in Berlin-Grunewald, behind Hagenstr. 41	31 WGA 611/51
Cecilie Sieverts, née Behrendt, Thiensville, Wisc., USA	Paula Werhahn, Berlin-Charlottenburg, Insterburg Allee 39	The property in Berlin Grunewald, Hagenstr. 39	31 WGA 612/51
Cecilie Sieverts, née Behrendt, Thiensville, Wisc., USA	Paula Werhahn, Berlin-Charlottenburg, Insterburg Allee 39	The property in Berlin Grunewald, Hagenstr. 43	31 WGA 613/51
Cecilie Sieverts, née Behrendt, Thiensville, Wisc., USA	Paula Werhahn, Berlin-Charlottenburg, Insterburg Allee 39	The property in Berlin Grunewald, Hagenstr. 45/47.	31 WGA 614/51

Cecilie Sieverts, née Behrendt, Thiensville, Wisc., USA	Paula Werhahn, Berlin-Charlottenburg, Insterburg Allee 39	The property in Berlin Grunewald, Hagenstr. 39a and 41.	31 WGA 615/51
Cecilie Sieverts, née Behrendt, Thiensville, Wisc., USA	Paula Werhahn, Berlin-Charlottenburg, Insterburg Allee 39	The property in Berlin Grunewald, Hagenstr. 43, 45, 47.	31 WGA 616/51

Some of the restitution demands linked to the property at Lützowstrasse 48/49

Betty Karger, Jenny Kuttner and Max Ascher resided on Lützowstrasse and it is their personal effects the demands concern. The demand from the Jewish Community concerns the actual property.

Claimant	Claim against	Item	Doc. No
JRSO (the Jewish Restitution Successor Organization) for Mrs Fanny Kuttner, née Levy, last known address: Berlin W35, Lützowstr. 49	The German Reich	Credit and securities held in Deutsche Bank.	52 WGA JRSO/875
Max Ascher (*28.03.1869, deceased), last known address: Berlin W30, Altersheim Lützowstrasse Claimant: Gertrud Ascher.	-	Gold, silver, jewellery, radio, household items.	21 WGA 2548-2549/57
The Jewish Community in Berlin, Berlin N65, Iranische Strasse 2	The German Reich	The property in Berlin W35, Lützowstrasse 49, except use.	52 WGA 290/51
The Jewish Community in Berlin, Berlin N65, Iranische Strasse 2	The German Reich	The property in Berlin W35, Lützowstrasse 48, except use.	52 WGA 291/51
Betty Karger (*06.10.1865), deceased, last known address: Berlin, Lützowstrasse, Jüdisches Altersheim	The German Reich	Gold, silver, jewellery.	52 WGA 1287/57

Selected interviews and memoranda
from the security police files

The memorandum is one of the earliest dated memoranda in Ekström's file verifying that Ekström collaborated with Calais and was a volunteer in the Waffen-SS. The security police still do not, however, have all the information. It is worth noting that according to this memorandum, Ekström held the rank of Unterscharführer (one above Rottenführer). Helmut Panzer also states that Ekström held the rank of Unterscharführer. However, according to interviews with Ekström, as well as other sources, he never made it higher than Rottenführer.

***

To
Herr Löjtnanten C.G Kagger
Defence Staff
Stockholm, 30 June 1943
Magnus Lemon

Classified memo on case Hd 1729/40

The case concerns Swedish citizen Hilding Gustaf Sigvard E k s t r ö m, engineer, born 9/10-07, most recently resident at 10 Kungsgatan. From existing registration cards and other documents, it is to be understood that for some years Ekström has been a member of and active in Swedish Socialist Unity (SSS) and formerly the National Socialist Workers' Party (NSAP), within which latter group, according to information received on 3/5-40, he was, when living in Örebro, S.A.

group leader for two years. It also shows that he purchased 5 shares worth 100 kr each in AB N.S. Press in 1937 and in 1938 sent Christmas greetings in Den Svenske Folksocialisten (the main organ of the Lindholm Movement). As far as we know, Ekström travelled from Sweden to Norway via Charlottenbern on 1/5-41 on Swedish passport No. A 7647, valid until 10/4-42. From Norway, he travelled to Berlin for academic study. In a memorandum from an interview with Swedish citizen Osborn Gerhard Stolpe, welder, dated 19/2-43 and drawn up by the Swedish consulate-general in Oslo, Stolpe claims that one Swedish "Rottenführer" Ekström was employed at the Waffen-SS's recruitment office in Oslo. This Ekström, according to Stolpe, is now living in Germany.

In an interview held on 5/2-43 in Gothenburg, Swedish citizen Erik Harald Jonsson, who had been recruited into the Waffen-SS but jumped from a German permittent train close to Gothenburg, claims to have encountered, amongst other people, a "Rottenführer" Gustaf Ekström, Kungsgatan 10, Lindesberg, during his stint with the Waffen-SS. Ekström, who had just been promoted to "Unterscharführer", worked at the Waffen-SS press office in Berlin, where he was put to studying and registering articles from Swedish newspapers about Germany in general and National Socialism in particular. Further, Ekström had told Jonsson that he had spent the Christmas and New Year holiday of 1942-1943 with commissioner Elof Thorwald Calais (this Calais fled from Sweden to Norway in the summer of 1942 and as far as we know here at the sixth department spied for the Germans).

By Ekström's own account, he returned from Oslo to Germany on 18/1-43, where as far as we know, he still lives.

Stockholm on 30 June 1943.
Magnus Lemon.

This interview was held shortly after Ekström arrived in Sweden. Although it gives a coherent description of his time with the Waffen-SS, much unfortunately remains unanswered. It is also full of details that do not tally with those from other mutually independent sources. For example, the dates of his time in Norway are wrong, and there is no mention of exactly what his business with Thorwald Calais was.

***

Malmö Police
Criminal Investigation Department

Memorandum
Wednesday 9 May 1945

Re: Swedish citizen Hilding Gustaf Sigvard Ekström and German citizen, widow Mrs Linnea Vilhelmina Ingeborg Calais.

Interview.

Copy sent to the sixth department for purposes of information. Malmö 14 May 1945.

While interviewing evacuated formerly Swedish now German citizens in Älmhult on Sunday 22 April 1945, Swedish citizen Hilding Gustaf Sigvard Ekström, engineer, was found at the centre in conversation with quarantined inmate and German citizen Linnea Wilhelmina Ingeborg Calais, widow of whom we now know to be the late former commissioner Elov Thorwald Calais, suspected of espionage against Sweden. Since Ekström and Mrs Calais seemed to be well acquainted and it was understood from their conversation that Ekström had been on the transport from Lübeck, which was subject to quarantine in Älmhult, he and Mrs Calais were questioned more closely, upon which Ekström was instructed to enter quarantine. County police superintendent Otto Rosengren was notified of Ekström's arrival by telephone.

Mrs Calais and engineer Ekström have each gave the following testimonies:

Mrs Calais: She was born on 23 October 23 October 1899 in the parish of Skön, Västernorrland county, the legitimate daughter of factory labourer Karl Johan Mattson and his now deceased wife Märta, née Erikson. She lived with her parents until the age of 22, during which time she attended elementary school. By the age of 22 she had married the then Swedish citizen Elof Thorwald Calais, a union that was dissolved with his death in a bomb shelter in Berlin in February 1945. She had then applied for and obtained permission to accompany the evacuation transports to Sweden. Her husband, Thorwald Calais, had been a national socialist as early as during Furugård's time, but had been a member of no other party than Lindholm's. In early April 1942 he left Sweden illegally and travelled to Norway, where he was in charge of propaganda for German and Norwegian authorities. On 10 July 1942 Mrs Calais also illegally travelled with their children to Norway, where she was met at Oslo railway station by her husband, who was in the company of the aforementioned Ekström. Mrs Calais was aware that Ekström had been Rottenführer for the Waffen-SS in Norway and was at that time also wearing a medal, probably indicating that he had fought at the Eastern Front. By the turn of the year 1942–1943 Ekström had travelled from Norway to Germany, where he was employed at some office in Berlin. Otherwise, Ekström's doings were unknown to Mrs Calais. On the journey from Lübeck to Copenhagen, Ekström has asked Mrs Calais to take care of his luggage as he intended to stay for a day or so in Copenhagen. He did not, however, mention what business he had there. Ekström's conversation with her in Älmhult had concerned Ekström's luggage, which had somehow been misplaced.

Ekström: He was born on 9 October 1907 in the parish of Färila in Gävleborg county, the legitimate son of the late gymnastics trainer Samuel Ekström and his surviving widow

Hilda, née Mickelson. On leaving school with secondary qualifications in 1923, he completed his military service in 1928. In early 1929 he travelled to America to study and gain practical laboratory experience. In 1932 he returned to Sweden. After his arrival he took a number of jobs at laboratories and drawing offices, most recently in 1939 with surveyor Albin Edlund in Sundsvall. In January 1940 he was called up for standby service with I3 in Örebro, which he left on completing his service in March 1941. He then tried to obtain civilian work in Sweden. Due to his political views and membership of the National Socialist party, however, work was denied him. In April 1941 he therefore visited the German consulate in Stockholm and inquired about opportunities for civilian work in Norway. The consulate promised to help him with this and issued the necessary visa for travel to Norway. He was told, however, that any work would possibly be of a military nature. At the end of April 1941 he obtained a German visa for travel to Norway and he arrived, probable via Charlottenberg, to Oslo on 30 April. He was told by the German authorities that there was no civilian work available but there was a position with the Waffen-SS open to him. Should he choose to decline this employment opportunity, he was free to return to Sweden. Ekström had then explained that he was willing to join the Waffen-SS and was promptly registered as a member of said organisation. On 6 May 1941 he took a permittent train to Germany via Trelleborg-Sassnitz. He then trained in Sennheim and Graz until 1 September 1941, when he was deployed at the SS-Hauptamt in Berlin to work as an interpreter and translator of Swedish newspapers.

On 1 November 1941 he was, at his own request "to do his bit on the Bolshevik front", sent by transport aeroplane to Helsinki. On 1 March 1942 he returned to Germany after having travelled through northern Sweden via Haparanda to Trondheim and Oslo and by permittent train to Germany via Trelleborg.

Between Haparanda and Östersund, the railway carriage containing Ekström's chest was broken into and raided, and his Swedish passport went missing. He later heard through the grapevine that the passport had been recovered and was now supposedly at some police station in northern Sweden, probably in Östersund.

After his return to Germany from the Eastern Front he was reinstated in his former office at the SS-Hauptamt in Berlin, upon which he was promoted to Waffen-SS Rottenführer. He was also then awarded the "eastern front medal".

In May 1942 he was given permission to travel to Norway, where he joined a permittent transport to Oslo, and upon arrival visited the Swedish consulate-general to apply for a passport to Sweden. The consulate told him that the Foreign Ministry had given instructions not to issue a Swedish passport for him; however, it was willing to issue a temporary passport for him to enter Sweden. When he thus realised that he would not be able to travel back out of Sweden legally he did not avail himself of the offer of a provisional passport. During his leave he therefore remained in Norway, where he spent most of his time in Lillehammer. At the end of his period of leave, he returned to his office in Berlin on a new permittent transport. After his arrival he was given the opportunity to study the politics, geography, literature, race relations, etc. of the Nordic nations at Berlin University alongside his work at the SS-Hauptamt.

On 1 September 1942 he was transferred to Oslo to serve with the "Waffen-SS Ersatzkommando, Norwegen". During this time, he worked as an interpreter for Swedes wishing to sign up with the Waffen-SS. He was thus employed to do registration work and other purely administrative tasks for the "Ersatzkommandot". On 1 November 1942 he was sent back to Berlin to complete his "Nordic studies" at Berlin University.

In February 1943 he handed in his resignation to the Waffen-SS in order to study at an institute of technology in Germany, which was granted in early April of that same year. He commenced his studies on 15 April 1943 at the Ohmpolytechnikum in Nuremberg, where he remained until 1 April 1945, when his studies came to an end.

On 5 April 1945 he travelled to Lübeck, where the Swedish consul in Nuremberg had told him that migrant Swedes had gathered for their journey home to Sweden. The Swedish consul in Nuremberg, Helander, had written to the Swedish legation in Berlin to confirm that Ekström was a Swedish citizen, which resulted in his being issued a temporary Swedish passport by the legation. From Lübeck he had joined a transport led by the Red Cross to Copenhagen, where he departed the contingent in order to exchange his German marks. After having gone in vain to the Copenhagen branch of the German national bank, he visited the offices of the Waffen-SS, where he spoke to one Hauptsturmfuhrer, a former colleague of his from Berlin, who arranged it so that Ekström received around 200 Danish kronor for 300 German marks, money he partly spent during his stay in Copenhagen, where he spent a night in the Swedish church and two nights in the Mission Hotel annex. He then flew to Malmö on 21 April 1945.

In 1926, Ekström joined Sveriges Fascistiska Kamporganisation, and remained a member until his trip to America. On his return from America he joined the Swedish National Socialist Party/Furugård Party/. In 1933 he left and jointed the N.S.A.P. /Lindholm/. During his time in Germany he was a member of Ortsgrupp Berlin until 1943. In 1935 he was secretary of Nordic Youth and in 1937 block leader in the N.S.A.P. Ekström still professed himself an adherent of national socialist ideas.

Ekström stated that after his quarantine, he would probably live with his mother in Lindesberg. Since there were suspicions that Ekström was the same person as the allegedly late commissioner Thorwald Calais, a description and a photograph were sent to the undersigned by the Malmö criminal investigation unit, upon which it could be established with certainty that Ekström and Calais were not the same person.

Malmö, as above

Knut G. Nilsson
Detective constable.

Gustaf Ekströms first application for a certificate of impunity.

***

Memorandum.
Cc. Rutqvist.

Nazi Hilding Gustaf Sigvard Ekström (Hd. 1729/40/)
applies for a certificate of impunity for travelling to South America.
Stockholm 9 Aug. 1947.

(J.W. Lönnerstam)

The second application for a certificate of impunity.

***

For travel to South America

CLASSIFIED

Information from the 3rd department of the national police concerning a person applying for a certificate of impunity. Doc. No 1721 I.D. 1948

1. Is it known whether the applicant, over the past two years, has been a member of a national socialist party? –
2. Might the applicant be suspected of acts of sabotage? –
3. Is the applicant suspected of having been engaged in any other kinds of act of sedition? –
4. Special information: The applicant has not been punished or prosecuted for a crime of the sort that is handled by the national police 3rd department.

Stockholm, 27 April 1948
Signature
Registry research conducted by M.B.

According to a foreign source, Gustaf Ekström is linked to the SRP and a blocked-out name that is probably that of Otto Ernst Remer, written incorrectly as Ernst Otto Remer, who was a leading member of the party.

***

CLASSIFIED
as per paragraph 4 of Act 1937:249
21 May 1953
DEFENCE STAFF

11/4 1953. _____

A foreign source has notified us that Gustav Sigvard Hilding Ekström, HD 1729-40, f. 9/10 1907 of Färila, Sweden, has received attention for his connections with radical right-wing West German circles, in particular the SRP.

E arrived in November 1952 to Karlsruhe, where he resides at Nebeniusstrasse 3.

He has apparently been staying in Nuremberg, where he also had close ties with the SRP. He has been in contact with E_____r.

E is also said to have assisted in the preparations of an international fascist congress.

The source maintains that E is known to Swedish anti-Semitic circles.

Signed: (Signature illegible)

Ekström is linked to another two far-right organisations in West Germany.

***

The National Police Board
Security Division
20 July 1976

According to information obtained, the board of West Germany's National Democratic University Federation (NHB) was in correspondence with Hilding Gustaf Sigvard Ekström, Kämnärsvägen 4:1045, 222 49 Lund.
Ekström admits to having contacts in the German-Rhodesia Association.

A brief and incomplete summary of Ekström's involvement in Nazism.

***

National Police Board/Security
Stockholm
PM 1976-07-23

Re. Hilding GUSTAF Sigvard EKSTRÖM, engineer, 071009-XXXX, unmarried, resident at Kämnärsvägen 4:1045, 222 45 Lund.

Ekström features in the National Police Board/Security ___ personal case file No HD 1729-40 and in section __ with _____ in accordance with the appended telegram.
EKSTRÖM has been involved in Nazi organisations since his teens.

1926 EKSTRÖM joined Fascistiska Kamporganisation (SFKO, roughly the Swedish Fascist Movement)
1932 the Swedish National Socialist Party (SNP)
1933 the National Socialist Workers' Party (NSAP)
1937 he was block leader in the NSAP
1938 leader for the party's SA group in Örebro.

Between 1941 and 1943 he was enlisted in the Waffen SS, where he attained the rank of Rottenfuehrer and served in Berlin, Helsinki and Oslo.

Ekström also maintained relations with the Sozialistische Reichpartei (SRP), which was dissolved in 1952.

(Signature unreadable)

Some key years

1907, Gustaf Ekström is born on 9 October in Färila.

1926 , Gustaf Ekström joins SFKO.

1933, Adolf Hitler takes power in Germany. The Jewish nursing home at 48/49 opens. Gustaf Ekström joins the NSAP.

1940, The Jews at the nursing home on Lützowstrasse are evicted and crowded into other properties and homes around Berlin with other evicted and deported Jews.

1941, The SS-Hauptamt moves into the seized premises at Lützowstrasse 48/49.
   Gustaf Ekström enlists with the Waffen-SS and serves at the SS-Hauptamt, Lützowstrasse 48/49, Berlin, in September–October.

1942, Jews from the nursing home at Lützowstrasse 48/49 are deported to the ghettos and killing fields in the east, and to Theresienstadt.

Ekström collaborates with Thorwald Calais in Norway and serves at the Waffen-SS Ersatzkommando Norwegen.

1943, Gustaf Ekström requests to be discharged from the Waffen-SS to study at the Institute of Technology in Nuremberg.
The last transports of Jews from the seized nursing home on Lützowstrasse leave Berlin.

1945, Germany capitulates. Ekström takes a seat on one of the Red Cross white buses and flees the Americans, aided by Nazi and Swedish consul Sven Helander.

1947/1948, Gustaf Ekström requests a certificate of impunity to travel to South America.

1949, Gustaf Ekström moves to Nuremberg, resumes his studies at the Institute and becomes politically active in several neo-Nazi and far right parties and organisations in Germany.

1977, Ekström visits the NPD executive in Germany.

1988, Ekström is elected auditor for the Malmö section of the Sweden Democrats at its first annual meeting in Malmö on 21 February 1988.

1989, Ekström is elected auditor for the party executive of the Sweden Democrats' national organisation.

1992, Gustaf Ekström is active at a Sweden Democrat rally.

1994, Gustaf Ekström takes part in the 30 November celebrations in Lund for the last time.

1995, Gustaf Ekström dies on 16 July 1995 and is buried in Färila.

Gustaf Ekström's political engagement

1926, SFKO – Swedish fascist movement, Sveriges Fascistiska Kamporganisation, member.

1932, SNSP – Swedish National Socialist Party (Birger Furugård's party), member.

1933–1950, NSAP/SSS – The National Socialist Workers' Party/ Swedish Socialist Unity (Sven Olov Lindholm's party), member, SA-man, block leader.

1935, NU – Nordic Youth, the NSAP's youth organisation, secretary.

1936, Sällskapet för Svensk Fostran (roughly: the Society for Swedish breeding), board member.

1937, NS-Press – the NSAP printing house, shareholder.

1941–1943, Waffen-SS, volunteer, SS-Rottenführer.

1943, NSDStB – NSDStB, the German National Socialist Student Organisation, member

1951, Sozialistische Reichspartei Deutschlands – the Socialist Reich Party of Germany, meeting participant, correspondent.

1951, Europäische Soziale Bewegung – the European Social Movement, aka the Malmö Movement, contact person in Germany.

1951, Deutsche Gemeinschaft/Bund der Heimatvertriebenen und Entrechteten – the All-German Bloc/League of Expellees and Deprived of Rights, meeting participant.

1976, Nationaler Hochschulbund – National Democratic University Federation, correspondent.

1976, The German-Rhodesia Association, correspondent.

1976, The National League of Sweden, member.

1977, Nationaldemokratische Partei Deutschland – NPD, meetings with the executive, subscriber to the party organ *Deutsche Stimme*.

1980s and 90s, 30 November Association, member, takes part in the 30 November demonstrations in Lund.

1988, Sweden Democrats, auditor for the party executive, member.

1996, HIAG, Hilfsgemeinschaft auf Gegenseitigkeit der Angehörigen der ehemaligen Waffen-SS, obituary in the organisation's organ *Der Freiwillige*, May 1996.

List of illustrations

1. Gustaf Ekström, in the municipal school in Lindesberg, 1923–1924. Ekström is in the middle row on the far left. Photo: Alfred Michelson, Lindesberg archive of cultural history. Page 57

2. Gustaf Ekström, school photograph, Örebro Technological Gymnasium, 1928. Photo: Örebro municipal archive. Page 58

3. Gustaf Ekström, third person sitting to the right. Family photograph, c. 1928, Lindesberg. Photo: Alfred Michelson, Lindesberg archive of cultural history. Page 59

4. Gustaf Ekström. Photograph from his visa to the USA, 1928. U.S. Department of Homeland Security, U.S. Citizenship and Immigration Services. Page 60

5. Gustaf Ekström, SA uniform, NSAP/SSS, c. 1935. Ekström is sitting in the bottom row to the far right. Photo: The Bosse Schön archive. Page 61

6. Sven Olov Lindholm leader of the Swedish Nazi party (NSAP/SSS) holds speech from the pulpit at a meeting probably around 1942. Photo: Pressens Bild/TT. Page 62

7. Swedish nazis on the march 1933. The flags were blue with yellow swastikas. Photo: TT. Page 63

8. Plans of the Jewish nursing home at Lützowstrasse 48/49. The plans were drawn by architect Gustav Bauer and approved by Ber-

lin's building inspectorate on 25 March 1933. To the left is the signature of Martin Salomonski, director of the nursing home. Landesarchiv Berlin. Page 64

9. Jüdisches Altersheim, Lützowstrasse 48, September 1933. Photo: Courtesy of the Leo Baeck Institute, New York. Page 65

10. Plaque commemorating the opening of the Jüdisches Altersheim, Lützowstrasse 48, September 1933. Photo: Courtesy of the Leo Baeck Institute, New York. Page 66

11. Painting of Adolf Jandorf (in whose memory the home was opened), Jüdisches Altersheim, Lützowstrasse 48, September 1933. Photo: Courtesy of the Leo Baeck Institute, New York. Page 67

12. Day-room (note the newspapers hanging on the wall), Jüdisches Altersheim, Lützowstrasse 48, September 1933. Photo: Courtesy of the Leo Baeck Institute, New York. Page 68

13. Dining room, Jüdisches Altersheim, Lützowstrasse 48, September 1933. Photo: Courtesy of the Leo Baeck Institute, New York. Page 69

14. Assembly room (note the leaded windows facing the street), Jüdisches Altersheim, Lützowstrasse 48, September 1933. Photo: Courtesy of the Leo Baeck Institute, New York. Page 70

15. Devotional niche in the assembly room, Jüdisches Altersheim, Lützowstrasse 48, September 1933. Photo: Courtesy of the Leo Baeck Institute, New York. Page 71

16. Single room, Jüdisches Altersheim, Lützowstrasse 48, September 1933. Photo: Courtesy of the Leo Baeck Institute, New York. Page 72

17. Nathan Baumgardt, one of the residents evicted from Lützowstrasse 48/49. Nathan Baumgardt was deported on Transport I/46 on 17 August 1942 to Theresienstadt, where he dies on 10 September 1942. Photo: Hall of Names, Page of Testimony for Nathan Baumgardt, Yad Vashem. Page 101

18. Doris and Moritz Holzheim, residents at Lützowstrasse 48/49, emigrated to Brazil on 19 August 1940. Photo: Immigration Cards, National Archives in Rio de Janeiro, Brazil. Page 102

19. Leopold and Regina Jablonowski, residents at Lützowstrasse 48/49, emigrated to Brazil on 7 June 1939. Photo: Immigration Cards, National Archives in Rio de Janeiro, Brazil. Page 103

20. Rosa Kalenscher, resident at Lützowstrasse 48/49, emigrated to Brazil on 25 December 1939. Photo: Immigration Cards, National Archives in Rio de Janeiro, Brazil. Page 104

21. Agnes Keiler, resident at Lützowstrasse 48/49, emigrated to the USA on 20 March 1940. Photo: U.S Citizenship and Immigration Services, USA. Page 104

22. Regina Abraham, one of the residents evicted from Lützowstrasse 48/49. Regina Abraham was deported first to Theresienstadt on 7 September 1942 on Transport I/60, and again to Auschwitz on 18 April 1944 on Transport Eb. Regina Abraham was murdered in Auschwitz. Photo: Hall of Names, Page of Testimony for Regina Abraham, Yad Vashem. Page 105

23. File and lists of the names of the 1,000 Jews deported from Berlin to Theresienstadt on transports I/60-I/64 and I/66-I/70 between 7 and 25 September 1942. Regina Abraham was deported on Transport I/60. Record/file YVA O.64/218, Yad Vashem.

Page 106

List of illustrations

24. Regina Abraham is number 6234 (third from last) on the list of the deported. The list states that she was unemployed (Beruf: Ohne) and residing at N. Schönhauser Allee 23/25 in Berlin at the time of her deportation on 7 September 1942. Record/file YVA O.64/218, Yad Vashem. Page 107

25. The SS-Hauptamt sets up at Lützowstrasse 48/49, 7 January 1941. NS 33 Bundesarchiv. Page 108

26. Address and telephone number of the Jüdische Altersheim. 1936 Berlin telephone directory. Authors' private archive.
Page 109

27. Address and telephone number of the SS-Hauptamt at Lützowstrasse 48/49. 1941 Berlin telephone directory. Authors' private archive. Page 110

28. Address and telephone number of the SS-Hauptamt at Lützowstrasse 48/49, department Amt VI at Hagenstrasse 39–47, Grunewald. Supplement to the 1943 Berlin telephone directory. Authors' private archive. Page 111

29. May 1941. SS-Hauptamt instructs building contractor Kurt Thiede to rebuild parts of the nursing home. Landesarchiv Berlin.
Page 112

30. September 1941. Cutaway view showing the rebuilding work and other changes to be made to the property by the SS-Hauptamt. Landesarchiv Berlin. Page 113

31. Hagenstrasse 39–47, Grunewald, 1940. At the time the photograph is taken, the building is a Catholic girls' home. One of the girls has marked the room she stayed in with an X and the words "Mein Zimmer" (my room). The buildings, which had made up the Jewish-run Sanatorium Grunewald (owned by the Behrendt

Meyer family) were expropriated by the Nazi authorities around 1938. Gustaf Ekström served in the building after it had been seized by the SS-Hauptamt. Photo: Authors' private archive.

Page 114–115

32. Kiestinki, ruins by the lake, 8 August 1941. Photo: SA-Kuva.

Page 116

33. Kiestinki, German vehicles bogged down in mud, 16 April 1942. Photo: SA-Kuva. Page 116

34. Der Untermensch. One of the SS-Hauptamt's best known anti-Semitic and racist publications. From 1942. Authors' private archive. Page 145

35. Max and Helene Behrendt Meyer, aunt of Cecilie Behrendt Sieverts and owner of Sanatorium Grunewald. C. 1928, Salinenpromenade in Bad Kissingen. Photo: The Sieverts Family private collection. Page 146

36. The Behrendts Sieverts family's last walk on 17 April 1938 before emigrating to the USA. From the left: Mrs Jaening, "Oma" Elise Behrendt (who later died in a Frankfurt clinic in 1940), Franz Behrendt (who also fled in 1939), "Oma" and "Opa" Sieverts, plus the children Henning and Arne. Photo: The Sieverts Family private collection. Page 147

37. Henning and Arne Sieverts playing on board SS Manhattan on 5 May 1938 en route to the security of the USA. Photo: The Sieverts Family private collection. Page 148

38. The Sieverts family in the USA c. 1945/1946. From the left: Cecilie, Laurie, Henning, Arne and Helmut. Photo: The Sieverts Family private collection. Page 149

39. Thorwald Calais's German passport. Photo: Authors' private archive. Page 150

40. Olof Sandström enlisted with the Waffen-SS at the same time as Gustaf Ekström and they were together during their first months of training. Olof Sandström was a die-hard Nazi and member of the NSAP, and worked for the Germans in the SS and as a civilian official at the SS-Hauptamt. In April 1945, as Ekström was fleeing the Americans, they met in Berlin. While Ekström was able to make his way back to Sweden on the white buses, Sandström had to flee by foot. Detail of Sandström's passport application, 10 August, 1942. Photo: Authors' private archive. Page 150

41. Ekström, Gustaf, Karteikarte des NSDStB, Bundesarchiv, Berlin. Page 151

42. Theresienstadt, doorway in the Small Fortress, concentration camp east, May 1945. Theresienstadt also used the slogan "Arbeit macht Frei" (work sets you free). Photo: Authors' private archive. Page 152

43. Auschwitz, May/June 1944. The photograph shows selection at the ramp in Auschwitz shortly after the arrival of a train containing Hungarian Jews. It is part of the famous Auschwitz album, which was found by Holocaust survivor Lili Jacob in Mittelbau-Dora concentration camp in 1945. Photo: Yad Vashem/United States Holocaust Museum. Page 153

44. Ruins, Lützowstrasse 1944. Photo: Authors' private archive.
Page 154

45. Ruins, Nuremberg, April 1945. Photo: NARA. Page 155

46. Party membership books of the "Sozialistische Reichspartei Deutschlands -SRP-, which translates as the Socialist Reich Party

of Germany, of which General Otto Ernst Remer, is vice-chairman, is distributed during an illegal party meeting in a forest near Nuremberg, Federal German Republic, 8 September, 1951. A black, white and red striped flag is hanging from the trees, the old flag of the German Empire. Gustaf Ekström was active in the SRP in the Nuremberg region. Photo: Associated Press. Page 156–157

47. Munich, Germany - Otto Ernst Remer gives a speech to his fellow Socialist Reich Party members at a rally 5 February 1951. Photo: Keystone Pictures/zumapress.com.   Page 158

48. The party conference of the Neo-Nazi National Democratic Party Germany (NPD) on 14 November, 1976, Frankfurt am Main. Party leader Martin Mussgnug sits in the middle. In August 1977 Gustaf Ekström pays a visit to the NPD executive and the circle surrounding Mussgnug. Photo: TT.   Page 159

49. Former members of the Waffen-SS have a look at pictures and information about members of the Waffen-SS who are missing since the end of World War II during a meeting of the "Hilfsgemeinschaft auf Gegenseitigkeit der Angehörigen der ehemaligen Waffen-SS e.V." (short: HIAG, translates as: "Mutual Help Association of Former Waffen-SS Members") in Gelsenkirchen, on the 16 November, 1952. HIAG was a lobby group and a denialist veterans' organisation founded by former high-ranking Waffen-SS personnel in West Germany in 1951. Its main objective was to achieve legal, economic and historical rehabilitation of the Waffen-SS. Photo: TT.   Page 160

50. The Sweden Democrats in Malmö, minutes of the annual meeting of 21 February 1988. §10 mentions Gustaf Ekström. Copy in the authors' private archive.   Page 193

51. At a rally with the Sweden Democrats, august 1994, the square of St: Knut, Malmö. 150 or so member of the Sweden Democrats

chant "Sieg Heil" and perform the Hitler salute. There is also men in uniform present in the crowd. Several of the members who attended this rally will later join Gustaf Ekström during the 30 November manifestations the same year. Photo: Martin Olson/Bilder i Syd. Page 194–195

52. Lund on 30 November 1994. Gustaf Ekström is standing by the base of the statue. He has doffed his hat for the laying of the wreath. Gösta Bergqvist dressed in a cap is seen to the left of Ekström. Photo: Jonn Leffmann. Page 196–197

53. Gustaf Ekström, passport photograph. Photo: Copy in the authors' private archive. Page 198

54. Lützowstrasse 48/49, 2015. Photo: Matti Palm. Page 199

55. Grunewald station, 2015. Röschen Silbermann lived on Lützowstrasse and was one of the thousands of Jews deported from Berlin. She was sent on Transport I/2 on 4 June 1942 to Theresienstadt concentration camp. The train departed from Grunewald, where a memorial has since been laid on platform 17. Photo: Matti Palm. Page 199

56. The Turkish motor vessel Asya, carrying 733 Jewish survivors arrives at Haifa, Palestine 3 April 1946, after being intercepted by a British destroyer near the coast. The Jews, who were attempting to enter Palestine illegally, were detained by immigration officials. The Hebrew name "Tel Hai" can be seen painted in Hebrew above the name "Asya". Renate Golinski were among the passengers. Photo: Dr Ernst Aschner/Keystone/Getty Images. Page 200–201

57. Renate Golinski and her son at the Kibbutz Ma'ayan Zvi in the town of Zikhron Ya'akov. Photo: Private. Page 202

58. The Obituray of Gustaf Ekström in Der Freiwillige, a journal

for former members of the Waffen-SS. He is mistakenly said to have belonged to 5. SS-Panzerdivision "Wiking". At the bottom of the page a version of the SS motto is printed, "Ihre Ehre heiß True". (their honour is loyalty). The loyalty is linked to the oath the members of the SS took when swearing their allegiance to Adolf Hitler. The motto is today banned in Germany according to the German Strafgesetzbuch (Criminal Code) in section § 86a. Photo: Antifaschistische Pressearchiv, Berlin. Page 203

Maps

Map 1. Europe 1942, Gustaf Ekström's travels, 1941–1942.
Page 204

Map 2. Europe 1942, Gustaf Ekström's travels, 1942–1945.
Page 205

Map 3. Transit camps and railway stations used for the deportation of Berlin's Jews, 1941–1945. Page 206–207

Map 4. Deportation of the residents of Lützowstrasse 48/49, 1941–1944. Page 208

All maps CC BY-SA 3.0, adapted from Wikimedia Commons.

References

Comments on references

One of the main references for this book has been Gustaf Ekström's file (Hd-1729-40) in the security police archive in the National Archive collection. Although the memoranda, notes, interview transcripts and registry extracts contained in this file are not comprehensive, they provided a solid platform on which to base our research. The information available to us – i.e. that is not marked as classified – comprised 42 pages; the material that the National Archive withheld is classified in accordance with Chapter 18 section 2 ("intelligence secrecy", maximum 70 years) of the Public Access to Information and Secrecy Act (2009:400). The content of the file must be judged from a source-critical perspective as it is largely dependent on information surrendered by Gustaf Ekström himself. Other information in the file comes from Swedish volunteers in the Waffen-SS and from various officials whom met Ekström or who handled cases concerning him. There is clearly much scope for misinterpretation and misunderstanding here (e.g. that a recorder missed a crucial piece of information.)

We are not the first to write about Gustaf Ekström. The earliest article we were able to track down about him in the Swedish was published in *Kvällsposten* on 28 April 1985 under the headline "The Swedes who fought for Hitler". It was part of a series of articles that the renowned journalist Mark Lippold wrote on Nazi Germany to commemorate the 40th anniversary of VE Day. In Lippold's article, Ekström claims to be living (now in 1985) a quiet pensioner's life in the university city of Lund, where he spends his time reading history books in the library.

In the 1990s, author and journalist Bosse Schön and researcher Tobias Hübinette continued to trawl the archives for SS veterans like Ekström. One of the magazine *ETC's* most widely circulated articles is Schön's account of the Nazis who were involved in the founding of the Sweden Democrats. Ekström was one of them.

Thanks to the letter that we obtained after contacting the Antifascist Press Archive in Berlin we found Helmut Panzer, a veteran from the 4th Parachute Division and Ekström's friend and fellow student from the 1950s in Nuremberg. Our interview with him and the manuscript he sent us gave us important information about Ekström's activities after the War that also filled in several lacuna in Ekström's war-time service. For example, Panzer's account led us on to Ekström's time at the Eastern front, which is otherwise given only cursory treatment in the security police file.

The letters that Gustaf Ekström sent to the German author Hans Werner Neulen helped us correct the erroneous but widely stated claim that Ekström served with the SS "Nordland" and "Wiking" divisions. This he never did. Ekström served with the 4th SS regiment "Der Führer", the SS-Hauptamt (Berlin and Oslo) and the SS "Nord" Division (in Kiestinki).

The interview with Gustaf Ekström in the documentary *Blågul Nazism* from 1993, two years before his death, was naturally a very important source, as it helped to flesh out Ekström's story with his own words. When making the documentary on the Sweden Democrats, we obtained a research copy from Swedish Television, allowing us to go back and scrutinise what he said.

The Bundesarchiv was also very helpful. Thanks to its highly engaged staff, we gained access to Gustaf Ekström's card index file from the NSDStB, the German Nazi student organisation, which gave us some new information about Ekström. His membership of the NSDStB was previously unknown. The card also confirms the date of his enlistment in the Waffen-SS. Another important document was the announcement concerning the SS-Hauptamt's new offices on Lützowstrasse dated 7 January 1941.

The 1936 and 1941 Berlin telephone directories (plus supplement) and the city's address books from 1931–1943 proved invaluable in our efforts to establish the addresses of different SS offices, properties and persons. Letterheads from the correspondence between various SS authorities and units also confirmed different addresses. The sharp-eyed reader has no doubt noted different German spellings for "Jüdisches Altersheim"; this is because we opted to reproduce the exact spelling as given in the respective sources. We have also used material published by the SS-Hauptamt to get a feel for the kind of propaganda that was being churned out by the authority at which Ekström worked. With the help of sundry year-books, address books and other lists published by the NSDAP (the German Nazi party), we have been able to refute information from other sources.

Without the public census that was taken in Nazi Germany in May 1939 and the memorial books for the victims of the Holocaust we would never have had the names of all the Jews living at Lützowstrasse 48/49. The most important of these books were *Gedenkbuch Berlins* (Berlin's memorial book), *Victims of the Persecution of Jews under the National Socialist Tyranny in Germany 1933–1945, Bundesarchiv,* and *The Memorial book of victims and prisoners in Theresienstadt*. Yad Vashem's enormous archive was also extremely valuable, containing as it does an exhaustive and searchable database of Shoah victims's names and survivors' testimonies. These personal details have sometimes been supplemented with the testimonies of relatives, adding another dimension to the fates of the 256 Jews on Lützowstrasse. Through Yad Vashem, we not only obtained information about those who were murdered but also gained a detailed picture of the paper trail that the Nazis left behind, such as copies of the Gestapo's transport lists and death certificates from Theresienstadt.

Other valuable archives were the Leo Beck Institute, where we discovered the photographs of the nursing home and the Centrum Judaicum, which helped up find the invoices for its telephone system. In the Central Archive for the History of Jewish People, Israel, we found three files which proved critical to establishing what had become of the property on Lützowstrasse. The archive and the database of restitution demands (WGA-Datenbank) in the Landesarchiv Berlin was also invaluable to our researches into the properties at Lützowstrasse 48/49 and Hagenstrasse 39–47, both of which were sequestered by the Gestapo and then utilised by the SS.

Tobias Hübinette's unpublished notes on Ekström, which he kindly let us use, was another important source. The groundwork he did led us further and made it easier for us to track Ekström in the civic registries.

One of the books that gave us best insight into the West German organisations in which Ekström was active after the War is Kurt Tauber's *Beyond Eagle and Swastika – German nationalism since 1945*. Despite its relatively early publication date (1967), it is still considered a standard work for anyone interested in German nationalism and neo-Nazism post-1945. HIAG, the revisionist SS-veterans' organisation, has been thoroughly analysed in Karsten Wilke's book of the same title from 2011. The book lifts the lid on the organisation and presents an important analysis of the effect of substantial historical revisionism that the organisation has promulgated about the Waffen-SS. It also deals with developments after 1967, which makes it a fitting complement to Tauber's work.

The booklet entitled *Germany's New Nazis* published back in 1952 provides a good, brief overview of the SRP.

Swedish Nazism is depicted best in Heléne Lööw's three-volume *Nazismen i Sverige*, published between 2000 and 2015.

The two books by Armas Sastamoinen, *Hitlers svenska förtrupper* from 1947 and *Nynazismen* from 1966, are valuable to anyone seeking names and general outlines of the NSAP/SSS and other smaller neo-Nazi parties or organisations in Sweden.

Holger Carlsson's *Nazismen i Sverige – ... ett varningsord* from 1942 must also be considered a standard work on the subject. Sven Olov Lindholm's own *Svensk Frihetskamp* from 1943 and his contributions to the newspapers *Stormfacklan* and *Den Svenske Folksocialisten* are first-hand sources for Swedish Nazi rhetoric in the 1930s and 40s. Max Pferdekämpfer is given exhaustive treatment in Anton Schulte's book *Menden im 19. und 20. Jahrhundert*.

Tobias Hübinette's directory of Swedish Nazis and Nazi sympathisers, *Den svenska nationalsocialismen – Medlemmar och sympatisörer 1931–1945*, published in 2002, includes not only Gustaf Ekström but also Sven Ekström, his brother, who is listed as a member of the Riksföreningen Sverige-Tyskland, a quasi-Nazi and pro-German organisation, in 1942 and 1943. In 1934, Bengt Ekström, Ekström's middle brother, was one of the 184 founders and original members of the Manhem Society, a pro-Nazi educational organisation aimed at the middle and upper classes that also kept a registry of Jews. We also found that Gustaf Ekström's sister's husband, Albin Edlund, sympathised with the National Socialist bloc, to whose organ he sent Christmas greeting.

Many books have been written on the SS, far too many of which fit into the pattern of the historical revisionism or idealisation that we described earlier. One example is the magazine *Siegrunen*, which includes Ekström in a list of Swedish volunteers in the Waffen-SS, albeit with incorrect details. Another is Eric Kaden's book *Das Wort als Waffe*, which whitewashes the SS propaganda units.

That said, there is of course a great deal of quality literature and research. An important book on the SS's educational programme is Hans-Christian Harten's *Himmlers Lehrer – Die Weltanschauliche Schulung in der SS 1933–1945* from 2014, which systematically covers all aspects of the extensive educational system that was erected to create the ideological base on which the SS stood. A major reference work on the development of the propaganda troops is *Ortwin Buchbender's Das tönende Erz – Deutsche Propaganda gegen die Rote Armee im Zweiten Weltkrieg*, published in

1978, which describes in detail how the Wehrmacht and SS propaganda troops were established during the War.

Akim Jah's comprehensive account of the deportations from Berlin in his *Die Deportation der Juden aus Berlin – Die nationalsozialistische Vernichtungspolitik und das Sammellager Grosse Hamburger Strasse* from 2013 is one of two German books that mention the nursing home on Lützowstrasse and its confiscation by the SS. The other is Susanne Willem's *Der entsiedelte Jude – Albert Speers Wohnungsmarktpolitik für den Berliner Hauptstadtbau* from 2000; it too is an exceptionally important work for anyone studying how properties were sequestered in Berlin during the Nazi era, and probes Albert Speer's role in the persecution of Berlin's Jews.

Two books which are still considered groundbreaking and extremely important accounts of Theresienstadt and the machinery of deportation are Hans Günther Adler's standard works *Theresienstadt, Das Antlitz einer Zwangsgemainschaft* and *Der verwaltete Mensch – Studien zur Deportation der Juden aus Deutschland*.

Grossman's horrific depiction of Treblinka appears in various published works, including *The Treblinka Hell* from 1946 and, in Swedish, in *Reporter i krig* (presented by Antony Beevor) from 2007.

In addition to the above, our research has drawn on a great many other writings, newspapers and archive material (see the list of references). All the material that we have gathered ourselves – hundreds of copies of documents from all archives, correspondence and photographs, we have saved in our own archive, which we intend to donate to the Labour Movement's Archives and Library.

Archive material

A3355, National Archives and Records Administration, Maryland, USA.

Archiwum Panstwowe w Leznie, Poland.

Anschriften Verzeichnis der Schutzstaffel der NSDAP, 1 Nov, 1944. Copy issue by Supreme Headquarters, Allied Expeditionary Force, National Archives and Records Administration, Maryland, USA.

Antifaschistische Pressearchiv und Bildungszentrum e.V. (apabiz), Berlin.

Berger, Gottlob, Public files declassified and released under Nazi War Crimes Disclosure Act, CIA.

Borg, Gösta's file in the security police archive, Swedish National Archives.

Calais, Thorwald Elof's file in the security police archive, Swedish National Archives.

Cederholm, Stig's file in the security police archive, Swedish National Archives.

Central database of Shoah victim's names, Yad Vashem, Israel.

Documents relating to the NSAP, security police archive, Swedish National Archives.

DP-Kartei 1945–1949, Jüdische Gemeinde zu Berlin (Displaced Persons Cards 1945–1949, Jewish Community of Berlin). Zentralarchiv zur Erforschung der Geschichte der Juden in Deutschland, Hrsgb, Berlin, 1949.

Ekström, Hilding Gustaf Sigvard's file in the security police archive, Swedish National Archives.

Ekström, Gustaf, Karteikarte des NSDStB, Bundesarchiv, Berlin.

Expo, Sweden.

Flossenburg Memorial Archive.

Forssman, Bertil's file in the security police archive, Swedish National Archives.

Hassel, Bengt's, file in the security police archive, Swedish National Archives.

Heinrich Stahl Collection, AR7171, Leo Beck Institute, New York, USA.

Hillblad, Thorolf's file in the security police archive, Swedish National Archives.

HL-Senteret, Norge.

Illegal Emigration of Nazis from Germany to Argentina, Public files declassified and released under Nazi War Crimes Disclosure Act, CIA.

Immigration Cards, National Archives in Rio de Janeiro, Brazil.

Institut Terezínské Iniciativy.

International Tracing Service, ITS, Bad Arolsen.

JRSO-Bln 600, Central archives of the history of Jewish people, Jerusalem, Israel.

JRSO-Bln 677, Central archives of the history of Jewish people, Jerusalem, Israel.

JRSO-Bln 683, Central archives of the history of Jewish people, Jerusalem, Israel.

Judgement of the International Military Tribunal, Avalon project, Documents in Law, History and Diplomacy, Yale Law School.

Kronvall, Svante's file in the security police archive, Swedish National Archives.

Krueger, Hans-Caspar's file in the security police archive, Swedish National Archives.

Landesarchiv Nordrhein-Westfalen, Abteilung Rheinland.

Lindesberg's property register.

Lindesberg archive of cultural history.

Lindesberg parish register.

Ma'ayan Zvi Kibbutz Archive.

Mauthausen Memorial Archive.

Memorial book of victims and prisoners in Theresienstadt, holocaust.cz, Czech Republic.

Microfilm of SS-enlisted men and officers, National Archives and Records Administration, Maryland, USA.

Military Archives, Stockholm.

Minutes, Sweden Democrats Malmö annual meeting on 21.02.1988, St Gertrud's hall 3.00 pm – 4.00 pm, doc. No 1357/88, Närradionämnden 12.04.1988.

Molund, Per Axel Olof's file in the security police archive, Swedish National Archives.

NS 33 SS-Führungshauptamt "Verlegung der Dienststellen des SS-Hauptamtes von Berlin SW 1, Prinz-Albrecht-Strasse 9, nach Berlin W35, Lützowstrasse 48/49, Jan. 1941", Bundesarchiv, Berlin.

Passenger lists, Swedish-American Line, 1929 and 1932, National Archives and Records Administration, Maryland, USA.

Population census USA, 1930, National Archives and Records Administration, Maryland, USA.

Remer, Otto Ernst, Public files declassified and released under Nazi War Crimes Disclosure Act, CIA.

Riedweg, Franz, Archiv für Zeitgeschichte, ETH Zürich.

Riedweg, Franz, Public files declassified and released under Nazi War Crimes Disclosure Act, CIA.

Rydén, Sven's file in the security police archive, Swedish National Archives.

Sieverts Family private archive.

Swedish National Archives Finland.

Swedish National Archives Norge.

Sandström, Olof's file in the security police archive, Swedish National Archives.

Schlussbericht, Stapo IV A 1 – 860/42g, 27. August 1942 (Baumgruppen), copy in the author's private archive.

Stockholm City Archive, the Roteman archive.

Stolpe, Osborn Gerhard's file in the security police archive, Swedish National Archives.

Stiftelsen Norsk Okkupasjonshistorie.

Swedish civic census 1910, Swedish National Archives.

Takman, John's collection, Labour Movement's Archive, Stockholm.

Telefonanlage Lützowstrasse 48, Stiftung Neue Synagoge Berlin – Centrum Judaicum, Berlin.

Umzug Germanische Leitstelle, badatelna.eu.

Volkszählung, May 1939, Tracing the past e.V.

Victims of the Persecution of Jews under the National Socialist Tyranny in Germany 1933 – 1945, Bundesarchiv, Berlin.

Verhandlungen des Deutschen Reichstags, 30.01.1939, reichstagsprotokolle.de.

WASt, Deutsche Dienststelle, Berlin.

WGA-Datenbank, Landesarchiv Berlin.

Örebro city archive.

Overview of National Socialism in Sweden, development and activities, 1 January 1935-5 October 1935, Memorandum, security police archive, Swedish National Archives.

Bibliography

Adler, Hans Günther, Theresienstadt. Das Antlitz einer Zwangsgemeinschaft. Geschichte. Soziologie. Psychologie., Mohr, 1955.

Adler, Hans Günther, Der verwaltete Mensch – Studien zur Deportation der Juden aus Deutschland, Mohr, 1974.

Allgemeine SS, Supreme Headquarters Allied Expeditionary Force Evaluation and Dissemination Section, G-2 (Counter Intelligence Sub-Division), 1944.

Aly, Götz (Hrsg.), Aktion T4 1939 bis 1945. Die „Euthanasie" Zentrale in der Tiergartenstraße 4, Berlin, Edition Hentrich, 1989.

Amtliches Fernsprechbuch Berlin, Ausgabe Juni 1941, Reichspostdirektion Berlin, 1941.

Amtliches Fernsprechbuch Berlin, Berichtigungsblatt 1, Ausgabe Oktober 1941, Reichspostdirektion Berlin, 1941.

Amtliches Fernsprechbuch Berlin, Nachtrag zur Ausgabe 1941, Ausgabe

März 1943, Reichpostdirektion Berlin, 1943.

Beevor, Antony, Andra världskriget, Historiska media, 2012.

Bekenntnis der Professoren an den Deutschen Universitäten und Hochschulen zu Adolf Hitler und dem Nationalsozialistischen Staat, 11 november, 1933, Überreicht vom Nationalsozialistischer Lehrerbund Deutschland, Gau Sachsen, Druckvermerk: Wilhelm Limpert, Dresden, 1933.

Bergen, Doris L., The Holocaust – a Concise History, Rowman and Littlefield Publishers, 2009.

Berlin – Allied Intelligence Map of Key Buildings 1945, After the battle, 2014.

Berliner Adressbuch, för åren 1931–1943, Verlag August Scherl, Deutsche Adressbuch Gesellschaft.

Binder, Dieter A., m.fl., SS-Kaserne Wetzelsdorf – Schiessplatz Feliferhof, Bundesheer, 2010.

Bohn, Robert, Die Deutsche Herrschaft in den "Germanischen Ländern" 1940–1945, Franz Steiner Verlag Stuttgart, 1997.

Browning, Christopher R., Helt vanliga män – Reservpolisbataljon 101 och den slutgiltiga lösningen i Polen, Norstedts, 2019.

Buchbender, Ortwin, Das tönende Erz – Deutsche Propaganda gegen die Rote Armee im Zweiten Weltkrieg, Seewald Verlag, 1978.

Carlsson, Holger, Nazismen i Sverige – ... ett varningsord, Federativs/Trots allt, 1942.

Czerniakow, Adam, Warzaw diary of Adam Czerniakow, Ivan R Dee, 1979.

Denazification (Cumulative Review), Report of the Military Governor (1 April 1947- 30 April 1948), No. 34, Office of Military Government for Germany (U.S) 1948.

Directive No.38 – The Arrest and Punishment of War Criminals, Nazis and Militarists and the Internment, Control and Surveillance of Potentially Dangerous Germans, Allied Control Authority, Control Council, 1946.

Dokumentation, Topographie des Terrors – Gestapo, SS und Reichssicherheitshauptamt auf dem Prinz-Albrecht-Gelände, Arenhövel, 1987.

Elmbrandt, Björn, Innan mörkret faller – Ska 30-talet hinna ifatt oss? Atlas, 2015.

Emigrationsutredningen, Kungliga boktryckeriet, 1913.

Englund, Peter, Brev från nollpunkten, Atlantis förlag, 1996.

Freunde des neuen Deutschlands, Ortsgruppe Brooklyn, 1934.

Franssen, Georg, Die Einwohner der Villenkolonie Grunewald 1943, Manuskriptdruck, 1992.

Friedländer, Saul, Förföljelsens år 1933-1939 – Tredje riket och judarna del 1, Natur och kultur, 1999.

Friedländer, Saul, Förintelsens år 1939-1945 – Tredje riket och judarna del 2, Natur och kultur, 2011.

Furuseth, Anne Kristin, Norske nazister på flukt – Jakten på et nytt hjemland i Argentina, Schibsted, 2013.

Galliner, Nicola, Wegweiser durch jüdische Berlin. Nicolai, Berlin, 1987.

Gedenkbuch Berlins – Der Jüdischen Opfer des Nationalsozialismus, Freie Universität Berlin, Zentralinstitut für sozialwissenschaftliche Forschung, Edition Hentrich, 1995.

Germany's New Nazis, Anglo-Jewish Association, Philosophical Library Publishers, 1952.

Gilman, Sander L., Katz, Steven T., Anti-semitism in Times of Crisis, NYU Press, 1993.

Glück, Emil, Hachschara and Youth Aliyah in Sweden 1933-1948, Sällskapet för Judaistisk Forskning, 2016

Golan, Ester, Auf Wiedersehen in unserem Land, Econ Verlag, 1995.

Goldhagen, Daniel Jonah, Hitler's willing executioners – Ordinary Germans and the Holocaust, Knopf, 1996.

Goñi, Uki, The Real Odessa – How Perón brought the Nazi War Criminals to Argentina, Revised edition, Granta, 2003.

Gottwaldt, Alfred, Mahnort Güterbahnhof Moabit – Die Deportationen von Juden aus Berlin, Edition Hentrich, 2015.

Grossman, Vasilij, The Treblinka Hell, Foreign Language Publishing House, Moscow, 1946.

Grossman, Vasilij, Reporter i krig – Dagboksanteckningar från andra världskriget, presenterad av Beevor, Antony och Vinogradova, Luba, Historiska media, 2007.

Grover, Warren, Nazis in Newark, Transaction Publishers, 2009.

Grüner, Wolf, The Persecution of the Jews in Berlin 1933-1945 – A Chronology of Measures by the Authorities in the German Capital, Stiftung Topographie des Terrors, 2014 (translation by Templer, William).

Guttman, Martin, Building a Nazi Europe – The SS's germanic volunteers. Cambridge University Press, 2017.

Gyllenhaal, Lars and Westberg, Lennart, Svenskar i krig 1914-1945, Historiska media 2008.

Harten, Hans-Christian, Himmlers Lehrer – Die Weltanschauliche Schulung in der SS 1933-1945, Ferdinand Schöningh, 2014.

Hirschfeld, Etty, Die Altersheime und das Hospital der Jüdischen Gemeinde zu Berlin. Schriftenreihe der Jüdischen Gemeinde zu Berlin, 1935.

Hitler, Adolf, Mein Kampf – Eine kritische Edition von Hartmann, Christian m.fl. Herausgegeben im Auftrag des Instituts für Zeitgeschichte Berlin-München, 2016.

Hübener, Kristina (Hg.), Hofmann, Wolfgang (Hg.), Meusinger, Paul (Hg), Fürsorge in Brandenburg Entwicklungen - Kontinuitäten - Umbrüche , be.bra Verlag, 2007.

Hübinette, Tobias, Den svenska nationalsocialismen – Medlemmar och sympatisörer 1931–1945, Carlssons, 2002.

In't, Veld, De SS en Nederland – Documenten uit SS-Archieven 1935-1945, 's-Gravenhage, 1976.

Jah, Akim, Die Deportation der Juden aus Berlin – Die nationalsozialistische Vernichtungspolitik und das Sammellager Grosse Hamburger Strasse, be.bra wissenschaft Verlag, 2013.

Jerk, Wiking, Rörelsen som dömdes ohörd – En historisk inblick i NSAP/SSS 1933-1950, Nordland, 2002.

Jüdisches Adressbuch für Gross-Berlin, 1931, Goedega Verlags-Gesellschaft m.b.H. Berlin, 1931.

Jäckel, Hartmut and Simon, Hermann, Berliner Juden 1941 Namen und Schicksale – Das letzte amtliche Fernsprechbuch der Reichspostdirektion Berlin, Stiftung Neue Synagoge Berlin, Hentrich & Hentrich, 2007.

Kaden, Eric, Das Wort als Waffe – Der Propagandakrieg der Waffen-SS und die SS-Standarte Kurt Eggers, Wienkelried-Verlag, 2009.

Klee, Ernst, Das Personenlexikon zum Dritten Reich, Frankfurt am Main, 2007.

Koehl, Robert Lewis, The SS: A History 1919-45, Tempus, 2004.

Kogon, Eugen, SS-staten – De tyska koncentrationslägrens system, Berghs förlag, 2002.

Kühnl, Reinhard, Die NPD – Struktur, Programm und Ideologie einer neofaschistischen Partei, Voltaire Verlag, 1967.

Ladwig-Winters, Simone, Anwalt ohne Recht: das Schicksal jüdischer Rechtsanwälte in Berlin nach 1933, be.bra Verlag, 2007.

Lanzmann, Claude, Shoah – De överlevande berättar, nyutgåva Alfabeta 2015, first edition 1985.

Larsson, Lars T., Hitler's Swedes – A history of the Swedish volunteers in the Waffen-SS, Helion, 2014.

Larsson, Stieg and Ekman, Mikael, Sverigedemokraterna – Den nationella rörelsen, Ordfront/Expo, 2001.

Lejenäns, Harald, The Severe Winter in Europe 1941–2: The large-scale Circulation, Cut-off Lows, and Blocking, Bulletin of the American Meteorological Society, March 1989, Vol. 70, No 3.

Lidner, Jörg, Den svenska Tysklandshjälpen 1945–1954, Acta Universitatis Umensis, 1988.

Lindholm, Sven-Olov, Svensk Frihetskamp, Första Upplagan, NS-Press, 1943.

Lindqvist, Hans, Fascismen idag. Eftersläntrare eller förtrupper..., Federativs förlag, 1979.

Lumsden, Robin, SS – Himmler's Black Order 1923–45, Sutton Publishing Ltd, 1997.

Lunde, Henrik, Finlands val 1941–1945 – Samarbetet med Hitler-Tyskland, Fischer & Co, 2014.

Lööw, Heléne, Nazismen i Sverige 1980–1999 – Den rasistiska undergroundrörelsen: musiken, myterna, riterna, Ordfront, 2000.

Lööw, Heléne, Nazismen i Sverige, 1924–1979 – Pionjärerna, partierna, propagandan, Ordfront, 2004.

Lööw, Heléne, Nazismen i Sverige, 2000–2014, Ordfront, 2015.

Nachama, Andreas and Hesse, Klaus (Hrsg), Vor aller Augen – Die Deportation der Juden und die Versteigerung ihres Eigentums, Fotografien aus Lörach, 1940, Edition Hentrich, 2015, 2nd edition.

Nationalsozialistisches Jahrbuch, 1941, Zentralverlag der NSDAP, 1941.

Nationalsozialistisches Jahrbuch, 1942, Zentralverlag der NSDAP, 1942.

Neulen, Hans Werner, An Deutscher Seite – Internationale Freiwillige von Wehrmacht und Waffen-SS, Universitas, 1985.

Nilsson, Gustaf-Adolf, Varulvar – Hur nazismen övervintrar, Federativs, 1947.

Ohm-Polytechnikum, Nürnberg, Jahresbericht 1934/1935-1935/1936, Tümmels Buchdrückerei, 1936.

Organisationsbuch der NSDAP, Zentralverlag der NSDAP, 1943.

Pries, Johan and Brink Pinto, Andrés, 30 november: kampen om Lund 1985–2008. Pluribus, 2013.

Richter, Pirn (Hrsg.), Die Grunewald Rampe – Die Deportation der Berliner Juden, Zentrum für audio-visuelle Medien, Landesbildstelle Berlin, Edition Colloquium, Berlin, 1993.

Sastamoinen, Armas, Hitlers svenska förtrupper, Federativs, 1947.

Sastamoinen, Armas, Nynazismen, 3rd edition, Federativs, 1966.

Schulte, Anton, Menden im 19. und 20. Jahrhundert – Bürger und Parteien Rat und Verwaltung im Wandel der politischen Verhältnisse, Selbstverlag, 1989.

Schön, Bosse, Svenskarna som stred för Hitler, Bokförlaget DN, 1999.

Schön, Bosse, Där Järnkorsen växer, Bokförlaget DN, 2001.

Schön, Bosse, Hitlers svenska SS-soldater – Brev och dagböcker, Fischer & CO, 2014.

Security services commission, report, SOU 2002:94.

Shirer, William, Tredje Rikets uppgång och fall – Det nazistiska Tysklands historia, Forum, 1984.

Silva Verkehrsplan von Berlin, Verlag für Heimatlich Kultur, c. 1935.

Smith, Arthur L., The Deutschtum of Nazi Germany and the United States, Springer, 1965.

Strauss, Herbert A., Biographisches Handbuch der deutschsprachigen Emigration nach 1933, Band I: Politik, Wirtschaft, öffentliches Leben. K. G. Saur, 1980.

Sweden's official year-book, 1950.

Tauber, Kurt, Beyond Eagle and Swastika – German Nationalism since 1945, Vol. 1–2, Wesleyan University Press, 1967.

Tjänsteföreskrifter (T.F.) för N.S.A.P., 2nd revised edition of 15 Jan. NSAP, 1937.

Tuchel, Johannes and Schattenfroh, Reinold, Zentrale des Terrors – Prinz-Albrecht-Strasse 8: Hauptquartier der Gestapo, Siedler Verlag, 1987.

Übersichtskarte zum 14. Verzeichnis der SF-Züge. Stand: 2. November 1942. Kursbuchbüro der Generalbetriebsleitung Ost (Hrsg.), Deutsche Reichsbahn, 1942.

Weale, Adrian, SS – En ny historia, Fischer & Co, 2013.

Welzer, Harald, Gärningmän – Hur helt vanliga människor blir massmördare, Daidalos, 2007.

Westberg, Lennart, Svenska krigsfrivilliga i tyska Waffen-SS 1941–1945 – Ett bidrag till den svenska frivilligrörelsens historia, Armémuseum meddelande XXXXV-XXXXVI, 1986.

Wilke, Karsten, Die "Hilfsgemeinschaft auf Gegenseitigkeit" (HIAG) 1950–1990 – Veteranen der Waffen-SS in der Bundesrepublik, Ferdinand Schöningh, 2011.

Willems, Susanne, Der entsiedelte Jude – Albert Speers Wohnungsmarktpolitik für den Berliner Hauptstadtbau, Edition Hentrich, 2000.

Wolf-Roskosch, Florian, Ideologie der Waffen-SS: Ideologische Mobilmachung der Waffen-SS 1942–45, Disserta Verlag, 2014.

Öhrn, Eric and Karlsson, Göran, Seklet då allt hände, Bergslagsposten tryck, 2001.

Printed matter published by the SS-Hauptamt

Aufbruch – Briefe von Germanischen Freiwilligen der SS-division Wiking, SS-Hauptamt, Nibelungen Verlag 1943 (första utgåvan april 1942).

Der Untermensch, SS-Hauptamt, 1942.

Rassenpolitik, SS-Hauptamt, Elsnerdruck.

Sennheim – SS-Ausbildungslager, SS-Hauptamt/Germanische Leitstelle/SS-Ausbildungslager Sennheim.

SS-Leitheft, 8. Jahrgang, Heft 3, 1942, SS-Hauptamt, 1942.

SS, Handblätter für die Weltanschauliche Erziehung der truppe, SS-Hauptamt N/0921.

Unpublished material

Ekström, Gustaf, letter to author Hans Werner Neulen, dated 28 August 1981.

Hübinette, Tobias, notes on Ekström, Gustaf.

Panzer, Helmut, letter to the authors, dated 01.09.2016.

Panzer, Helmut, manuscript, dated 01.09.2016.

Sieverts, correspondence with the family.

Films

Jansson, Karl-Axel and Schmid, Ingemar, Blågul nazism, documentary 1993, broadcast on SVT 1995.

Lanzmann, Claude, Shoah, 1985.

Magasinet, on Bevara Sverige Svenskt, SVT, 8 December, 1980.

Nelson, Erik, Engineering Evil, 2011.

Reklamfilm, M/S Gripsholm, the Archival Film Collections.

Sands, Philippe and Evans David, What our fathers did – a Nazi Legacy, 2015.

Sverigedemokraterna, Ett parti som alla andra? A film produced by the Swedish Trade Union Confederation (LO), 2015.

Newspapers

Aufbau, 09.11.1945, 16.11.1945, 23.11.1945, 30.11.1945, 07.12.1945.

Aftonbladet, 19.05.1945, 01.12.1994, 14.01.2011.

Amtsblatt des Kontrollrats in Deutschland, 7 maj 2004 – 7 juni 2004.

Arvika Tidning, 24.11.1944, 20.02.1945, 14.03.1945.

Arbetarbladet, 01.02.2009.

Arbetet, 04.12.1944, 23.05.1945, 18.07.1945.

Associated Press, 01.05.1939.

Central-Verein-Zeitung, 08.05.1937.

Dagens Nyheter, 11.12.1931, 29.04.1942, 17.02.1945, 09.12.1945, 27.03.1945, 09.12.1945, 27.03.1946, 14.12.2014.

Dala-Demokraten, 28.09.2015.

Den Svenske Nationalsocialisten, 1934-1938.

Den Svenske Folksocialisten, 1939-1942.

Der Spiegel, Nr. 28/1961, Nr.38/1957, Nr. 7/1967, Nr. 51/1999.

ETC, 04.04.2014.

Expressen, 17.02.1945, 19.05.1945, 01.12.1994 , 04.11.2013.

Friends Journal, 15.12.1975.

The Guardian, 23.01.2008.

Göteborgs Handels- och Sjöfartstidning, 10.03.1945.

Göteborgsposten, 09.11.1997.

Hela Hälsingland, 17.02.2016.

iDAG (Malmö), 01.12.1994.

Jüdische Gemeindeblatt, Nr. 9, september 1933, Nr. 11, november 1933.

Jüdisch-liberale Zeitung, 01.09.1933.

Jüdische Rundschau, 17.04.1935.

Kvällsposten, 28.04.1985, 01.12.1983, 01.12.1984, 01.12.1985, 01.12.1986, 01.12.1987, 01.12.1988, 01.12.1989, 01.12.1990, 01.12.1991, 01.12.1994.

Lappland-Kurier, Nr 22, 04.09.1941, Nr 50, 10.11.1941.

Marshall Evening Chronicle, augusti 1931.

Nerikes Allehanda, 12.02.1938, 16.02.1938, 17.02.1938.

New York Daily News, 31.05.1998.

The New York Times, 19.02.1930, 27.04.2004.

Nya Dagligt Allehanda, 27.04.1942.

Ottawa Citizen, 22.11.1952.

The Pittsburgh Press, 07.07.1943.

Portsmouth Herald, 19.02.1930.

SD-Kuriren, nr 7-8, 1989.

Skånebladet, SD-Skåne, nr 1-5, 1992.

Skånska Dagbladet, 01.12.1994.

Spöknippet, 1926.

Stormfacklan, 1934-1939.

Svenska Dagbladet, 13.03.1945.

Sverigedemokraternas medlemsbulletin, juli 1989.

Sydsvenska dagbladet, 01.12.1983, 01.12.1984, 01.12.1985, 01.12.1986, 01.12.1987, 01.12.1988, 01.12.1989, 01.12.1990, 01.12.1991, 01.12.1994.

Trots Allt, 23.02.1945.

Ungt Folk, 1937-1944.

Wermlands-tidningen, 14.03.1945.

Zeit, 20.03.1952, 17.03.1961.

Magazines

Der Freiwillige, 30. Jahrgang, Heft 9, September 1984.
Der Freiwillige, 30. Jahrgang, Heft 10, October 1984.
Der Freiwillige, 42. Jahrgang, Heft 5, May 1996.
Populär Historia, January 2002.
Sverige-Tyskland, Volume 1, February, 1938.
Siegrunen #57, 1994.

Authorities

U.S Citizenship and Immigration Services, USA.
Statistics Sweden (SCB).

Other sources

Katolische Schule Herz Jesu, Berlin.
Panzer, Helmut, Auch noch Ehre der deutschen Wehrmacht besudelt, Leserbrief, Preussiche Allgemeine Zeitung, Nr 23 – 08.06.2002.
Panzer, Helmut, Erinnerung an nicht-deutsche Kameraden, Leserbrief, Preussiche Allgemeine Zeitung, Nr 30 – 25.07.2009.
Åkesson, Jimmie, Sagan om SDU-Sölvesborg, SDU-south, Medlemsblad, 1997.

Testimonies

Baldwin, Ruth, Testimony, Deportation from Berlin to Theresienstadt in March 1943. Interview conducted by the USC Shoah Foundation Institute, Yad Vashem.
Coffield, Abraham, Meine deportation am 23 juni, 1942 nach dem K.Z. Theresienstadt, manuscript, April 1957, Yad Vashem.
Henschel, Hildegard, wife of the Chairman of the Jewish community in

Berlin, 1940–1943, Testimony regarding Jewish community activities 1941–1943 and the fate of the community leaders, 1943–1945, Yad Vashem.

Lachman, Walter, Testimony describing his deportation from Berlin, the conditions during the trainride and the arrival to Riga in January 1942. Interview conducted by the USC Shoah Foundation Institute, Yad Vashem.

Messerschmidt, Hans-Peter, Bericht über miene KZ-Zeit 1943–1945, manuscript, June 1945, Yad Vashem.

Salz, David, Testimony of David Salz, describing his deportation from Berlin, the conditions during the trainride and the arrival to Auschwitz in March 1943, Yad Vashem.

Schindler, Henry, (Född Heinz Schindler) Testimony, describing his deportation from Berlin, the conditions during the trainride and the arrival to Theresienstadt in June 1942. Interview conducted by the USC Shoah Foundation Institute, Yad Vashem.

Steinhagen, Frieda, Testimony, Documentation on the trial of Bovensiepen and others, 1969, Yad Vashem.

Stransky, Salo, Testimony, Documentation on the trial of Bovensiepen and others, 1969, Yad Vashem.

Vogel, Wolfgang Josef, Testimony, Documentation on the trial of Bovensiepen and others, 1969, Yad Vashem.

Interviews

Bergquist, Gösta, interview conducted by the authors on 25.08.2016.

Golan family, interview conducted by the authors on 5.12.2018.

Panzer, Helmut, interview conducted by the authors on 25.08.2016.

Sieverts, Henning, interview conducted by the authors August, 2017.

Snyder, Laurie, interview conducted by the authors August, 2017.

Plus several other people who wish to remain anonymous.

Acknowledgements

Many people have helped us in the production of this book. We would like to thank all of you. We reserve a special word of thanks for Bosse Schön, who gave us tips and a copy of the significant photograph of Ekström from around 1935, which is in his personal archive. Tobias Hübinette made valuable comments during the writing of the manuscript. Ulli Jentsch at the Antifascist Press Archive in Berlin also deserves a mention. We would also like to thank the Sieverts and the Golan family for opening their family album to us.

Index

4th Parachute Division, 211, 300

4th SS regiment "Der Führer", 77

30 November parades, 220

1939 census, 85

Abraham, Regina, 105, 106, 107, 179, 181, 215, 291, 292

A. F. Kriegersvej, 138

AG Gesellchaft für automatische Telephonie, 37, 91

Allgemeine-SS, 82, 218

Alternative für Deutschland, 12

Anti-Comintern, 185

Anti-Semitism, 31, 38, 136

Argentina, 209, 306, 310

Arlt, Johann, 129

Ascher, Gertrud, 81, 215, 272

Ascher, Max, 81, 86, 140, 163, 175, 177, 215, 272

Auschwitz, 6, 105, 127, 153, 164, 178, 179, 180, 181, 185, 187, 190, 191, 217, 241, 242, 244, 246, 249, 250, 251, 254, 256, 257, 259, 261, 265, 266, 291, 294, 319

Auschwitzprocess, Der, 191

Austria, 85, 97

Åkesson, Jimmie, 226

Älmhult, 170, 187, 229, 275, 276

Bauer, Gustav, 64, 242, 289

Baumgardt, Nathan, 101, 163, 215, 291

Baum, Herbert, 143

Bayway Refinery, 31

Beer Hall Putsch, 32, 45

Behrendt, Auguste, 175

Behrendt, Cecilie, 131, 146, 293

Behrendt Hochstaedter, Elise, 132

Belzec, 6, 172, 173, 181

Berenbaum, Michael, 230, 231

Berger, Gottlob, 84, 94, 189

Bergqvist, Gösta, 197, 296

Berlin Landesarchiv, 81

Bernadotte, Folke, 186

Bernhard, Lina, 178

Bevara Sverige Svenskt (Keep Sweden Swedish), 220, 315

Black Thursday, 29

Blagovshchina, 129

Blågul nazism, 13, 14, 40, 315

Borchardt, Elisabeth, 122, 124, 127

Bovensiepen, Otto, 124, 125, 144, 190, 191

Buchenwald, 242

Bundesarchiv, 80, 86, 93, 94, 108, 151, 168, 183, 240, 292, 294, 300, 301, 305, 307, 308

BVG (Berlin public transport company), 142

Bütow, Selma, 87

Calais, Linnea, 185, 187

Calais, Thorwald, 150, 168, 169, 170, 171, 185, 187, 188, 229, 274, 275, 276, 279, 286, 294

Calvary, Johanna, 129

Casparius, Siegfried, 175

Catholic Gesellschaft Heiligen Herz Jesu (Society of the Sacred Heart), 135

Cederström, Gustaf, 20

Clarté, 43

Coffield, Isaak, 162

Cohn, Margarete, 127

Crescent Avenue, 30

DAF (Deutsche Arbeitsfront), 42

Davidowsky, Jenny, 175

Den Svenske Folksocialisten, 46, 274, 303, 316

Den Svenske Nationalsocialisten, 49, 50, 316

Depression, 30

Derfflingerstrasse 17, 91, 243, 244, 246, 250, 252, 255, 260, 268

Deutsche Dienststelle, 94, 308

Deutsche Hypothekenbank, 134, 135

Deutsche Reichsbahn, 6, 123, 127, 141, 163, 164, 181, 230, 314

Dickstein, Samuel, 33

Directive No 38, 233

Drammensveien, 54, 169, 170

S/S Drottningholm, 34, 39

Eastern Front Medal, 118

Edlund, Albin, 23, 51, 277, 303

Eichmann, Adolf, 164

Einsatzgruppen, 83, 96, 123, 137, 173, 189, 218, 231, 232

Ekström, Johan Sacharias, 19

Ekström, Samuel, 19, 20, 276

Ekström, Sven, 24, 303

Ellingsen, Harry, 56

Emigration Report, 27

Engdahl, Per, 23, 24, 186, 216

Ewige Jude, Der, 73

Fabian, Laura, 142, 143

Fabrikaktion, 164

Falk, Clara, 127

Feige, Marie, 175

First World War, 21, 22, 25, 76, 99, 163

Flossenbürg, 178, 181, 249

Franco, Fransisco, 53

Free Society of Teutonia, 32

Freiwillige, Der, 203, 218, 219, 288, 296, 318

Fresenius laboratories, 183

Fried, Hédi, 187

Friedländer, Saul, 45

Friends of New Germany, 33

Furugård, Birger, 25, 39, 40, 287

Furugård, Gunnar, 25

Furugård, Sigurd, 25

Färila, 19, 21, 226, 232, 276, 282, 285, 286

Generalplan Ost, 96

German American Bund, 33

Germanische Leitstelle, 10, 136, 308, 315

German-Rhodesia Association, 219, 283, 288

Gerstein, Kurt, 174

Gestapo, 16, 79, 83, 84, 90, 120, 121, 122, 124, 125, 127, 135, 141, 143,

144, 161, 162, 163, 164, 165, 168, 180, 240, 301, 302, 309, 314

Gissibl, Fritz, 32

Globocnik, Odilo, 173

Goebbels, Joseph, 25, 73, 143, 161, 213

Golan, Ester, 87, 242

Golinski, Paula, 178

Golinski, Renate (Devorah Golan), 87, 88, 178, 181, 201, 202, 227, 228, 296

Gothenburg, 28, 34, 39, 40, 41, 43, 50, 274

Graz, 77, 277

M/S Gripsholm, 28, 315

Grosse Altertransport, 141, 163, 164, 242

Grossman, Vasily, 175

Grunewald, 7, 9, 98, 111, 115, 121, 122, 124, 127, 128, 129, 130, 131, 134, 136, 138, 139, 146, 164, 183, 199, 207, 270, 271, 292, 293, 296, 310, 313

Grunewald railway station, 121, 124

Gustaf V, 22

Göring, Hermann, 79

Hackenholt, Lorenz, 172

Hagelberg, Jenny, 175

Hagenstrasse 39–47, 9, 111, 115, 130, 131, 135, 183, 270, 292, 302

Haid & Neu, 215

Haifa, 201, 227, 296

Hanning, Reinhold, 191

Hartmannsweilerkopf, 76

Hedin, Sven, 22

Heim, Irene, 7, 96, 97, 98, 119

Helander, Sven, 186, 187, 236, 286

Hersby gymnasium, 23

Herzog, Sally, 175

Heydrich, Reinhard, 83, 97, 120

HIAG, 160, 216, 217, 218, 219, 288, 295, 302, 314

Hillblad, Thorolf, 42, 93, 209

Himmler, Heinrich, 41, 42, 83, 96, 130, 161, 173

Hirschberg, Joseph, 127

Hitler, Adolf, 14, 18, 25, 32, 33, 37, 40, 41, 44, 45, 53, 74, 75, 76, 77, 88, 95, 96, 99, 100, 132, 137, 164, 173, 186, 188, 195, 203, 213, 220, 224, 285, 296, 297, 299, 309, 310, 311, 312, 313

Hitlerjugend, 73

Holocaust, 17, 230, 309

Holzheim, Doris, 87

Holzheim, Moritz, 87, 102, 103, 291

Holzheim, Pauline, 127

Horst Wessel Lied, 45

House of Representatives Special Committee on Un-American Activities, 34

Hübinette, Tobias, 13, 56, 300, 302, 303, 320

Höss, Rudolf, 190

I2 regiment, 26

I3 regiment, 24, 51, 56, 78, 188, 277

IG Farben, 178, 181

International Tracing Service, 17, 87, 306

Jablonowski, Leopold, 87, 103, 291

Jablonowski, Regina, 87, 103, 291

Jacobsen, Rudolf, 73, 84

Jacoby, Helene, 127

Jacubowski, Michael, 87

Jah, Akim, 90, 304

Jandorf, Adolf, 35, 37, 67, 290

Jeckeln, Friedrich, 123, 190

Jersey City, 30, 31, 34

Jud Süss, 73, 74

Jüdische Altersheim e.V, 35, 36, 240

Jüdische Gemeinde, 35, 305

Jülich (Atomic research centre), 216

KaDeWe, 35

Kalenscher, Rosa (Rose), 87, 104, 291

Karger, Betty, 215, 272

Karlsruhe, 215, 216, 282

Karlstad, 13, 26

Karl XII, 20, 220, 226

Keiler, Agnes, 87, 104, 291

Kiestinki, 99, 116, 117, 118, 293, 300

Kirstein, Luise, 162, 175

Konow, Jan von, 218

Kreuger, Hans Caspar, 209

Kristallnacht, 89

Kuhn, Fritz, 33, 34

Lachman, Walter, 126

Lack, Dorothea, 161, 162

Lappland-Kurier, 100, 317

League of Nations, 23

Lebensraum, 74, 75, 76

Leo Beck Institute, 36, 302, 306

Levin, Louis, 175

Levy, Ada, 178, 179

Levy, Mathilde, 175

Lewinson, Gustav, 175

Lewy, Johanna, 127

Lewy, Richard, 128, 138

Lidingö, 23

Life Grenadiers Regiment, 23

Lindesberg, 20, 21, 22, 26, 47, 49, 57, 59, 93, 167, 188, 232, 274, 279, 289, 306

Lindholm, Sven Olov, 23, 39, 40, 41, 42, 44, 47, 50, 62, 237, 287, 289, 303

Lippmann, Regine, 178

Litvinov, Maxim, 100

Litzmannstadt (Ghetto), 97, 98, 119, 241, 251

LO, 11, 43, 50, 316

Lützowstrasse 48/49, 7, 12, 15, 16, 35, 36, 64, 79, 80, 81, 86, 90, 97, 101, 102, 103, 104, 105, 108, 110, 111, 122, 124, 129, 130, 131, 140, 161, 165, 199, 207, 208, 240, 272, 285, 289, 291, 292, 296, 297, 301, 302, 307

Lützowstrasse 77, 91, 244, 245, 250, 251, 253, 255, 256, 257, 260, 261, 263, 265, 266, 268

Lööw, Heléne, 42, 237, 302

Ma'ayan Zvi, 181, 202, 227, 296, 306

Madison Square Garden, 33, 34

Makt, 48

Malmö Movement, European Social Movement (ESB), 216, 288

Malung, 46, 237

Maly Trostenets, 129, 241, 245

Manasse, Regina, 127

Mauthausen, 87, 181, 227, 249, 306

Mein Kampf, 44, 99, 311

Messerschmidt, Hans Peter, 179, 180, 181

Meyer, Max, 131

Michaelis, Sophie, 175

Michelson, Alfred, 21, 22, 26, 57, 59, 289

Michelson, Hilda, 19

Minsk (Ghetto), 120, 129, 141, 241, 245

Mussgnug, Martin, 159, 219, 295

Mussolini, Benito, 23, 53

Nationaldemokratische Hochschulbund, 219, 283

Nationaldemokratische Partei Deutschland (NPD), 12, 159, 219, 220, 286, 288, 295, 312

Neulen, Hans Werner, 54, 74, 189, 300, 315

Neuthal, Natalie, 175

New Deal, 32

Nordiska Rikspartiet, 216

Nordisk Ungdom (Nordic Youth), 41, 42, 43, 44, 45, 48, 49, 97, 220, 279, 287

NSAP/SSS, 12, 47, 50, 51, 55, 56, 61, 62, 78, 93, 168, 184, 188, 192, 207, 209, 216, 220, 236, 237, 273, 287, 289, 302, 311

NSDStB (German National Socialist Student Organisation), 151, 183, 288, 294, 300, 301, 305

NS-press, 49

Nuremburg, 25, 45, 49, 85, 89, 217

Nuremburg Laws, 49, 85, 89

Nycop, Carl-Adam, 48

Oath of loyalty to Adolf Hitler, 76

Operation Reinhard, 93, 173, 178

Oppenheim, Martin, 127

Orbach, Frieda, 179, 180, 181

Ordower, Salomon, 175

Ordower, Scheindel, 175

Oslo, 54, 55, 56, 118, 166, 168, 169, 170, 171, 183, 274, 276, 277, 278, 284, 300

Örebro, 20, 22, 23, 47, 49, 50, 51, 58, 188, 273, 277, 284, 289, 308

Panzer, Helmut, 211, 212, 232, 273, 300

Permittenttrafik, 55

Pferdekämpfer, Max, 41, 42, 303

Preussische Allgemeine Zeitung, 211

Prinz Albrecht Strasse, 79, 83

RAF (Royal Air Force), 92, 184

Rassenpolitik (Racial Policy), 136, 315

Rat lines, 192

Red Army, 93, 175, 184, 185

Reichsfluchtsteuer (Reich Flight Tax), 132

Remer, Otto Ernst, 157, 158, 212, 214, 215, 282, 295

Riedweg, Franz, 84, 94, 189

Riefenstahl, Leni, 184

Riga (Ghetto), 120, 122, 123, 124, 125, 126, 127, 128, 141, 190, 241, 244, 246, 247, 249, 250, 251, 252, 253, 256, 257, 260, 262, 263, 264, 266, 267, 268, 319

Riksposten, 51

Ring, Laura, 144

Rockefeller, John D, 31, 32

Roosevelt, Franklin Delano, 32

Rosenbaum, Sophie, 175

Rosenthal, Amalia, 87

Rosenthal, Ida, 127

Rosenthal, Rosa, 175

Rothschild (Family), 32

Russian revolution, 22

Rystedt, Elsie, 29

Rystedt, Sven, 29

Röll, Josef, 210, 212

SA, 15, 33, 48, 50, 61, 88, 116, 284, 287, 289, 293, 297

Salinger, Minna, 175

Salomonski, Martin, 35, 36, 64, 241, 290

Salz, David, 180, 181, 319

Sammellager (Transit camps), 121, 304, 311

Sanatorium Grunewald, 9, 115, 131, 134, 146, 292, 293

Sandström, Olof, 55, 150, 294

Sastamoinen, Armas, 48, 302

Scheidemann, Edith, 123

Schenectady, 29, 30

Schindler, Henry, 144, 161

Schwammberger, Josef, 209

Schön, Bosse, 13, 42, 61, 289, 300, 320

Sennheim, 55, 73, 74, 75, 76, 77, 93, 277, 315

SFKO, 12, 23, 24, 25, 39, 279, 284, 285, 287

Shoah, 88, 126, 240, 301, 305, 312, 315, 318, 319

Siegmann, Helen, 178

Sieverts, Cecilie, née Behrendt, 270, 271

Sieverts, Henning, 133, 134

Sieverts, Rudolf, 132

Silbermann, Röschen, 199, 296

SNFP, 25

SNSP, 39, 40, 287

Sobibór, 172, 173, 174, 178, 181, 191, 241, 242, 269

Social Democrats, 23

Sohjana river, 118

South America, 13, 192, 209, 210, 280, 281, 286

Sozialistische Reichspartei Deutschlands (SRP), 12, 157, 210, 212, 213, 214, 215, 216, 220, 282, 284, 288, 294, 295, 302

Speer, Albert, 90, 122, 304

Spöknippet, 24, 317

SS-Hauptamt, 7, 10, 15, 16, 78, 79, 80, 81, 84, 90, 91, 92, 93, 94, 95, 108, 110, 111, 112, 113, 115, 130, 135, 136, 137, 138, 145, 150, 167, 170, 171, 183, 185, 187, 189, 207, 224, 277, 278, 285, 292, 293, 294, 300, 301, 315

SS-Leitheft, 137, 315

SS-Schule, 55

SS-Sonderkommando, 83

SSU, 43

Staaf, Karl, 22

Stahl, Heinrich, 36, 161, 241, 306

Stalin, Joseph, 18, 210

Stangl, Franz, 172, 173, 174, 191

Steinhagen, Frieda, 144

Sternberg, Emelie, 161, 162

Stern, Willy, 127

Stormfacklan, 41, 43, 49, 303, 317

Stransky, Salo, 124

Sudetenland, 85

Sundsvall, 51, 277

Svensk Socialistisk Samling (SSS), *See* NSAP/SSS

Sveriges Nationella Förbund (SNF), 192

Sverige-Tyskland, 186, 303, 318

Sweden Democrats (SD), 3, 8, 9, 11, 12, 13, 15, 193, 195, 222, 223, 224, 225, 226, 227, 236, 237, 286, 288, 295, 300, 307

Sällskapet för Svensk Fostran, 49, 287

Söder, Björn, 237

Takman, John, 41

Tauber, Kurt, 214, 217, 302

Tel Hai, 201, 227, 296

Theresienstadt, 6, 7, 87, 101, 105, 106, 129, 140, 141, 142, 143, 144, 152, 161, 162, 163, 164, 165, 171, 172, 174, 177, 178, 179, 187, 199, 240, 241, 242, 243, 244, 245, 246, 247, 248, 249, 250, 251, 252, 253, 254, 255, 256, 257, 258, 259, 260, 261, 262, 263, 264, 265, 266, 267, 268, 269, 285, 291, 294, 296, 301, 304, 306, 308, 318, 319

Topographie des Terrors, 16, 79, 309, 311

Totenkopf SS, 190

Tracing the past e.V., 85, 240, 308

Transport Workers' Union, 50

Treaty of Versailles, 23, 31

Treblinka, 6, 83, 172, 173, 174, 175, 177, 178, 181, 191, 215, 217, 241, 242, 243, 245, 246, 247, 248, 250, 251, 253, 254, 255, 257, 258, 259, 260, 261, 262, 263, 265, 269, 304, 310

Triumph of the Will, 184

Typographical Association, 50

UN, 23

Untermensch, Der (The Subhuman), 137, 145, 293, 315

Via Nord, 209

Vitt Ariskt Motstånd (White Aryan Resistance), 223

Vogel, Wolfgang Josef, 125

Volk ans Gewehr, 45

Voxenkollen, 55

Waffen-SS, 12, 14, 15, 16, 42, 52, 53, 54, 55, 56, 74, 77, 78, 82, 83, 84, 93, 94, 99, 117, 120, 136, 150, 160, 166, 167, 168, 169, 171, 183, 184, 187, 203, 217, 218, 219, 229, 232, 233, 234, 235, 273, 274, 275, 276, 277, 278, 279, 285, 286, 287, 288, 294, 295, 297, 299, 301, 302, 303, 312, 313, 314

Waffen-SS 4th war correspondent platoon, 99

Waffen-SS division "Nord", 99, 120, 184

Wagner, Amelie, 127

Walles, Erik, 47, 236, 237

Wannsee conference, 120

Warsaw (Ghetto), 120, 128, 138, 141, 173, 184, 241

Wasa, *See* Nordisk Ungdom

Wehrmacht, 84, 99, 100, 212, 217, 304, 313, 318

Werhahn, Paula, 135, 270, 271

Westberg, Lennart, 218

Westenberg, Selma, 127

Wetzelsdorf, 77, 93, 309

White Buses, 12, 186, 187, 229, 236

Wiklund, Gösta, 48

Wirth, Christian, 172

Wulff, Selma, 128, 138

Yad Vashem, 88, 96, 101, 105, 106, 107, 124, 128, 129, 142, 153, 161, 162, 164, 178, 215, 240, 291, 292, 294, 301, 305, 318, 319

Zikhron Ya'akov, 202, 227, 296

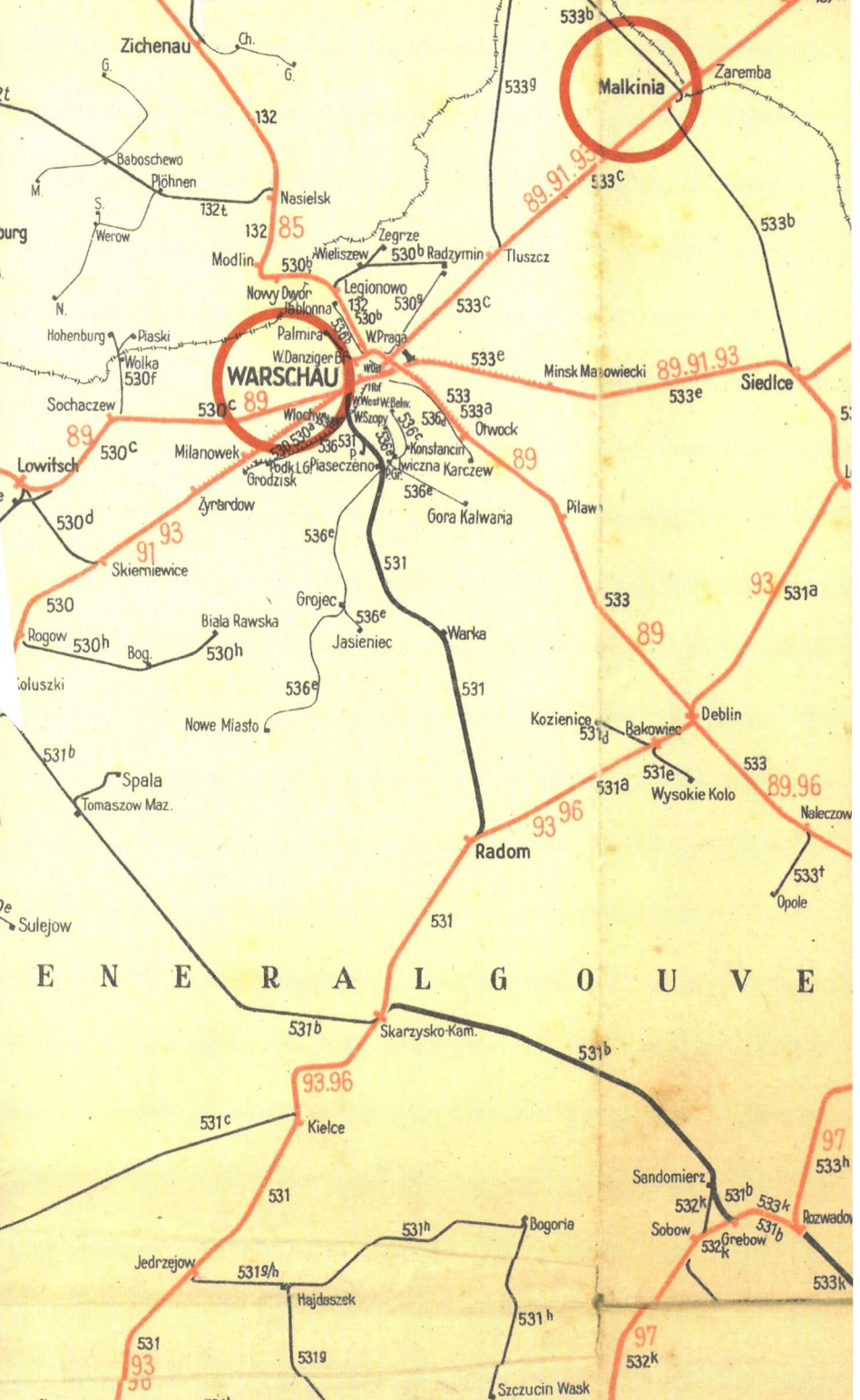